A Pack of Idle Sparks

Letters from Hexham on the Church, the People, Corruption and Scandal, 1699-1740

Edited by
Greg Finch

HEXHAM LOCAL HISTORY SOCIETY
2013

Hexham Local History Society
Hexham, Northumberland

www.hexhamhistorian.org

First published 2013

ISBN: 978-0-9565078-4-6 softcover

Front cover: Design by Peter Rodger includes William Hogarth, The Sleeping Congregation, London, 1736 engraving, © Trustees of the British Museum, collection number 1868,0822.1540.

Rear cover illustration: St. Andrews, Hexham by S. Grimm, 1778, British Library, Add.MS 15543

Printed by Lightning Source UK, Milton Keynes, MK11 3LW

Contents

Figures

Foreword

Thanks to the work of Hexham Local History Society this collection of fascinating letters, describing the gossip, intrigue and political machinations of early 18th century Hexham from the perspective of its clergy, is gathered together for the first time.

When the Society's treasurer, Greg Finch, came across this remarkable collection, which has lain in an archive in York for three hundred or so years, he had the vision of making the letters available to a wider audience. This led to a five year project which brought together a team of Hexham Local History Society members to transcribe the church correspondence and related material and prepare it for publication, set in the context of Greg's Introduction and biographical notes. It is a remarkable team effort and congratulations should be offered to all involved.

By its very nature of being correspondence largely to do with Church courts, this book tends towards those negative attributes of the people of Hexham and how, as the *Book of Common Prayer* puts it, they 'erred and strayed from thy ways' following 'too much the devices and desires of their own hearts'. It gives us insights into personal ambitions alongside underhand dealings and petty squabbles; genuine mistakes alongside human frailties. Centuries later, we gain a glimpse of the texture and personality of these characters. On one level you can read of similar contemporary stories as you turn the pages of the *Hexham Courant*! However, what was different in the early 18th century was the power and control of the local established church; its influence extended into every sphere of human living and well-being.

I believe that this book asks of us at least two contemporary questions. First, what does it mean to live together as a community? One of the privileges of being Rector of Hexham is trying to mirror back to the town its hidden stories and those that go below the genteel surface. At a time of economic crisis many are struggling and we must always be asking ourselves how we can better pitch our tent together so that the lost, the least and the lonely are supported and cherished.

The picture of the disciples painted in the Gospels is of a group of ordinary men and women who were captured by the extraordinary life and teaching of Jesus. In baking sun and through pangs of hunger they sat and listened to him and were sent out to share with strangers something of what they had learnt. They were so bound up in that life that slowly, as the penny dropped and with many failings along the way, they were to make Jesus' life their own; to model his beliefs, his actions, his attitudes. In other words they learnt to pitch their tent together and through their actions brought hope to all around them.

Secondly, the letters ask us to explore how we might, or might not, be maintaining a treasure trove of primary sources for future historians researching the life of the church and the community of Hexham in the early years of the 21st Century. Communication has never been as easy; we can receive the answers to our questions from the internet, read extensive documents on the screens of our phones, and, at the press of a button, send emails to all and sundry. Yet, there are things that are lost in this fast approach; things can be less considered and less reflected upon in our rush to expect an instant response, and we have yet to really work out a way to keep some of this material so that future generations can glimpse where we too have 'erred and strayed'.

This book is an important contribution to a wider insight into a particular period in the history of church and town. I hope that its stories will delight readers and resource historians in equal measure.

The Revd Canon Graham Usher
Rector and Lecturer of Hexham
Holy Cross Day 2013

Acknowledgements

This has been a collaborative effort by members of the Hexham Local History Society over several years. At the core of it were a number of transcribers, including Sonja Bailes, Mark Benjamin, Steve Casson, Jim Hedley, Susan Ketelaar, Yvonne Purdy, Ted Wall, and especially Jennifer Britton and Ian Hancock, without whose dedication and diligent work this edition would have not have appeared. Susanne and Chris Ellingham were extremely thorough and efficient in checking the entire set of transcripts. Peter Rodger provided a secure technical foundation for the project, from the creation of a web-based document control system ideal for the distributed nature of the transcription work, through to the final assembly of the material ready for printing, and design of the cover. Mark Benjamin picked out the quote from Thomas Andrewes which gives us our title. I am also indebted to Colin Dallison for help on Hexham House, and to Stan Beckensall for the image of Hexham House (Figure 8) and to Patrick Lindsay for obtaining a high quality image of Figure 3. We are grateful to the British Library for granting permission to use the image in Figure 4 and on the rear cover, and likewise to the British Museum in respect of the image used on the front cover. Val Bott, chair of the Hogarth Trust, responded swiftly to a request to help track it down.

In common with all works of this nature, the support and assistance of dedicated archivists has been crucial, and I would like in particular to thank Dr. Paul Dryburgh and Danna Messer at the Borthwick Institute of Archives, Carol Scott and Keith Gilroy of the Northumberland Archives at Woodhorn, Donna Marshall, Assistant Archivist at The Worshipful Company of Mercers in London, Julian Reid, Archivist at Corpus Christi College, Oxford, and Michael Riordan, Archivist at The Queen's College, Oxford. The permission of the Borthwick Institute to publish transcripts of the material in their care, and to allow reproduction of the images in Figures 10-12, is gratefully acknowledged. Likewise, our thanks go to the Society of Antiquaries of Newcastle upon Tyne and their librarian Denis Peel for granting permission to include transcripts of their documents.

The Introduction has been greatly improved thanks to the suggestions of Dr. Adrian Green of Durham University and Professor Jim Sharpe of York University, who readily made available their specialist expertise. Their valuable contribution to our project is much appreciated. I would also like to thank Professor Bill Purdue of

Northumbria University for his input on part of an earlier version of the Introduction, and Jennifer Britton and Ian Hancock for their insights. The final version is also much the better for Liz Sobell's usual high standard of editing suggestions, proof reading and content review. For this, and other support to the project, including our initial visit to York to obtain the main body of document images, assisting with guidance to the transcription team (some of whom were new to archival work), and the Bewick engraving (Figure 9) I am greatly in her debt, as is the Society as a whole. Errors that remain despite the contributions of those who gave their time to review the work so willingly are entirely my fault. Hilary Faulkner has been very efficient in indexing the book. We also greatly appreciate the willingness of Revd Canon Graham Usher to provide the foreword.

Finally, for putting up for so long with the obscure activities of Messrs Ritschel, Andrewes and others, I give my deep thanks and love to Julie, Jenny and Rosie.

Greg Finch, Hexhamshire, September 2013

A Transcriber's view

When the opportunity arose to do some transcribing for the Hexham Letters project I jumped at it. My main reason for doing so was simply that I love transcribing! It's a challenge sometimes rather akin to doing a cryptic crossword or even a jigsaw. The struggle to identify that elusive word: searching for similar characters in other words, looking at the overall sense of the sentence. Sometimes the answer is to leave well alone for a while: a couple of hours later the mysterious word suddenly becomes crystal clear and obvious.

Little did I realize, however, that transcribing the letters would also open up a whole new world to me: Ecclestiastical Courts, Visitations, Presentments and Admonitions; vexatious attorneys; priests of 'unquiett temper'; injunctions against 'a new method of singing'; 'busy and imperious' Lady Blackett; the 'implacable malice' of Thomas Allgood; the ruinous state of the Abbey, infested with pigeons; I could go on and on. Suffice to say that it's been not only a steep learning curve but also a fascinating voyage of discovery!

Jennifer Britton, Hexham, August 2013

Abbreviations

AA	*Archaeologia Aeliana*
ABN	Additional Biographical Notes (in this volume)
BIA	Borthwick Institute for Archives, York
DUL	Durham University Library, Special Collections
HH	*Hexham Historian*
HPR	Hexham Parish Registers. Originals at NRO EP/184/1-5. Transcripts available at Hexham Library and Newcastle City Library
NCH III	A.B.Hinds, *History of Northumberland*, Vol III, Hexhamshire part 1, (1896)
NCH IV	J.C.Hodgson, *History of Northumberland*, Vol IV, Hexhamshire part 2, (1897)
NCH VI	J.C.Hodgson, *History of Northumberland*, Vol VI, Bywell St. Peter, Bywell St. Andrew, Blanchland, and Slaley, (1902)
NRO	Northumberland Record Office, now Northumberland Archives, Woodhorn
ODNB	H.Matthew and B. Harrison ed. *Oxford Dictionary of National Biography,* (2004)
Smith	M.G.Smith, *Pastoral Discipline and the Church Courts: the Hexham Court 1680-1730*, University of York Borthwick Paper, No. 62, (1982)
Shuler	J.C.Shuler, The Pastoral and Ecclesiastical Administration of the Diocese of Durham 1721-1771; with Particular Reference to the Archdeaconry of Northumberland, unpublished Ph.D thesis, Durham University, (1975)
Till, *Courts*	B.D.Till, *The Church Courts 1660-1720: the Revival of Procedure*, Borthwick Papers, No.109, (2006)
Till, Study	B.D.Till, The Administrative System of the Ecclesiastical Courts in the Diocese and Province of York. Part III: 1660-1883 A Study in Decline. BIA unpublished study/ Leverhulme Research Scheme, (1963)
TNA	The National Archives

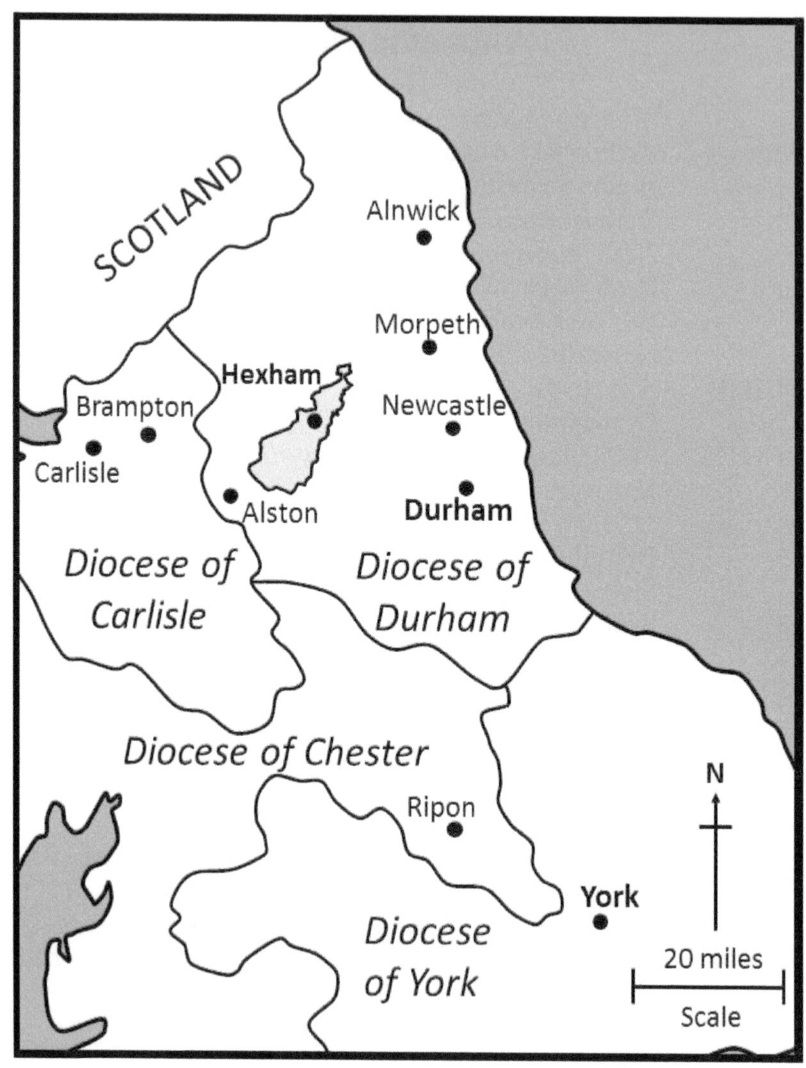

Figure 1: Diocesan boundaries in Northern England, c.1700
(Peculiar of Hexhamshire lightly shaded)

1. Introduction

Direct observations of the lives and misdemeanours of ordinary people in the early modern period are few in number. Letters sent from Hexham in Northumberland between 1699 and 1740 therefore offer rare and vivid insights into the life of a small northern town and its surrounding countryside before the industrial revolution. Most were written by successive senior church ministers in Hexham, the Reverend George Ritschel junior and the Reverend Thomas Andrewes, and were addressed to church officials within the archbishopric of York. They made their way into the Borthwick Institute for Archives at the University of York with other ecclesiastical papers.[1]

The ability of the church to influence the moral behaviour of ordinary people was in decline by this time, but in the Hexham area at least it was not for want of trying, and the correspondence sheds a great deal of light on local life and on the operation of the church courts. Marriage licences, wills, inventories and administration grants might be known territory to family historians, but the Hexham correspondence provides a much rarer insight into the way the processes which created them operated, formally and informally, in one jurisdiction at least.

While the correspondence has been researched before and a valuable short study produced,[2] it is now published for the first time in full. To support readers in making their own use of the material, this introduction provides context on Hexhamshire, the Church, the principal correspondents and the documents.

Hexhamshire and the Church

Hexhamshire in 1700

Hexhamshire, a civil administrative 'liberty and regality' separate from the county of Northumberland until 1572, occupied ninety two square miles of land on either side of the river Tyne. It lay twenty miles west of Newcastle (see Figures 1 and 2), and was centred on the market town of Hexham. Nominally it was a single parish, Hexham, but by 1700 the two parochial chapelries of

[1] BIA, Pec.Hex/2.
[2] Smith.

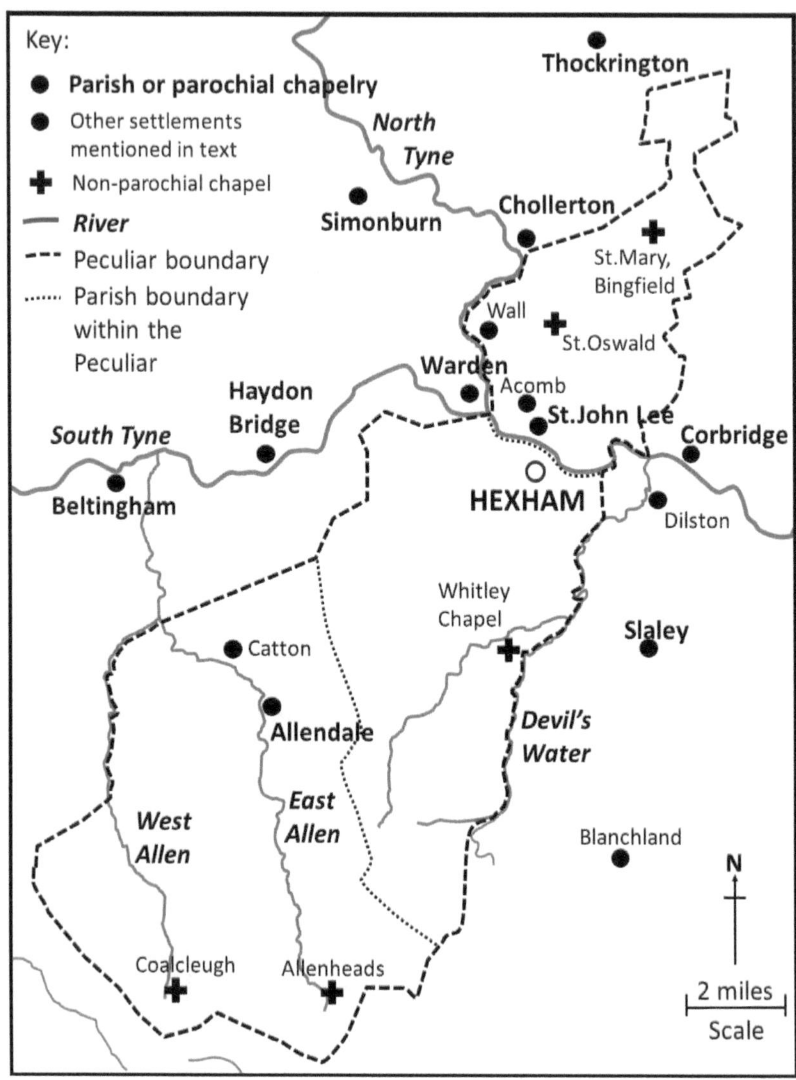

Figure 2: The Peculiar of Hexhamshire and adjacent parishes

Allendale and St. John Lee operated as separate parishes, served by their own curates, and kept their own registers. Allendale lay to the west of Hexham parish across the open common, centred on Allendale Town above the East Allen river. St.John Lee was north of the Tyne in a narrowing triangle of land crossing the line of Hadrian's Wall, and included the villages of Acomb and Wall. What remained as Hexham parish included the town and a large rural area to the south, the only part of the old Liberty still known as Hexhamshire today.[3] The town's recorded population was around 2,000 in 1700, and a further 4,000 or so people were spread around the rural parts of the Liberty.[4]

Apart from the narrow lowland corridor alongside the Tyne, the land was of poor quality, much of it unenclosed waste fit for little more than rough grazing. Large expanses lay above 1,000 feet in altitude, rising to 2,200 feet at Killhope Law on the southern boundary with County Durham. Hexham's streets ran outwards from the market place, set on a bluff above the river, hemmed in to the south by the town's open fields and the bleak commons on the hills above. The whole area was often seen by outsiders as isolated, poor, unruly and backward. In 1688 over a dozen Hexham people were bound over in the wake of a riot, and between 1689 and 1697 12% of those bound over to appear at Northumberland's Quarter Sessions were from Hexham. The town accounted for around 2% of the county's population.[5] While this might simply reflect a relatively

---

[3] To avoid confusion, references to Hexhamshire in this Introduction are to the entire Liberty. The rural southern part of Hexham parish is referred to as 'the Shire', the term familiar today and which was also used on occasion during the period covered by the correspondence. 'Hexham' refers to the town.

[4] These estimates can only be an approximate guide as they are derived from annual average baptisms recorded in each Anglican parish register between 1700-11, and therefore do not take account of any under-registration due to non-conformity or other reasons. Furthermore, they have also been scaled up using the blunt instrument of the national crude birth rate of 32 per 1,000 given in Wrigley and Schofield, *The Population History of England 1541-1871*, (1981), p.533.

[5] Northumberland Archives (NRO) QSO/2 *passim,* 1688: QSO/2, f18. A new estimate of 98,700 for Northumberland's population in 1700 is provided in E.A.Wrigley, *Early English Censuses*, (2011), Table A2.6 (excluding 16,000 for Newcastle included in the original total). I am grateful to Professor Wrigley for an early sight of this data ahead of publication.

youthful population, it seems disproportionate enough a share to perhaps underwrite a reputation for local unruliness. As Ritschel observed ruefully in one of his letters that 'there are many rakes in this town'.[6] Regarded from afar as a nest of dangerous papists, there was also much suspicion of Hexhamshire's people at the time of the 1715 Jacobite Rising. The rebels engaged in this attempt to overthrow the previous year's succession of George I of Hanover to the throne raised the standard of the Stuart claimant, James III, in Hexham market place that October. The archbishop of York expressed concern afterwards both for Ritschel's person and his *conduct.* In his measured reply, Ritschel conceived his conduct 'to be such as no man can justly condemn.' So few Hexham people joining the rebels was 'testimony of our good affection to the present Goverm't at least that we are not enemys to it.'[7]

The archbishop's suspicion seems reasonable given the actions of Robert Patten, the curate of Allendale. He joined the rebels, preaching for them all the way to their surrender to Hanoverian forces at Preston in November, before turning himself in to provide evidence for the Crown in the subsequent trials. Rewarded with a pension in addition to his reprieve, he wrote the first history of the rebellion and returned to his curacy.[8] While few people from the area appear to have joined the rebels, lingering pro-Jacobite feeling and sullen resentment drove Patten out of his Allendale curacy by 1718.[9] A fight in a Hexham pub in September 1718 turned into a much bigger Jacobite inspired brawl in the marketplace. Similarly inspired intimidation was directed towards those in Hexham foolish enough openly to support the loyalist Whig candidate during the election campaign of 1723.[10]

Unruly as Hexham might have been however, it was not isolated, and the local economy grew strongly in the late seventeenth

---

[6] Ritschel to Jubb, 26 Oct 1713, doc. **66**.

[7] Ritschel to Pearson, 20 Jan 1716, doc. **89**.

[8] L.Gooch, *The Desperate Faction? The Jacobites of North-East England 1688-1745*, (2001), pp. xi-xii, 121.

[9] 28 people from Hexham and St. John Lee are listed amongst those captured at Preston: Gooch, Appendix, pp. 182-8. Andrews to Jubb, 6 Sept 1718 refers to Mr Lowes as the curate of Allendale.

[10] Gooch, *op cit*, pp. 131-2, NRO QSB 50 pp175-177, NRO QSB 59 pp85 – 100. The Hexham vote was, however, split evenly between the two candidates: *The poll book of the contested election for the northern division of the county of Northumberland* (Newcastle, 1841), pp. 147-70.

century. The town's population probably rose by more than a third in the three decades before 1700.[11] This growth was driven primarily by immigration. Only around half of the fathers registering their children in the 1690s had been baptised in the town themselves, and a similar proportion of people marrying in that decade also came from outside Hexham.[12] The reason is not hard to find – the huge engine of economic development on Tyneside, driven on mainly by London's demand for coal. The various leather trades employed up to half of Hexham's workforce in 1700, an industrial specialisation servicing demand across the whole region rather than meeting purely local needs. Although overshadowed by the leather industry trades, cloth making also flourished in the area, accounting for nearly a fifth of the town's workforce in the 1710s.[13] The diversity of occupations within the town is also impressive. Forty seven were counted in the 1690s by Anna Rossiter, nearly double the number typically found in the smaller English market towns in this period.[14] Market stall holders were frequently reminded by the manor court not to sell to people from outside the town until the needs of residents had been met, evidence both of Hexham's importance to regional trade, and the ineffectiveness of such decrees.[15] Population continued to rise through the eighteenth century, reaching approximately 2,500 in the 1740s. 3,400 people were enumerated in the town in the 1801 census.[16]

The surrounding area shared in the town's growth during the late seventeenth and early eighteenth centuries. Demand for food and

---

[11] Applying the commonly used ratio of 4.3 people per household, the 320 households listed in the 1673 hearth tax assessment and exemptions for Hexham town wards suggest a population of around 1,400: E179/158/110/r28,r33, T.Arkell, 'Multiplying Factors for Estimating Population Totals From the Hearth Tax', *Local Population Studies*, 28 (1982). 1700-11: 2,000, as given before.

[12] A. Rossiter, *Hexham in the Seventeenth Century*, (2010), p.65.

[13] From a survey of occupational detail for townspeople in HPR, 1710-8.

[14] A. Rossiter, 'Death in Hexham in the 16th and 17th Centuries. What we can learn from the Records', *HH*, 12 (2002), p.56.

[15] For example NRO 672/A/3/40 (from 1702).

[16] 1740: NRO ZAL/84/16, an undated population count of the town taken apparently for ecclesiastical purposes, for it distinguishes those older and younger than 16, the normal age for taking church communion. From internal evidence it appears to date from around 1740. 1801: A.B.Wright, *An Essay towards a History of Hexham..*, (1823), p.23.

industrial raw materials such as hides and wool fostered an intensification of agriculture. Land was nibbled away from the extensive wastes and commons to provide more grazing, such as in the late 1680s at Harwood Shield, twelve miles south of Hexham.[17] Many of the remaining areas of open strip fields were enclosed, either in piecemeal fashion by individual farmers or by collective agreement. Acomb's open fields were enclosed in 1694 by local agreement; their neighbouring farmers across the river at Nether Warden followed suit just a year later.[18] The greater flexibility this allowed to individual farmers led to an increasing focus on pastoral farming, to which most of the land was better suited. Ritschel complained to the Quarter Sessions in 1703 that land in St. John Lee parish had lately been laid to grass, thereby reducing the value of the tithe on corn.[19]

Contrary to the stereotype of rural depopulation following enclosure, the rate of population growth in Hexham's rural hinterland roughly matched that of the town in the late seventeenth century. A network of spinners and weavers fed the cloth industry and new fulling or 'walk' mills for thickening woven cloth were erected on the fast flowing streams feeding northwards into the Tyne.[20] A marked increase in lead mining in the late seventeenth century must largely explain the dramatic increase in the population of Allendale of around 50% between the 1673 hearth tax assessment and the first decade of the eighteenth century.[21] Lead was also mined above Acomb in St. John Lee parish, and the same period witnessed the development of a cluster of lead smelting mills on the Rowley Burn and Devil's Water in the Shire and in Slaley parish. The lead industry was financed largely by investment from Newcastle

[17] Documented in a Chancery Court case: TNA C10/346/10.

[18] NCH IV, pp. 139-40; Nether Warden: NRO 672/A/16/60.

[19] NRO QSB 19, Easter Sessions, Morpeth, 1703, doc. **8**.

[20] For example a fulling mill was established at LambShield by at least 1709 and there were two at Blackhall by 1706, and possibly earlier in both cases (HPR baptisms and burials), both located in the Shire on tributary streams of Devil's Water.

[21] Adjusting the number of households assessed or exempted from the 1673 hearth tax by an allowance for those excluded altogether on grounds of poverty, and comparing with the average number of baptisms in the 1670s suggest a total population of around 1,300: TNA E179/158/110 r29,33d-34; annual average registered baptisms of 60.8 between 1700-11 would indicate a population of around 1,950 in Allendale during that decade.

merchants, further tightening trading links between Tyneside and this supposedly isolated and backward inland area.

The structure of local society was not heavily dominated by the aristocracy and gentry. The Radcliffes, Earls of Derwentwater, were rich and prominent landowners with a principal seat nearby, Dilston Hall, and significant estates to the east, west and south of Hexhamshire, but they had little land within the Regality and, as Catholics, took no part in the county's government through the Quarter Sessions. The same was true of lesser gentry such as the Erringtons of Beaufront Castle. The lord of Hexhamshire certainly had influence given the size, property, mineral rights, market tolls and manor court fees of the manor. Between 1632 and 1689 it was owned by the Fenwicks of Wallington. The family's fortunes had been ailing for some decades before Sir John Fenwick sold out to the 'new money' of the astute businessman Sir William Blackett II, a member of the foremost of the Newcastle merchant families developing the lead industry and establishing themselves as Northumberland gentry.[22] However, while the manor's landed property was extensive, most was let on customary terms, which gave great security of tenure to its occupiers, the 'copyholders.'

The numerous copyholders within Hexhamshire therefore carried a great deal of weight within local society. While many of them occupied holdings of land or houses within the town too small to make them well off, they paid fixed 'ancient rents' typically already far below their market value a century before, and as we have seen Hexham grew and prospered over the course of the seventeenth century.[23] They therefore shared a degree of independence with the 110 Hexhamshire freeholders who appear in the poll books as owning enough property to vote, an independence that might go some way to explain the rumbustious reputation of the town. Some of this middling group of independent farmers,

---

[22] In the period covered by this correspondence there were two Blacketts of the same name, father (William II) and son (William III). See ABN.

[23] A survey of the manor for James I in 1608 concluded that the true value of the land was nearly four times the rent paid to the manor: NCH III, p. 103. The success of Hexhamshire's copyholders in resisting subsequent attempts to change their tenancies to terms more favourable to the manor preserved their independence, and distinguished them from those of many other communities elsewhere in Northumberland: S.J.Watts, *From Border to Middle Shire: Northumberland 1586-1625* (1975), p.164.

craftsmen and traders felt confident enough to style themselves 'Mr', pushing themselves alongside the local lawyers, land agents, teachers, and physicians on the verges of respectable society.

It is beyond the scope of this work to assess the relative size of this 'middle class' compared to the precarious wage labourers and the poor. The numbers of the latter group can be assumed to have risen as a result of inwards migration in the decades before 1700. However, while economic dynamism does not preclude widespread poverty, the nature and pace of Hexhamshire's development, and the ability of the town to support a Grammar School and a range of professions at the turn of the century, give reason enough to treat claims of abject local want with some caution. In 1712, in Ritschel's view, there were about 120 poor people in the town deserving of annual payment from a recently established charity.[24] Even if this is taken to mean households rather than individuals, it would represent perhaps a quarter of the town's population. In the context of the times this is not consistent with Smith's view that the inhabitants were 'miserably poor for the most part'.[25] A measure of quiet prosperity is reflected in the number of contemporary buildings which survive around Hexham town centre today. When she passed through in 1698 Celia Fiennes described it as 'built of stone and looks very well' and thought it the best in Northumberland except for Newcastle.[26]

Hexhamshire might have been perceived in an earlier age as suffering from the depredations of border reivers' lawlessness and banditry, but if this diverted elsewhere the attentions of tax-seeking authorities, the local population would have seen little reason to gainsay it. Faced with fiscal demands from York, Ritschel used a similar tactic. His frequent references in the 1710s to 'the late decay in the lead trade' might give the impression of terminal decline, but almost certainly reflected no more than one of the periodic downturns in a volatile industry that was still in the early stages of long term local expansion.

---

[24] Notes given in the parish register in respect of the 1707 bequest of Margaret Allgood to the poor of Hexham: NRO EP 184/5. This is followed by lists of those in receipt of the charity in each of the four town wards between 1712-9, from which more could be learned of the incidence of poverty in Hexham at the time.

[25] Smith, p.12.

[26] C. Morris (ed), *The Illustrated Journeys of Celia Fiennes*, (1982), p.175.

During this period Hexham was the most important town and market between Newcastle and Carlisle. It was never a chartered urban borough, perhaps because of its distinctive administrative past as a Liberty independent of Northumberland. Instead its civil affairs were run by a combination of the Hexham parish vestry, generally known as the 'Four and Twenty', and the manor, the surviving remnant of the Liberty. Their precise division of responsibilities remains unclear although the Four and Twenty levied the rates and – amongst other things- the manor courts regulated the market, attempted to licence 'incomers', and dealt with minor public order offences and bye-law infringements.[27] It was a confusing and vaguely defined hybrid of bodies and geographic boundaries, but saved from utter dysfunction by being largely in the hands of a small and self-perpetuating body of men. Hexham's independent middle class, the long established leather trade guilds, and other leading tradesmen and minor gentry dominated membership of the Four and Twenty.[28] They were criticised by Ritschel as 'the grand predominant clan in town' from whom the governors of the Grammar School were also selected.[29]

With his varied business interests centred on Newcastle and position as an MP, William Blackett II had little direct involvement in the manor of Hexham. Local power was devolved to the bailiff, who presided over the manor courts. This comprised a number of sub-courts, one of which, the self-styled 'borough court' was responsible for the town. Its jury was typically drawn from or selected by the same small group that ran the Four and Twenty. For much of the seventeenth and early eighteenth centuries the office of bailiff passed between just two families – the Carrs, many of whom were Catholics, and the Allgoods, influential lawyers in Hexham and later of Nunwick.[30] They were effectively the leaders of Hexhamshire's tight knit 'grand predominant clan'. According to Andrewes 'the [Manor] Bayliff as deputed by the vestry of 24 Receives what [rates] the churchwardens collect; they account to him; the people murmur at the great abuses that are made of this parish fund; and that no publick account is ever made of it.' [31]

---

[27] Rossiter, *Seventeenth Century*, *op cit*, pp.172-5.

[28] *ibid*, p. 221.

[29] BIA Pec.Hex/4/3

[30] Rossiter, *Seventeenth Century*, *op cit,* pp.173-4. See ABN.

[31] Andrewes to Jubb, 30 July 1719, doc. **109**.

The Archbishop's Peculiar of Hexhamshire

For church purposes most of Northumberland lay within the diocese of Durham but Hexhamshire had long been associated with the archbishop of York. The manor was part of the archbishop's estate until 1545 when Archbishop Holgate was obliged by Henry VIII to exchange it for land elsewhere.[32] Ecclesiastically, however, it remained the direct responsibility of the archbishop of York, one of the geographic outliers of diocesan jurisdiction known as peculiars. As we have seen, the Hexhamshire Peculiar comprised the parish of Hexham itself and the parochial chapelries of Allendale and St. John Lee, effectively independent parishes by 1700, served by their own curates.

The parish clergy had a contemporary importance beyond their spiritual duties. England's comprehensive map of parishes might have encompassed a wide range of sizes, and idiosyncrasies in the appointment of their clergy, not to mention their calibre, but nothing else could provide as standard a pattern replicated at local level across the country. It was an important network through which the tendrils of government could reach down to monitor, police and tax its people. Local clergymen therefore acted as recorders of baptisms, marriages and burials, as the licencing authority for education, marriage, death and inheritance, and –it was hoped-providers of a moral compass to their flock. Parish vestries, churchwardens and constables were responsible for levying rates, moving on the poor from other parishes, and –it was also hoped-mending the roads. The parish clergy were the district commissioners of a remote central state. Joining their ranks could for some mean the prospect of a comfortable life and an elegant parsonage house. For the more numerous it held out the hope of at least being able to exploit the right to secure a variety of fees from a captive local market. Amongst them must also have been those with a sense of vocation who took a close pastoral interest in their parishioners' spiritual lives and welfare.

---

[32] C.Cross,'The Economic problems of the See of York: Decline and Recovery in the Sixteenth Century' in J.Thirsk (ed), *Land, Church and People, Essays presented to Professor H.P.R.Finberg*, (1970), p.64. The origins of York's involvement with this distant estate in Northumberland are explored in R.Walterspacher, *The Foundation of Hexham Priory, 1070-1170*, North East of England History Insituitute, Paper no. 11 (2002).

The clergy might have been expected to act on behalf of the distant state, but they were appointed through a bewildering range of 'presentation' rights, the ownership of which were the accident of history, inheritance and sale. Even those that remained in the gift of the church itself might have no connection with the diocese to which the parish belonged, and the only control exercised by the church's own elaborate chain of command was to licence the men presented to the various parishes or living. In the absence of a labour market to match aspiring clerics with vacant positions, appointments were inevitably a matter of personal connection, favour, or purchase.

Before its dissolution in 1537 Hexham Priory held the right to appoint the parish priests. They were 'perpetual curates', whose appointment could not subsequently be revoked. These rights of presentation of the curates formed part of the dissolved priory's Hexhamshire property which was sold by the Crown in 1579 and ended up with the Fenwicks, and thence to the Blacketts.[33] Sir William II was disappointed to discover in 1699 that he could not turn Ritschel out of his position as perpetual curate of Hexham.[34] The church could do no more than grant their licences– and it wasn't always clear that the curates actually had them. John Laidman, presented as perpetual curate of Hexham in 1717 by his wife's cousin Sir William Blackett III, was unlicenced and absent from Hexham for long periods.[35] James Laing, curate of Allendale, was presented to the church court by his churchwardens in 1725 for 'officiating without a licence and refusing to Exhibit his order'. He was dismissed and according to Andrewes that summer 'frequently visits Hexham and marrys persons … in our publick houses.'[36]

The tithes, that tenth of all produce which was due to each English parish ostensibly to support the fabric of the church and its ministers, had also been granted to Hexham Priory. They too ultimately made their way into private hands, but as a gesture towards the needs of the local church, the Crown grant of 1579 reserved a portion of its residual annual income or fee farm rent on the estate to provide for the curates in Hexham and its dependant

[33] The curacy of Allendale was, however, in the gift of the Radcliffes of Dilston: Gooch, *op cit*, p. ix.

[34] NCH III, p.170.

[35] Andrewes to Jubb, 6 Sept 1718, doc. **93**, Fenwick et al to Jubb, 29 March 1719, doc. **98**.

[36] BIA Pec.Hex/1, Andrewes to Jubb, 19 July 1725, doc. **150**.

chapelries. In 1703 Ritschel wrote to Archbishop Sharp with a survey of the income of each parish within Hexhamshire and several others nearby, a transcript of which is included in this volume as it gives us a valuable summary of the position then. In Allendale this amounted to some £20-£25 each year in total, in St. John Lee to £18, and in Hexham £13 6s8d. The St. John Lee stipend was achieved by adding the £4 left under the Crown grant in respect of the then derelict chapels of St. Mary at Bingfield and St. Oswald at Heavenfield.[37] In each case the curate would also have taken the surplice fees for baptisms, marriages and burials, but these were carefully regulated by the parish vestries and in Hexham's case even carefully documented by the manorial borough court jury.[38]

Such meagre sums are hardly likely to have attracted clergy of high calibre, and it is unlikely that John Laidman and James Laing were the only unlicenced and unsatisfactory curates to have tried their chances in Hexhamshire. Not all were unlearned. Robert Patten, the Allendale Jacobite, was a graduate of Glasgow University, as was Leonard Bentham, curate of St. John Lee for forty years before his death in 1720.[39] His successor there was the recently ordained Edward Twedale, who supplemented his income with the curacies of Corsenside and Thockrington and later the mastership of Hexham Grammar School. While pluracy (the concurrent holding of multiple parishes and the non-residence it implied) was officially frowned upon, it was at least more acceptable than the practice of undertaking swift marriages by private arrangement and personal fee, for which Twedale was presented to the church court in 1720.[40] In this he was following Bentham's long established practice, many examples of whose corruption feature in the correspondence to York.

On the other hand, the will of John Toppin, Allendale's curate from around 1728 to 1756, reveals an interest in the spiritual welfare of his flock, in the form of bequests of money for books to Allendale School, of which he was the master. The school was a recent charitable foundation, established with local support in 1704. Toppin had hoped to found another school at Ninebanks in the West

---

[37] NCH IV, p.129.

[38] For example in 1702: NRO 672/A/3/40.

[39] Patten: Bishop Gomme, 'Bishop Nicholson's diaries', *Cumb. and West. Antiq. and Arch. Soc.* N.S. ii., (1902) 20 Sept 1702. Bentham: NCH IV, p.131. He was ordained in York in 1676: BI, Inst. AB 7, Episcopal Act Book.

[40] NCH IV, p.134. He was also presented for repeated drunkenness in 1725.

Allen valley. He was another cleric who spread himself thinly, however, being also the minister at Alston in the diocese of Durham, some distance and a difficult journey away across the fells.[41] In Hexham, the evidence of George Ritschel's letters and various appeals to York suggest that Ritschel too had some genuine interest in his parishioners. He was an Oxford graduate, as was Thomas Andrewes, who came to Hexham after Ritschel's death. Neither of them had to rely upon the meagre curate's stipend and surplice fees, for they held the much more lucrative post of Lecturer of Hexham. This had been established in 1628 thanks to a bequest from the Mercers' Company of London to Hexham and other northern parishes to support 'the preaching of the word of God'. It was worth some £80 per year, the income derived from a variety of tithes purchased through the original bequest, and made the Lecturer of Hexham easily the best remunerated clergyman in Tynedale.[42] The stature of the Lecturer made him the obvious person in the Peculiar to oversee the administrative responsibilities of the church, and act as the local link into the elaborate hierarchy of the national ecclesiastical establishment.

Church Business in Hexhamshire

In addition to the registration of baptisms, marriages and burials, the church exercised official responsibility over considerable swathes of everyday life. This work included both routine administration and the holding of the ecclesiastical courts. The survey given here simplifies the complicated ecclesiastical structures and procedure in order to give sufficient context to the correspondence, much of which is concerned with court and routine administration. For those wishing to explore the rich social and family history potential of church court documents in greater depth, Anne Tarver's reference book is an invaluable guide.[43]

---

[41] Shuler, p.399; NCH IV, p.84; E. Mackenzie, *View of the County of Northumberland*, second edition, Volume 2, (1825), p.303.

[42] G. Huelin, *Think and Thank God, the Mercers' Company and its contribution to the Church and religious life since the Reformation*, (1996), pp. 51-3; NCH III, pp. 166-7.

[43] Anne Tarver, *Church Court Records, An introduction for family and local historians*, (1995). Smith, *op cit*, pp. 16-22 describes these responsibilities in his study of the Hexhamshire correspondence but in view of the scarcity

Routine Administration

Routine administration included the issue of marriage licences and the management of probate business. **Marriage licences** were attractive to those seeking speed or secrecy, thereby avoiding the publicity following from banns being called in church on three successive Sundays. A marriage licence was obtained from the diocesan authorities. One of the parties appeared before the bishop's chancellor or official and swore upon oath that there was no impediment to the marriage, and that they belonged to the diocesan jurisdiction. The oath was backed up by a bond entered into by two witnesses as guarantors.[44] In the case of Hexhamshire, the diocesan officials in distant York appointed the Lecturer as their 'commissary' to verify that the happy couple lived within the Peculiar, take the oath and bonds, and collect the fee. Although apparently sometimes open to negotiation, the fee appears to have been around £1, a sum which put marriage by licence beyond the means of most people. Between August 1708 and December 1710, a period for which a complete account of such licences is given in an abstract of court business in Hexham of 1710, there were 16 in total. This was just 15% of the 105 marriages registered in the Peculiar during the same period.[45] A portion of the fee was retained by the commissary for his trouble and the rest sent to York with the oaths and bonds. Licences were then returned to be issued prior to the marriage. As with all legal documents, they incurred stamp duty under the 'temporary' tax introduced in 1694 to prosecute the war with France. Blank stamped licences were issued to the commissary to simplify the process. It is no surprise, given their intrinsic value, and with stamp tax paid, that these were doled out from York sparingly. Many of the letters in this collection ask for more 'blanks' or 'stamps' from York.

The role of the church in overseeing last wills and testaments, and the disposal of the goods and chattels of the

---

of the booklet they are summarised again here. The first few pages of his work are available online in Google Books: http://www.books.google.co.uk.

[44] A useful guide to the process as it was administered in the adjacent diocese of Durham can be found at http://www.durhamrecordoffice .org.uk/Pages/MarriageLicencesBondsandAllegations.aspx.

[45] Doc. **36**; HPR, and St. John Lee, Allendale: NRO EP 1/2.

deceased, has been discussed extensively elsewhere.[46] **Probate business** within the diocese of York was a matter for the exchequer court, presided over by the chancellor, but most routine work was delegated to his 'surrogate'. Acting as the court's agent, the Hexham surrogate took the oaths and bonds of the deceased's next-of-kin and executors along with the inventories they were expected to have taken, proved wills, took the fees and sent documents and money to York. The court registrar then sent back the grants of probate, or letters of administration in the absence of a will, to be given to executors. The settling of estates was a much valued service provided by the church, forestalling family disputes and settling up debts. As with marriage licences, the evidence of the Hexham correspondence is that the fee was around £1, with a negotiable portion for the surrogate.

The Church Courts

Church of England courts operated under canon law. While this was subordinate to English common law it was wide ranging in its scope, dealing with disputed wills and administrations, moral offences, and the spiritual discipline of the personnel of the church and their parishioners. This extended to non-payment of church rates and not attending church on Sunday or otherwise "profaning the Sabbath", as well as sexual misconduct. Church courts were therefore one of the means available through which social order might be maintained. The records which survive today contain vivid examples of the eternal frailty of human nature. [47] Cases –strictly termed causes- brought by the church or its officers were termed 'office causes', but people could use the church court machinery to

---

[46] See for example, Karen Grannum and Nigel Taylor, *Wills and Probate Records* (2nd ed, 2009), or T.Arkell, 'The Probate Process', in T. Arkell, N. Evans and N. Goose, (eds), *When Death Do Us Part.* (2000). A simple online guide to the process and records for the diocese of Durham is provided at http://familyrecords.dur.ac.uk/nei/index.htm.

[47] The large quantity of cause papers from the early modern period retained in diocesan registries are a rich research source. Those in York have recently been opened up and made far more accessible through the creation of the Cause Papers Database, available at http://www.hrionline .ac.uk/causepapers. This also includes a succinct guide to the operation of the church courts both at local level and the higher courts in York itself. See also J.A.Sharpe, *Defamation and Sexual Slander in Early Modern England: The Church Courts at York*, Borthwick Papers, 58, (1980).

bring their own cases, 'instance causes', as long as the charges brought had a moral dimension within the meaning of canon law. This could include defamation, but not theft or assault, which came under the common law and civil courts.

Because the Hexham correspondence is from ministers and officers of the church, the focus is on office causes. They originate from 'presentments' of alleged wrongdoers, mostly brought forward by each parish's churchwardens. The court judge, registrar, or his delegate then decided whether to issue a citation to the accused committing them to appear at the next court sitting. This was often enough to persuade those cited to settle out of court and mend their ways, to avoid the expense of court fees and proctors (church lawyers) and the inconvenience of appearing at what could be distant court sittings. For causes pursued to successful prosecutions the punishments available under canon law were restricted to penance and excommunication. The deliberate public humiliation of penance remained common practice in the 18th century, remaining a channel for community regulation of moral behaviour. This Hexham example from 1720 is one of many. See also Figure 9.

> 'The said Jane Simpson shall be present in the church …in the Time of Divine Service ... In the presence of the whole Congregation …being bare-head, bare-foot, and bare-leg'd, having a White Sheet wraped about her from the Shoulders to the Feet, and a White Wand in her Hand, where … she shall stand upon some Form or Seat before the Pulpit …and say after him as followeth. Whereas I good people forgetting my Duty to Almighty God, have committed the Detestable Sin of Fornication with John Davison of the parish of Hexham and thereby have justly provoked the heavy wrath of God against me, to the great danger of my own Soul, and evil example of others, I do earnestly repent, and am heartily sorry for the same..' [48]

John Davison did not appear. The penalty for such contempt, or contumacy, was temporary exclusion from church services. Repeated contumacy led to excommunication. This took two forms. Lesser excommunication meant exclusion from the church and all its sacraments for a time, normally a few weeks, sometimes for years, and could mean denial of the right to burial on consecrated ground.

[48] BIA, Pec.Hex/1, Visitation Court papers, 22 May 1720.

Those subject to greater excommunication were excluded from the company of all Christians; anyone having dealings with them could also be subject to lesser excommunication.

The church court for the Archbishop's Peculiar of Hexhamshire sat twice each year. A Visitation Court was held at Whitsun, which the clergy and churchwardens were expected to attend. This was the occasion for the annual appointment of new churchwardens in each parish. Before the outgoing churchwardens were released from their duties they were to attend the court to give answers to the articles of visitation, 'pre-inspection' questions regarding the state of the Peculiar, its churches and clergy.[49] They also handed in their presentments of offenders for the court to consider citation and, most importantly, paid their 'dismission fees,' collected from the church rate assessments of the previous year. The amount expected, and their payment by the churchwardens, were bones of some contention between Hexham and York. There was a particularly acrimonious dispute between 1712 and 1714.[50] Churchwardens can perhaps be forgiven for trying their best to avoid this periodic duty of having to collect money from their neighbours and send them to court.

People thus cited, including delinquent outgoing churchwardens, were normally summoned to a sitting of the Correction Court, usually held in November. Tracking them down fell to the court summoner, the apparitor, who was often another local clergyman. The Hexham courts were traditionally held in the church itself, presumably the better to impress upon those who transgressed the sombre importance of canon law and the omnipotence of the established church. However in one of his letters Ritschel makes clear that sittings had also been held in the town's post house, and he suggested holding them in his own house to save expense.[51]

The key officials who operated the court machine were the spiritual chancellor of the diocese and the registrar. As the most senior lawyer, the chancellor presided over the church courts and was responsible for the entire machinery of diocesan administration.

---

[49] An example of these 'Books of Articles' is given as doc. **42**, with the largely anodyne responses set out in Ritschel's hand and countersigned by the outgoing churchwardens.

[50] Docs. **49**, **50**, **60-1**, **67**, **72**, **74-5**, **77-8**. See also Smith, pp.19-22, on this dispute.

[51] Ritschel to Jubb, 13 April 1713,doc. **58**.

As Shuler put it in his study of the diocese of Durham, the chancellor was 'almost always a man of some distinction, with connections in the intricate worlds of the temporal and ecclesiastical law, and his presence in London may not unfairly be assumed for the vast majority of the time.'[52] The York chancellor between 1673 and 1713 was Dr. Henry Watkinson of Leeds, succeeded on his death aged 83 by his son-in-law William Pearson.[53] This was a position of sufficient grandeur to be worth keeping in the family, although in 1716 it passed to the relatively youthful qualified ecclesiastical lawyer Dr. John Audley, possibly through the good offices of the Duchess of Ormonde. He was an absentee chancellor for much of his long reign.[54]

The registrar –often referred to as the 'register' – was the clerk of the church courts, issuing citations, maintaining the court records, including the vast amount of probate documentation, and charged with collecting the expected diocesan revenue from fees and licences. The York registrar was responsible for a number of courts across the diocese and diligent occupants of the office required a great deal of stamina and administrative efficiency, as well as a keen understanding of canon law. This is evidently not what John Aislaby had in mind when he succeeded his father George as registrar in 1675. Aislaby senior had married the widow of the previous registrar, and 'improved' the value of the office from £500 to £2,000 a year – a substantial inheritance for his son, in addition to a landed estate near Ripon. Aislaby junior sub-let the office, concentrating on his estates and his later role as an MP.[55] By the time of our correspondence the deputy registrar overseeing the work was Thomas Empson. [56] His successor was the efficient Thomas Jubb, a biography of whom is given later in this Introduction.

For men such as Watkinson, Pearson, and the Aislabys, senior church positions in a rich bishopric such as York were seen as marks

---

[52] Shuler, p. 248.

[53] R.V.Taylor, *The biographia leodiensis; or, Biographical sketches of the worthies of Leeds and neighbourhood*, (1865), p.18. See ABN

[54] W. Gibson, ' "Good Mr. Chancellor," The Work of Dr. John Audley, Chancellor of York, 1710-1744', *The Yale University Library Gazette*, Vol. 73, No. 1/2 (1998), p. 32; Till, Study, pp. 221-2.

[55] Till, *Courts*, pp. 17-8. Aislaby went on to become Chancellor of the Exchequer until disgraced by his part in the South Sea bubble.

[56] See ABN.

of distinction for the second or third generation of prospering merchant families, and – for the registrars at least- a valuable source of income. Actually sitting in the courts as chancellor and registrar was to be delegated, especially if it could avoid visiting an outpost as far-flung as the Peculiar of Hexhamshire twice a year. The chancellor's 'surrogate' who presided over his courts was usually the Hexham lecturer, and the deputy registrar of York came to an arrangement with John Rowell, for nearly forty years one of the Durham registrars, to visit Hexham in his place in return for half the registrar's fees.[57] On the very day of Rowell's death one of the Durham proctors, Peter Burrell, wrote to Empson to offer his services, so great was his eagerness for the post. Over the years that followed, Burrell and Ritschel each tried to persuade York to dispense with the other's services and allow them free reign in Hexhamshire, reflected in several letters in the correspondence in this volume. Thomas Andrewes, as Lecturer and surrogate judge, appeared to have a much more harmonious working relationship with York registrar Jubb, who even visited Hexham on a few occasions, and might at other times have trusted Andrewes with dispatching the registrar's role.

The State of the Church of England

Having set out the structure of the church court machinery, it is important to understand the problems which beset its operation locally against the background of the state of the church in the late seventeenth and early eighteenth century. Nationally, this was a period of declining influence for the Church of England. While the church might still have provided the 'architectural centrepiece to the community' across an England where over 90% of the population might formally be considered members, many were increasingly disengaged from its ministry, especially the labouring poor.[58] The pace and nature of this might vary across the country but one of Ritschel's laments in 1712 allows us to hazard a guess as to its extent in Hexham. 'Before ye late unhappy civil wars … always about a thousand communicated at Easter, but now we have not halfe ye number.' [59] As we have seen, the population of the parish had

[57] Shuler, p.288, Smith, p.18.

[58] J.Hoppit, *A Land of Liberty? England 1689-1727*, (2000), p. 208; K.Wrightson, *English Society 1580-1680*, (1982), pp.218-20.

[59] Ritschel to Jubb, 25 Feb 1712, doc.**47**.

increased greatly during this time. If Ritschel was right then Easter attendance fell from around four fifths of the adult population in the 1640s to under a quarter by 1712.[60] Attendance at this later date was, if anything, slightly better than other examples quoted by Hoppitt from Pewsey in Wiltshire (20%) and the diocese of Ely (12% in 1728.)

It is unsurprising to find that the business of the church courts was also in decline. The number of causes tried at the Chester Consistory Court halved between 1680 and the 1730s, and by as much in just a few years in Hereford in the immediate aftermath of the Glorious Revolution of 1688/9. 'Instance work', causes brought by members of the public, was especially vulnerable since the common law courts offered an alternative to the slow and potentially costly church courts. This left the church's own causes, including those instigated by presentments by churchwardens, as a means to sustain its own level of business. However, in an era when the legitimacy of the church to continue governing the daily lives of the population was increasingly questioned, churchwardens can be forgiven for neglecting to denounce every last sin of the people they lived amongst. Presentments at Carlisle fell by nearly 40% between the 1700s and 1720s.[61]

The Hexham evidence is mixed. Looking back to 1689 from a quarter of a century later, Ritschel noted in the parish register that 'the Parish affairs [began] to run into confusion when both churchwardens and jurors takeing advantage of the distraction of the times and liberty of conscience began to despise our visitation court.' The surviving papers show that many did not turn up at the court. Doubtless there were many who shared the lack of concern of Thomas Hemsley of St. John Lee in 1715 who was 'saucy & sd If he had the Excom[munication] he wd have burnt it.' Far from living in awe of the moral authority of the established church, offenders in Hexham, according to Ritschel, 'regard us no more than we do the thunder of the Vatican.' [62] Such local vignettes lend support to Till's

---

[60] The population of Hexham parish in the 1640s is estimated from burial and marriage totals in the parish registers and the ratios calculated by the Cambridge Group. Nationally, some 30% of the population was under the age of communion: E.Wrigley and R.Schofield, *The Population History of England, 1541-1871*, (1981), pp. 216, 565-6. For 1712 see page 3 above.

[61] Hoppit, *op cit*, p.225, Till, *Courts*, p.30.

[62] Hemsley: Ritschel to Jubb, 31 Mar 1715, doc. **83**; Vatican thunder: Ritschel to Jubb, 13 April 1711, doc. **40**.

conclusion in his study of the period that 'the Church of England had ceased to be the church of the nation and had become a sect.'[63]

There were, of course, other sects offering a different path to God for those who still sought it. A century and a half after the Reformation, Catholicism remained active, if only accounting for perhaps 1% of the population nationally. Northumberland was seen as a traditional hotbed of 'popery' and the influence in Tynedale of gentry families such as the Swinburnes of Capheaton, the Erringtons of Beaufront and especially the Radcliffes of Dilston might have sustained the ancient faith in the area. In Hexhamshire, Catholicism must have accounted for more than the 1% of the population which Gooch estimates for the Durham diocese as a whole, for this would have meant only fifteen or so families.[64] In 1743 they were said to have accounted for nearly 6% of the families in Hexham parish.[65] Whatever the actual number, they did not constitute an isolated seditious sect. Catholics witnessed the church baptisms of their neighbours and occupied manorial offices. The Erringtons of Beaufront offered in 1714 to help repair the dilapidated chapel at Bingfield, and the Hexham minister thought it worth noting in the churchwardens account book that one of the church rate collectors had done his job well "tho a papist".[66] For all the religious overtones of the 1715 Jacobite rebellion it was not a Catholic plot. As we have seen, it was the protestant curate of Allendale who led the preaching.

Protestant dissenters might have been accorded undue national influence by the prominence of large congregations in and around London, and long memories of the explosion of religious dissent and myriad sects during the disruptions of the civil war and Commonwealth period. A recent survey suggests that the number of nonconforming dissenters rose by over 50% nationally between 1680 and 1720, accounting for around 6% of the population by the latter date.[67] The view from inside many of the more established dissenting

---

[63] Hoppit, *op cit*, p.209; Till, *Courts*, p.11.

[64] Gooch, *op cit*, p. 23.

[65] S.L.Ollard, P.C.Walker, (eds), *Archbishop Herring's Visitation Returns, 1743, Volume 3*, Yorkshire Arch Society, Record Series, Vol LXXV (1929), p.249.

[66] NRO EP 184/68.

[67] C.D.Field, 'Counting Religion in England and Wales: The Long Eighteenth Century, c. 1680–c.1840', *The Journal of Ecclesiastical History*, Vol 63, Issue 4 (October 2012), pp.710-11.

faiths was, however, more often of concern over falling numbers of adherents, and for their future.[68] In the Hexham area small congregations of Baptists had been present since the 1650s, and Quakers were active in Allendale, where 21 were convicted for non-payment of tithes in 1711.[69] As with the Presbyterians in the 1690s, other dissenting faiths in Tynedale might have been sustained by connections with Newcastle. The Presbyterians had established a meeting house in Hexham by 1703 and were moving further westwards.[70] The little evidence we have suggests that the dissenters accounted for perhaps 5-8% of Hexham's population in the 1710s.[71] In 1743, however, the visitation returns for Hexham counted 83 Presbyterian families alone, nearly 11% of the total.[72]

Despite the reach of the Church of England's hierarchical structure down through the network of parishes by which the state operated locally, its bishops were keenly aware that their traditional role at the centre of English society was under threat. It is worth sketching the outline of how national political developments affected the church during this period for they were not lost on the inhabitants of Hexham. Permissive legislation was blamed by many churchmen for allowing people increased freedom of expression. Successive royal declarations of indulgence under Charles II and James II, although intended to give a degree of toleration to Catholics and dissenters, also signalled to others that they need not attend any church at all on Sundays. And while the accession of the protestant William III in the 'Glorious Revolution' of 1688 appeared to remove the threat to the church of resurgent Catholicism, the following year's Act of Toleration disturbingly granted freedom of worship to all protestants who pledged allegiance to the new regime.

---

[68] Hoppit, *op cit*, pp. 219-20.
[69] NCH IV, p.83.
[70] A.Yeo, 'The diary of Elizabeth Gill', *HH*, 19 (2009), pp. 2-37. Elizabeth Gill was the daughter of a Presbyterian minister in Hexham and her diary gives an interesting insight into dissent in the town during this period, and into her own religious fervour. See Ritschel to Sharp, 6th March 1704, doc. **9**, on their meeting house.
[71] 25 dissenting wives of childbearing age in 1712 were listed in the Hexham parish register, amounting to perhaps 5-8% of the total equivalent households: NRO EP 184/5. Further study might reveal whether the religious affiliations of the leading tradesmen nevertheless gave dissenters influence beyond their small numbers.
[72] Ollard and Walker, *op cit,* p.249.

Fear that the church was in danger stimulated a vigorous reaction over the next two decades. A focus on the theatre of politics through which to achieve this was perhaps natural given the bishops' membership of the House of Lords. Some attempt was made to reach 'hearts and minds', such as through the Society for Promoting Christian Knowledge from 1698, and some of the new bishops appointed by William III sought to improve pastoral provision.[73] The Queen Anne's Bounty fund was set up in 1704, through which revenues collected from richer clergy were placed in a fund to be distributed amongst the poorer, with the intention of improving the ability of the latter to minister to their parishes.[74] Intellectual and theological arguments for the primacy of the Church of England were made with confidence by 'High Church' leaders, whose number included Archbishop John Sharp of York. It helped to delineate national political affiliations, with the Tory party championing the active protection and promotion of the church in distinction to the Whigs, who were portrayed as far less zealous in support of the traditional order. The impeachment and trial by the Whig government of the outspoken High Church preacher Dr Henry Sacheverell in 1709 for railing against the Act of Toleration, the growth of 'heresy and schism', Whigs and dissenters, ignited strong popular reaction which led to a Tory ascendancy in Parliament during the final years of the reign of Queen Anne. The same period witnessed a growth of various societies for the 'reformation of manners', self-appointed guardians of moral standards driving miscreants to the disciplines available through the church courts. In an attempt to reverse the drift from the church, an act outlawing 'occasional conformity' was passed in 1711. Ultimately, however, the association of some Tories with the Jacobite rebellion following the accession of George I in 1714 discredited the party, and under the longer Whig ascendancy which followed the influence of the church on the national political stage went back into gentle decline.[75]

All of this had a great deal of resonance in Hexham. Ritschel blamed the decline in respect for the church on the declarations of Indulgence and the Act of Toleration. He claimed to have been

---

[73] T.Claydon, *Europe and the Making of England 1660-1760*, (2007), p.327.

[74] Hoppit, *op cit*, pp. 237-8, 240. Ritschel's letter to Archbishop Sharp, 2 March 1704, doc. **10**, was his grant application to this new fund on behalf of Tynedale.

[75] Hoppit, *op cit*, pp.231-40 gives a useful summary of the church and national politics during this period.

victimised by the staunch Whig Sir William Blackett II and his Hexham bailiff Thomas Allgood for daring to vote for the Tory William Forster in the 1698 general election instead of Sir William's relative Sir Edward Blackett, heroically adding that 'I shall not desert Mr Forsters interest so long as he is for the Ch[urch]s interest.' [76] As we have seen above, election campaigns could be intimidating and highly charged affairs in Hexham, where the pattern of property ownership developed over previous generations had given more than 100 men the vote in elections of Northumberland's M.P.s.[77] The troubled 1723 by-election saw Whig supporters in the town accused as 'King killers and kirk sellers', combative allusions demonstrating continued popular anger at the execution of Charles I eighty years before and of presbyterian threats to the established church.

With the state and prospects of the Church of England remaining a contentious marker of respectability and political affiliation in Parliament and in the nation, it is hardly surprising that the bishops saw legislation as a suitable means to compel religious adherence. Few appear to have recognised that putting their own houses in order might also help, and those who did were unable to make much progress.

At York since 1691, Archbishop John Sharp witnessed the corruption and inefficiency that ran through the elaborate system of courts within his diocese. In 1698 the practice of the deputy registrar of the York Exchequer court, Robert Oates, of raising extra money in return for promising to annul excommunications became a public scandal. Oates needed to raise £450 each year to pay the registrar, a Mrs. Whichcott, for the privilege of using his lucrative office. She was making a very handsome return on her own investment in the post of just £1,000 in 1684.[78] Oates claimed that the case against him had been engineered by Thomas Empson, our deputy registrar for the

---

[76] Ritschel to Watkinson, 13 Feb 1699, doc. **3**. It turned out later that Forster's interest was in the restoration of King James, and he led the Jacobite army in 1715.

[77] 113 Hexham men were listed in the 1710 poll book, 9% of the county total. In that year Robert Dawson of Hexham claimed he dared not vote for the Whig Lord Hertford having been 'threatened wth prejudice in his trade and to pull down the front of his House as an Encroachmt.' Sir William Blackett III was a Tory. Hertford gathered just sixteen votes in Hexham that year. *Poll book, op cit,* (1841), pp. 9-45.

[78] Till, *Courts*, p.31.

Hexham courts, with whom he had been feuding over the registrarship of the archdeacon of the East Riding's court.[79] Sharp launched an investigation into the operation of his courts the following year, including such pointed questions as whether the fees were made clear, and whether extra fees were asked for in return for rapid despatch of business. In his vague reply, Chancellor Henry Watkinson either did not know what was going on in the courts over which he had presided since 1673, or had his own reasons for not saying. William Mawde, one of the York proctors, had given up being deputy registrar of the Exchequer Court, presumably because Mrs Whichcott's fee had gone up, and now felt the practice to be an abuse, but Empson thought there was no harm in it. The enquiry dragged on for six years and ended in 1705, rather lamely, with the instruction that the archbishop should approve all deputy registrar and surrogate appointments and that a new table of registrars' fees be made clear in the courts. While Oates was removed, the small and introspective community of church lawyers clustered around Minster Yard continued in place, jostling for such fees as they could take from the shrinking pot offered by church court business. The outbreak of a further extortion scandal in 1728, involving a deputy registrar, showed how limited was the ability of even the archbishop of York to reform his own court machinery and how strong the vested interests which relied upon it.[80] Wholesale change would have to wait until Parliament acted in the 1850s.

Such was the example offered to Hexham by their ecclesiastical superiors. No wonder that Leonard Bentham at St. John Lee felt so little compunction at offering additional paid services to those seeking speed and discretion. For a fee he would mumble the marriage banns in Latin during Sunday service, and was often willing to offer a discount on the cost of licences quoted elsewhere. Challenged by George Ritschel's sister, he 'alleged his place was small and he must make the best of it', which he did for forty years.[81] Neither could it help the image of the church for each visitation and correction court sitting to be followed by a dinner for officials, ministers and churchwardens, which the visiting Peter Burrell was

[79] Till, Study, p.220. See also entry for Empson in ABN.
[80] Till, Study, pp.191-7, 205-12.
[81] Ritschel to Jubb, 17 Dec 1714, doc. **81**, Andrewes to Jubb, 13 Oct 1718, doc. **94**, Ritschel to Jubb, 23 Sept 1714, doc. **79**.

expected to pay for from the fees he had collected as the registrar's delegate.[82]

Another dubious but common practice was to offer the option to those proceeded against in court to have their penance commuted for a monetary consideration. There is evidence enough in his letters that Ritschel's fine judgement of character extended to the associated wallet, and that this had some bearing on the cases he decided to pursue. Ritschel collected £5 from William Pearson in 1715 to 'prevent his being exposed to the world' and asked Jubb if he could keep it to offset fees incurred in another case, swearing that he had had 'not so much as a bottle of wine or pair of gloves' on Pearson's account. [83] The church had claimed it wished to clamp down on the abuse of penance commutation, but it is clear from Ritschel's letter that, in this case at least, he felt under pressure to justify to the York chancellor his reasons for not asking for more money.[84]

In general then, the energies of the church seem to have been devoted more to preserving its vested interests and seeking a legislative route to adherence, rather than the renewal of a spiritual appeal or improved examples of piety. While churchmen such as Sharp might have grasped the need for such reforms, it is likely that a more common attitude was that of the complacent Lancastrian preacher who felt that if the people learnt little, it 'cannot be imputed to the want of good preaching but to the want of good hearing.' [85] It is small wonder that, in an increasingly rational age, a rising proportion of those still seeking God found solace outside the gilded paraphernalia of the established church.

Church finances in Hexhamshire

This difficult background might have been easier for the church to cope with in Hexhamshire had its financial position been more comfortable. As we have seen, the stipends of the curates of the three parishes amounted to slightly under £40, although this could be

[82] See for example Burrell's moan to Jubb on 27 Dec 1711, doc. **45**. The bibulous nature of these dinners is evident from the receipt for November 1714 , doc. **80**.

[83] BIA, Hex/1, Visitation Court papers, 19 Jan 1716; Ritschel to Jubb, 9 Oct 1716, doc **92**.

[84] Ritschel to Chancellor Pearson, 20 Jan 1716, doc **89**.

[85] Quoted in Wrightson, *op cit*, p.216.

added to by various additional fees, legitimate and otherwise. By way of contrast, a rental of the Blackett estate in 1735 shows that the tithes, diverted away from the church, were let for £261 per annum, being worth even more to the 'farmer' who rented these rights.[86]

One of the purposes of tithes was the upkeep of the fabric of the parish church, and if the tithe income moved into private hands so too did this responsibility. Much depended upon the inclinations of the owner. In St. John Lee parish both St. Mary at Bingfield and St. Oswald were derelict. The vast priory church of St. Andrew had served Hexham parish as well as the priory in medieval times, and maintenance responsibility was apparently shared between the parishioners and the inheritor of the priory estate – the lord of the manor.[87] Given this confused situation it is perhaps not surprising that by Ritschel's time there were holes in the roof, cracks had appeared in the masonry and the nave had collapsed completely, leaving the three sided church of early illustrations, sealed up at the west end of the tower (see Figure 4). 'Poor St.Andrew' he wrote,

> 'which a thousand years ago exceeded all the minsters in England; nay all the churches on this side of the ALPS for stately magnificence, through the injuries of time and weather, become a proper object of Christian Compassion; like a poor disconsolate widow in distress, imploring our good Etheldreda and St. Wilfrid, the Crown and Mitre, which first erected it out of the dust, to preserve it from falling down again into it.' [88]

Ritschel launched various restoration initiatives and even laid out money of his own on urgent repairs, only to come up against the disapproval of both the four and twenty of the vestry, and the manor bailiff, effectively claiming that it belonged to the lord of the manor.[89] The vestry was, however, prepared to levy church rates to

---

[86] Uncatalogued Allendale documents.
[87] C.C.Hodges, *The Abbey of St. Andrew: Hexham*, (1888), p.48.
[88] G.Ritschel, *An account of certain charities, containing a catalogue of several benefactors, who have given or left anything to pious and charitables uses, in Tyndale-ward*, (1713), p.62.
[89] In 1700 Ritschel was paid by the vestry for recent work but was forced to agree that 'the sd Mr Ritschell shall not hereafter meddle with the repaires of the church or make any bargaines for repaires or other work' Hexham churchwardens' account book: NRO EP 184/68 p.19.

Figure 3: private pews and galleries in the Church choir, c.1813 (reproduced in Hodges, *Abbey of St. Andrew, op cit,* Plate 7)

raise funds for maintenance of the fabric, but the church remained in a precarious state until major restoration work in the 1720s.[90]

Workmen were certainly busy inside the church in a flurry of activity around 1720 – building private pews and galleries within the Choir, marks of status for the leading townspeople. This was part of a national trend seen with misgiving in some quarters for reasons summed up well by Sir Christopher Wren in 1708: 'A church should not be so filled with pews that the poor may have some room in the alleys to stand and sit in; for to them equally is the Gospel preached. It is to be wished that there were no pews but benches. But there is no stemming the tide of profit, and the advantages of the pew keepers.' [91] As seen in the Hexham correspondence this was also a topic of some concern locally, and it led to presentments of pew builders to the church court in 1723. Andrewes' worry was that pew building was a presumptuous encroachment by Sir William Blackett where ecclesiastical permission and licence should have been obtained. If he additionally had any concern that the poor might feel even more excluded as the public space within the church walls was built over for private use, he did not write to York about it. Andrewes was keen to build his own private pew within that frail cavern of the ancient church before all available space was taken by others (see Figure 3).

A more positive picture emerges from Allendale. The parish church of St. Cuthbert was extended in the second half of the seventeenth century as the population increased, and chapels were built in the higher reaches of the dales to serve the lead miners at Allenheads in 1703, and at Coalcleugh in the West Allen the following year.[92] Sir William Blackett II contributed to the building of the Allenheads and Coalcleugh chapels, but it is striking that there was direct support for the clergy from the local population. The miners gave half a day's wages each month to pay for a curate to preach at Allenheads and Coalcleugh, which was said to have raised upwards of £70 per year when the mines were flourishing. This would have made the curate better remunerated than all but the Hexham lecturer.[93] As it was orchestrated by Blackett's mine agent some caution is called for regarding how voluntary an arrangement

[90] Wright, *op cit,* (1823), p.82.
[91] Quoted in Till, Study, p.237.
[92] NCH IV, p.79; Ritschel, *charities*, *op cit*, pp.58-9.
[93] NCH IV, pp.99-100.

this was, but it was still in place in the 1760s.[94] It seems to have superceded an earlier arrangement whereby four men of the East Allen collected money to pay for a lay reader to lead prayers and the litany at Allenheads. We know this only because the population was unhappy in the 1660s with the performance of the then reader, John Heatherington, and the manor court jury was asked to investigate.[95]

The point here is that money was forthcoming where people could see some direct benefit to their own communities. It was the demand for fees and fines to support remote church officials and lawyers that stoked resentment. And demands there were. Thomas Jubb might have been competent and hard-working compared with previous occupants of the registrar's desk in York, but his outlook towards collecting the church's customary dues was just as zealous, as we have already seen in respect of the churchwardens fees. Andrewes found Edward Foster, outgoing churchwarden of St. Oswald's in 1719, to be insolent when handing over his fees, uttering 'some expressions of reproach and contempt against the [Peculiar] jurisdiction. .. there was noe occasion for all this bustle and trouble we gave them; and that twas only to bring grist to your [ie. Jubb's] mill.' [96] As Peter Burrell started finding his way around the jurisdiction he had been so eager to take on in 1705 he was dismayed to find that the fees hardly made it worth his while, and resorted to sniping about how much Ritschel was accustomed to claiming.[97] The latter was presumably well used to the minimal additional income available from local church administrative work, and somewhat insulated from it by his income as Lecturer. Smith calculates that Ritschel received less than £2 a year from court business, derived from issuing marriage licences, and that this was probably outweighed by expenses it is unlikely he was ever able to recover.[98]

As the local clergy went scrabbling around for additional business they came up against the difficulty that Hexhamshire was a

---

[94] Archdeacon Sharp's survey of the Peculiar, NRO SANT/GEN/ECC/3/3/ 10.

[95] NCH IV, p. 79. It is interesting to note that the local collectors were called proctors, as if in deliberate rustic imitation of remote and lofty church lawyers.

[96] Andrewes to Jubb, 30 July 1719, doc. **109**.

[97] For example, Burrell to Empson, 8 Dec 1705, doc. **18**.

[98] Smith, pp.14-5. See Ritschel's account of his expenses in 1713-4: Ritschel to Jubb, 29 Nov 1714, doc. **80**.

small Peculiar surrounded by the diocese of Durham, populated by ministers equally keen to drum up trade. In 1720 John Coatsworth and Margery Carr were cited to the Correction Court by Andrewes for ante-nuptial fornication, but they produced a licence showing that they had been married at Ovingham under a Durham licence. Andrewes protested to York that they were Hexham people and therefore the Durham surrogate should not have granted the licence. 'I hope you will make them sensible of it; or we shall soon have less use for Licences, If Durham can adopt our people into what parish they think fitt.' [99]

The problem of competing local jurisdictions in the marriage licence market was further complicated by the fact that 'clandestine marriage' was not actually illegal before 1753. Canon law was very clear regarding conditions for church weddings. Banns had to be read or a licence obtained, the wedding had to be in the church of residence of one of the couple, and between 8am and noon, and any party under the age of 21 was to have parental consent. However, either verbal promises to marry (ie. engagement followed by consummation) or the public exchange of vows anywhere remained legal marriages under ecclesiastical law, a confused situation taken advantage of by unscrupulous clergymen such as Edward Twedale, mentioned earlier.[100] None of this, however, prevented the continued vigorous citation of many couples to the Hexham courts for clandestine marriage during the period of our correspondence.

Following the decline in both church attendance and respect for its institutions in the second half of the seventeenth century, the church appears to have been on a more stable footing from the early 1720s in Hexham. On Ritschel's evidence, the number of Easter communicants in 1712 was just under a quarter of Hexham parish's adult population, a figure still matched at Easter 1743.[101] A sample of the Hexham correction court papers from 1729-34 shows that of sixty people presented for various offences some two thirds did actually appear. And for all the complaints about the much higher

[99] Andrewes to Jubb, April 1720, doc. **116**.
[100] L.Stone, *The Family, Sex and Marriage in England 1500-1800*, (Abridged Edition, 1979), pp. 30-2. This was not tidied up until Hardwick's Marriage Act of 1753. A delightful 1560s Allendale example of the earlier folk tradition of 'handfasting' as an accepted betrothal ritual is given in the form of a long description in a church court case quoted in NCH IV, p.82.
[101] Ollard and Walker, *op cit*, p.249.

level of churchwarden dismission fees imposed in the 1710s, the higher amounts were paid, according to fee accounts surviving from the 1720s, and appear not to have been accompanied by much further comment from Andrewes in his letters.[102] The Church of England might have become principally the church of 'respectable' society, of the establishment, but it was now more stable in Hexhamshire, and able still to sustain some respect for its role in maintaining the social order, howsoever grudging. Perhaps this can be explained by the change in the leading personalities at work in the Peculiar, to whom we now turn.

The Hexham correspondents

The main correspondents at the centre of these conflicting pressures were the Hexham Lecturers George Ritschel and Thomas Andrewes, the Durham commissaries Peter Burrell senior and junior, and the recipients of most of the letters in York, court registrar Thomas Jubb. Shorter notices are given in the following chapter of other individuals who come to our attention within several letters or have a significant influence on the subjects addressed. Others, of more fleeting appearance but for whom some contextual information might assist in using the correspondence, are dealt with in annotations to the text in the main body of this volume.

Reverend George Ritschel, 1657-1717

George Ritschel is the most colourful of the leading figures in this work. An outspoken, energetic, resourceful and combative minister, it is unlikely that any of his parishioners and society failed to hold a strong opinion of him, good or bad. The reader is given ample opportunity by the material presented in this volume to form a view of his character and abilities, but given that much is from his own pen it will be helpful to provide here some balance from other sources.

He was born in Newcastle in 1657, the son of George Ritschel senior, headmaster of the Royal Grammar School since 1648. Ritschel senior was born to a German Lutheran family in Bohemia in 1616, and will therefore have known war and chaos during his formative years in the maelstrom of the Thirty Years War.

[102] BIA Pec.Hex/1 (Court papers), Hex/3 (Fees).

Persecution of the Bohemian protestants by the Habsburgs after 1640 drove him to the Netherlands and Denmark. He was an intellectual, a philosopher, and was taken up by Jan Comenius, the Czech educationalist and scientist renowned across much of protestant Europe. Comenius sent Ritschel to England to collect material for a textbook on metaphysics, and he resided at Oxford in the mid-1640s. When Comenius rejected the work as too sophisticated, Ritschel published the book under his own name. Leibniz was amongst several European philosophers who held it in high regard.[103]

To the strict Presbyterian leaders of Commonwealth Newcastle, Ritschel senior's learning and impeccably protestant credentials will have made him a prized appointment. He achieved much at the Royal Grammar School, repairing the fabric of the building, creating a library, and increasing the number of University entries from the school.[104] He was a practical man, as well as a learned one. Given his reputation and achievements, then, it might seem surprising that in 1657 he gave up the school to move westwards to Hexham as perpetual curate and Lecturer, not least because there is no trace of his ever taking Holy Orders. The headship, however, paid just £50 per annum.[105] As we have seen the Hexham lectureship was worth around £80 per annum. Furthermore, he already had a family of young children and his wife was from Carlisle. Having been a supporter of the Presbyterian elite in Newcastle, Ritschel moved quickly after the Restoration to demonstrate support for the established church. His *Dissertation de Ceremonil Anglicanae*, a strong defence of the Anglican church and critical of puritanism, was published in June 1661 with a dedication to Bishop Cosin of Durham.[106] It is likely that he was the most sophisticated, well-

---

[103] R. Howell Jr, 'A Bohemian Exile in Cromwell's England: The Career of George Ritschel, Philosopher, Schoolmaster and Cleric', *Puritans and Radicals in North England,* (1984), pp.162-71. See also John T. Young, 'Ritschel, Georg (1616–1683)', *ODNB.* A biography of Ritschel junior by Margot Johnson can also be found there, and both men are included in T.Corfe (ed) *Hexham Lives*, (2006).

[104] Howell, *op cit*, p.170.

[105] B.Mains and A.Tuck (eds) *Royal Grammar School, Newcastle upon Tyne*, (1986), p.30.

[106] *ibid*, p.33; Howell, *op cit*, p.170. Cosin, whose principles had seen him spend the Cromwellian interregnum in exile, might have viewed this sudden ardent support with some scepticism.

travelled and intellectually renowned Hexham resident since St. Wilfrid, a millennium before.

With his father comfortably installed at Hexham, George Ritschel junior attended the Royal Grammar School and then St. Edmund Hall at Oxford. He had failed to obtain a scholarship to Corpus Christi College, Oxford, and it is perhaps illustrative of a pugnacious family spirit that this rejection was challenged all the way to the Privy Council, though to no avail.[107] He came back to Hexham after graduating in 1679 to assist his father until the latter's death four years later, and then followed him as perpetual curate. The Mercers' lectureship came a year later.[108] He was just 27 and will have known the town well. He never married, and lived in the Lecturer's house in the shadow of the old Priory church for the rest of his life, mostly with his mother and sister.

Taking up his effectively inherited post in a town with a strong vestry, manor court and lordship, the young George Ritschel could have been forgiven for settling for a quiet and comfortable life, collecting books, tending his beehives, and accommodating his pastoral duty to the realities of local political power. [109] Instead, as demonstrated throughout his correspondence, he set out to improve the moral character of his flock, take on what he saw as the corrupt management of the town's grammar school, and to restore the fabric of the ancient but crumbling old Hexham priory church. In all this his sense of mission, responsibility, and (not least) entitlement, appeared to run well ahead of local respect for his qualities and qualifications.

The examination papers of the callow youth propelled by his father to Corpus Christi College in the summer of 1674 are revealing. Young Ritschel, the Oxford dons found, had a poor command of Latin, the grammar so 'guilty of gross errors … as induced us to conclude him destitute of the qualification. … Considering the advantage of his education under his Father, his dullnesse and the small proficiency, we conceived him to have no claime.' He also suffered from a 'great impediment of speech which himself

---

[107] T.Fowler, *History of Corpus Christi College*, (1893), pp.250-1. There is evidence that Ritschel senior used his old Oxford contacts to seek the Corpus scholarship for his son.

[108] Huelin, *op cit*, p.52.

[109] His two moveable beehives were left in his will to his successor as Lecturer. BIA, PCY George Ritschell of Hexham, December 1717, Probate Register 72, f. 124. A transcript is given in NCH III, p.171.

confessed to be natural & therefore not easily if at all to be removed & which they conceived was not the tone of his country, but proceeded from such defect in his organs as rendred him unfit.' [110] The future Lecturer of Hexham must have struggled to lecture – the basic requirement of his well remunerated post. If a complaint to the Mercers' Company lodged within four months of his appointment is to be believed, however, he had at least made enough progress in his public speaking abilities to 'use vile stories in his sermon fitter for a bawdy house than a pulpit.' It was further alleged that 'since he had some hopes of succeeding his father he hath lorded it over his parishioners' and that he claimed to be their minister 'by Lineall descent.' [111] They sought his removal, and no doubt there was lingering resentment that the attempt failed. Over the long years of his incumbency some took consolation in baiting him instead.

In the late 1680s Ritschel had fallen into theological debate with a Catholic, Thomas Ward, who had been taken in by the Radcliffes at Dilston.[112] Ward's contribution to the debate was published at a later date. After goading Ritschel that he came 'from the veins of an unknown alien', presumably calculated to raise a Ritschel temper in defence of his great father, the respected European philosopher, Ward went on to express surprise that

> 'the learned Vicaress dowager, that critical and sagacious lady your mother, should never discover the absurdity [of your ideas], when she revised and examined your writings, as she assured me she did.' [113]

In 1703 the precocious Thomas Stackhouse, scarcely two years out of Cambridge and already headmaster of Hexham Grammar School, composed an apparently scurrilous Latin verse about Ritschel which caused some amusement to the friends he passed it amongst in the town. It was probably little more than a joke by some bright young turks, but a highly-strung Ritschel was soon launching common law and church court cases for defamation. His targets were

---

[110] Corpus Christi College, Oxford, A/5/3/2.

[111] Mercers' Company, Act Book, 3 Oct 1684; Huelin, *op cit*, pp. 52-3.

[112] G. Scott, 'Thomas Ward (1652-1708) and Hexhamshire. Catholic Apologetics in the Tyne Valley', *Northern Catholic History*, 41, (2000), pp.32-7.

[113] T. Ward, *An interesting controversy with Mr Ritschel, vicar of Hexham*, (1819), p.16. She was Jane, the daughter of John Cope of Carlisle.

Stackhouse and a young Hexham lawyer John Rowell, who was reported to have been laughing about it in the market place as he passed it on to further acquaintances. Amongst the deposition questions submitted for his defence witnesses Rowell could not resist suggesting that Ritschel had to ask the Haydon Bridge schoolmaster to translate it for him, so poor was his Latin.[114]

In the face of such idle sport at his expense, and more overt hostility from the likes of Sir William Blackett II, his bailiffs and members of the town's 'grand predominant clan', Ritschel's tenacity at pursuing his pet projects has to be admired. Likewise, he recognised that taking his pastoral responsibilities seriously was rarely popular but his duty nonetheless; 'I shall take the same care of this Peculiar as if I made some considerable benefit of it, for we must do somewt for conscience sake.' [115] If his evident resilience, efficient record keeping, and enthusiasm had been consistently accompanied by a matching level of tact, he might have made life easier for himself. We have already seen that he was adept in squeezing a few pounds for the church from the commutation of penance and sometimes, as in the case of the dying John Heron, the implicit blackmail was more blatant.[116] Ritschel seemed to use the church court machinery and undoubted knowledge of canon law in his own way based, on the one hand, on what Hexhamshire would tolerate, and –on the other- what distant York and the infrequent visits from their Durham based appointees would never know or be able to change. On one of his early visits Peter Burrell might have complained that Ritschel was 'soe forward & dexterous in business tht as he thinks he needs noe assistance' but there was little Burrell

[114] BIA York Consistory Court cause papers CP/1/90. Thomas Stackhouse, a native of the North-east, left Hexham the following year, went into the church and was a religious writer of minor renown in London in later life. Scott Mandelbrote, 'Stackhouse, Thomas (1681/2–1752)', *ODNB*. Rowell, not to be confused with the John Rowell, Durham Registrar who died in 1705, remained and raised a family in Hexham.

[115] Ritschel to Jubb, 29 Nov 1714, doc. **80**.

[116] Ritschel to Jubb, 5 Oct 1713, doc. **65**. This episode might also reveal a vindictive streak in Ritschel for Heron was a member of the town's 'grand predominant clan'.

Figure 4: St. Andrews, Hexham from the west, with the Abbey house to right, by S. Grimm, 1778 (British Library, Add.MS 15543)

Figure 5: Hexham Grammar School (photo by Greg Finch)

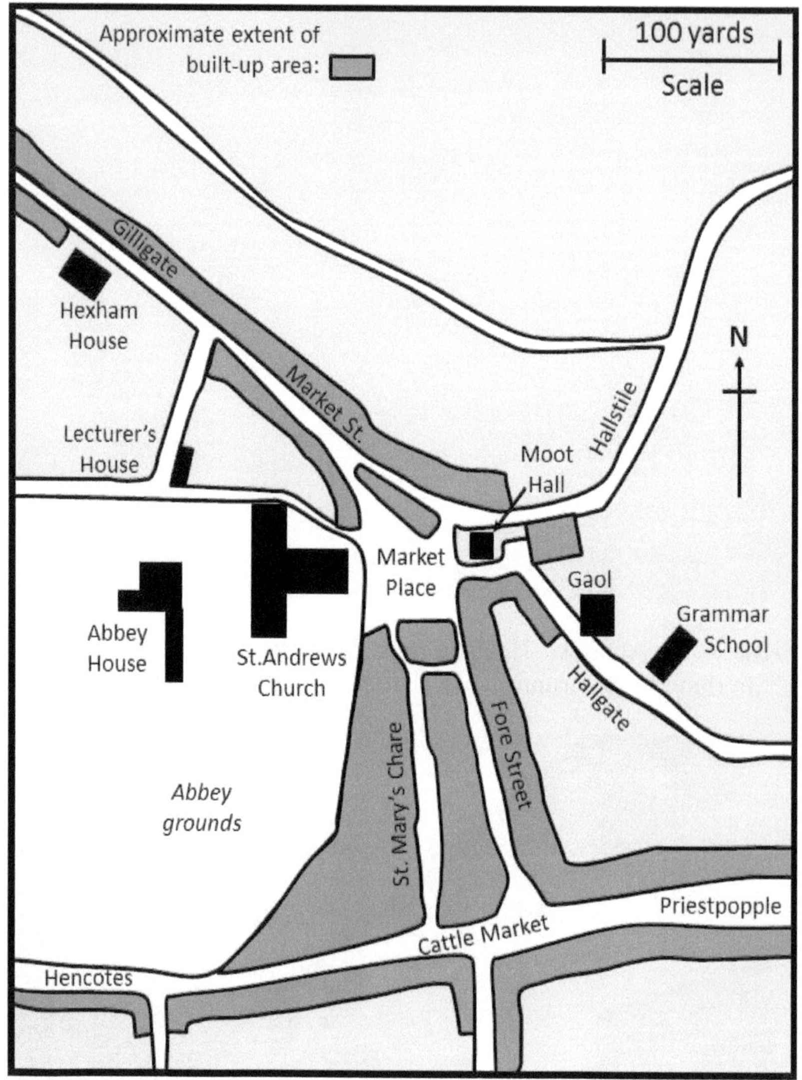

Figure 6: Hexham town c.1700

could do about it.[117] Conducting himself in this way with a flock already jaundiced with the church, Ritschel might have dreaded his dealings with more parishioners than just the fierce Mary Carnaby, whose church rates 'being only 6d wch I had rather pay 10 times out of my own pocket than be lickt with the rough side of her tongue.' [118]

However dubious his means, and arrogant his approach, Ritschel's motives do appear to have been genuine. His objectives in publishing his book on the Hexham charities in 1713 were to goad patrons into action, and to raise funds to support repairs to the ancient church, through sales and new bequests.[119] From the correspondence left to us this was the main purpose of the permission he sought from York to use the penance commutation fines extracted from his straying parishioners. His concern was not limited to bricks and mortar. The rules he devised in 1712 for the fair distribution of existing charity money to the poor of Hexham show thoughtfulness and care, and it is clear he supervised the annual Christmas payments in his final years.[120] His will included provision for annual payments to poor widows in Newcastle, and Carlisle (in his parent's memory), and also in Hexham, the Shire, and Slaley.[121]

Ritschel's will was written in June 1717, a few months before his death and burial near his father in the Hexham church Choir. His long standing projects do not appear to have met with much success in his lifetime. The school went on in much the same way, the archbishop having declined to exercise his rights of visitation and enquiry. Parochial status for Whitley Chapel lay nearly half a century in the future. There was no significant work on the church fabric until a few years after Ritschel's death. It was as if the vestry and lord

---

[117] Burrell to Empson, 13 Nov 1705, doc. **17**. However, when Ritschel found himself in difficulty in 1715 over his handling of the case of John Jackson, Pearson and Jubb got their own back by providing only belated and half-hearted support. The nature of the case appears to have required otherwise. See letters between Ritschel, Pearson and Jubb, docs. **85-7**. See also Smith, pp. 23-5, on this case.

[118] Ritschel to Jubb, 29 Nov 1714, doc. **80.**

[119] Ritschel, *charities, op cit*, (1713), preface. The second edition of this work, published in 1780, gives an interesting account of Hexhamshire in the early eighteenth century and can be found in http://books.google.co.uk/.

[120] HPR, NRO EP 184/5.

[121] NCH III, p.171.

of the manor waited until it could literally be done over his dead body.

Reverend Thomas Andrewes, 1677-1757

Much less is known about Ritschel's successor as Lecturer, Thomas Andrewes (as he signed himself, rather than Andrews), and there is little to draw upon beyond the correspondence itself. He was a southerner from a London mercantile family, the son of Gerrard Andrews, gentleman, of Battersea, and attended the Queen's College, Oxford where he graduated in 1703 and took his MA in March 1706. Ordained as a church deacon in the same month, he was appointed shortly afterwards to Jesus Chapel within the parish of St. Mary's in Southampton, across the River Itchen from the city. He was ordained as a priest in 1709.[122]

The appointment of an outsider to succeed Ritschel as Lecturer was attractive to the Mercers' Company. Ritschel's decline in the year before his death had given early warning of an impending vacancy to those circling the lucrative position and the Company received two recommendations from Hexham – John Laidman, the new perpetual curate swiftly installed by his wife's cousin Sir William Blackett III, and John Cowling, a curate at St. Nicholas in Newcastle. The Mercers, it was reported, decided that 'to return either of them, must disoblige a great part of the town, and therefore they would send a third to whom they thought the town could find no exception.' [123] The 40 year old compromise candidate Thomas

---

[122] Foster, *Alumni Oxoniensis 1500-1714*, Vol 1, (1891), Oxford County Record Office, MS Oxf. Dioc. Papers c. 266 (Register), Hampshire Record Office, 21M65/F1/6 (Subscription Book). The relatively new Church of England Clergy database (http://www.theclergydatabase.org.uk/jsp/search/index.jsp) is a valuable resource for researchers. Foster is mistaken in showing Andrewes as the vicar of Burbage, confusing him with another near contemporary of the same name. The Jesus Chapel appointment fits the known chronology: D. Corps, The Story of Jesus Chapel, http://southernlife.org.uk/ peartree_church.htm, (extracted 11 March 2013).

[123] Ritschel's distinctive handwriting became shakier through the winter of 1716-7 and disappeared from Hexham's parish registers in March, more than six months before his death. The Lectureship candidacies and outcome is given in 'The Diary of Rev. John Thomlinson', entry for 17 Nov 1717: J.C.Hodgson (ed) *Six North Country Diaries*, Surtees Soc, Vol 118, (1910), p.69. Archives of the Mercers' Company, Act Book 1716-9.

Andrewes appealed to the Mercers in offering relief from the divisiveness of Ritschel's time.

How Andrewes, the Londoner ensconced on the outskirts of Southampton, even knew of the vacancy and then came to the Mercers' Company's attention is not immediately apparent, but the baptism in Hexham in October 1715 of a daughter of Gerrard Andrewes provides a compelling clue. He was Thomas's brother, a 'commissary or muster-master', or civilian auditor of the size of army regiments for pay purposes, and the baptismal date places him in the town very soon after the Jacobite rebels had left.[124] He was still there four years later when another child was baptised, so would have been ideally placed in the meantime to alert his clerical brother to the impending availability of the Lectureship. The family's mercantile background in London might have provided connections in the city able to influence the Mercers' decision regarding his appointment.

Smith portrayed Andrewes as a detached functionary.[125] He was certainly another lofty High Church Tory, voting for William Wrightson in the 1723 election, and for Lancelot Allgood in that of 1747.[126] The conditions of the Hexham lectureship did not require permanent residence and he was often absent for extended periods of time. This included several months early in 1719 when the presence of his austere authority might have calmed tense bickering in the wake of the dismissal of the villainous John Laidman and subsequent confusion.[127] His calm demeanour and emollient style were doubtless a pleasant change to that of his predecessor. There is a languid self-assurance in the dry detachment with which he reported the petty abuses and encroachments into church authority in the year after Ritschel's death.[128] He was careful not to stray outside the bounds of his own position, and was driven to mild irritation when he felt the need to defend himself to Jubb in 1733 against an accusation from Lady Blackett that he was imposing himself. This arose in the course of a spat over Psalm singing in church:

---

[124] HPR.

[125] Smith, *op cit*, p.35.

[126] Poll book, *op cit*, (1841), p.157, *The Northumberland poll-book... in the years 1747-8, 1774, and ..1826*, (1826), p. 40.

[127] See the sequence of letters to Jubb between March and June that year: docs. **97-108.** For Laidman, see ABN.

[128] Andrewes to Jubb, 6 Sep 1718, doc **93**.

> 'and if it has been too great a streach of the surrogates power, to give directions to the parish clark, in the absence of the minister, what Psalms he should sing for one day, tis the only instance I have made use of it in this 15 years.' [129]

He showed no interest in taking that ministerial position for himself during his long years in Hexham, yet it was surely his for the taking after Laidman was drummed out of the curacy in 1719. Unused as we might have become by now to such diffidence in the pursuit of further church incomes, it is clear that Andewes was already financially independent. Within six years of his appointment he had built himself a mansion, now Hexham House, in place of the meaner dwelling previously occupied by the Lecturer (see Figures 7 and 8).[130] Personal financial security, and the renovations to the church, might also have made penance commutation less attractive than before. Even though the persistent moral offender John Coatsworth could apparently easily afford to commute his latest punishment in 1722, Andrewes was resolved that

> 'The punishment and amendment of bold, sturdy, insolent offenders in order to deterr others from their examples, will be of good use to this place, and I desire no other advantage than what with the publick I shall partake in it, except the obtaining some credit to this jurisdiction, and the proveing myself observant of your needfull commands' [131]

Andrewes might not have been well known or liked by many within the Peculiar, but his detached consistency was probably respected well enough, and might go a long way to explaining the sustained residual influence of the church courts well into the eighteenth century. Certainly there was the mutual respect of competent administrators between him, Registrar Jubb and Chancellor Audley in York, on whom he could call when passing through York on his

---

[129] Andrewes to Jubb, 26 March 1733, doc. **168**. This Lady Blackett was the wife of Sir Edward Blackett, to whom the Abbey House had been let by his 'Wallington' Blackett cousin.

[130] An oval stone plaque on the inside lintel of doorway under the projecting south porch on piers, reads: *T.A. / Has Aedes struxit/ 1723* (TA built this house in 1723). I am grateful to Colin Dallison for this.

[131] Andrewes to Jubb, 12 July 1722, doc. **128**.

Figure 7: Hexham Lecturer's house, c.1900, with white gable end in front of the church, looking south-east (J.P.Gibson, reproduced in A.Bradley, *The Romance of Northumberland*, 1927)

Figure 8: Hexham House, built by Thomas Andrewes in 1722 (Photograph courtesy of Stan Beckensall)

extended journeys to the south. There is no evidence that Andrewes sought to run the Hexham courts other than in the regular pattern expected by York, another change from the days of Ritschel.

Smith felt that Andrews was more amused by the people around him than he was concerned for them, but this seems harsh. He fended off Jubb's suggestion that Hexhamshire offenders should be cited to appear in the Chancery court at York, recognising the inconvenience this would cause, and felt that a Shire churchwarden was over-vigilant in presenting to the court a widow's son for driving home straying sheep on the common when there were blatant cases of fornication closer to hand that merited his attention.[132] He was alert to sharp practice against vulnerable parishioners and willing to engage in the detail of cases where such exploitation was suspected.[133] No leniency was shown to the more affluent members of the local community. Andrewes made examples of a 'pack of idle sparks' in 1732, seeking to 'doe something towards their reformation, or at Least to shew the world, that discipline is not only intended to expose the poorest of sinners.' [134] Marriage licence abuse by the likes of Leonard Bentham and Edward Twedale was another of his frequent concerns. His haughty bearing might have set him apart from the local population, but arguably set an example of personal conduct which helped shore up the reputation of a tarnished church after Ritschel's long period of divisive familiarity, especially among the more respectable members of local society, who now constituted the solid core of reduced church attendance.

Andrewes remained unmarried, and various members of his family joined him in Hexham, enough of them eventually to join him in a family vault in the parish church. He died in 1757, having been Lecturer for forty years. One of his nieces became the wife of a later Lecturer.[135] They are all commemorated on plaques in the north transept of the church.

---

[132] Andrewes to Jubb, 10 Oct 1726, doc. **156**.

[133] The handling of William Younger's will is an example: docs. **140**, **142**.

[134] Andrewes to Jubb 19 Feb 1733, doc. **167**.

[135] In addition to Gerrard, mentioned earlier, a brother Henry was left holding the fort for a while in 1719. Robert, Thomas' executor, was in Hexham from at least the 1740s and, like a further brother Laurence and sister Sarah, was buried in the church. Robert's daughter Honour was later the wife of Lecturer Revd. Sloughter Clarke. The 'family vault' was the

Peter Burrell senior (d. 1708) and junior (d.1720)

Many of the early letters in the York correspondence are from Peter Burrell, the Durham registrar appointed by Empson to save him the bother of thinly rewarded visits to the Hexham church courts, and to act on his behalf. We have seen already the indecent haste with which Burrell moved to be appointed to the Hexham post, scarcely waiting until the body of his predecessor John Rowell had been fished out of the River Wear. Burrell's actions probably would not have surprised many in Durham, if the views noted by the Swedish industrial spy Angerstein half a century later are anything to go by.

> 'To the question of what trade is carried on in the city, the answer is 'Law and Gospel', as the great majority of the population consists of lawyers and priests. Those who do not enjoy any of the ample profits regard these people as a plague, as there are too many of them.' [136]

Burrell was probably busy with other letters on the same day, for he was appointed registrar of the Archdeacon of Northumberland in succession to John Rowell in 1705 and deputy registrar for the Durham diocese as a whole.[137] Addresses on inventories in the Durham probate registry show that he was at work in the diocesan registry from at least 1689, and this was presumably his chance of promotion.[138] His wife, Elizabeth Hilton, was from a landed County Durham family, one of her brothers was a Durham registrar, and

---

crypt of St. Wilfried, rediscovered in 1725-6, and granted to Andrewes as a vault in 1737: R.N.Bailey, 'The Anglo-Saxon Church at Hexham', *AA*, 5th ser, Vol 4, (1976), p.63.

[136] T and P Berg (trans), *R.R.Angerstein's Illustrated Travel Diary, 1753-1755, Industry in England and Wales from a Swedish perspective*, London, Science Museum, 2001, p.240.

[137] Shuler, *op cit*, pp. 289, 306.

[138] He possibly followed his father into the registry, for an earlier Peter Burrell worked there from at least 1681. Probate was granted to this older Peter Burrell's widow in 1690: Durham University Library Special Collections catalogue, Durham Probate Records: pre-1858 original wills and inventories, 1681-99, 1700-1725: http://reed.dur.ac.uk/xtf/view?docId=ead/dpr/dpr1-1-1725.xml. For further insights into the Durham Probate Registry, see K. Wrightson, *Ralph Tailor's Summer. A Scrivener, His City, and the Plague,* (2011).

there were at least two other Peter Burrells at work in the Durham registry and as proctors during the early eighteenth century. The small rarified world of ecclesiastical law around Durham Cathedral was very much a family specialisation. The first Peter Burrell died in October 1708 and, doubtless to Ritschel's dismay, was succeeded by his nephew, also a proctor and notary public (ie. a commissioner of oaths).[139] He found Hexham no more welcoming or remunerative than did his uncle. The court held in 1714 was the occasion of his last visit to the town. Ritschel contrived to pack it with a host of poor people who had gathered nuts on a Sunday, the smell of whom Burrell found obnoxious, no doubt to much local hilarity at the expense of the Durham registrar.[140]

Thomas Jubb (d.1736)

There are very few letters from Jubb in the York collection but he was the recipient of most of them, and the occasion of much of the work documented in the letters. Compared to the grand Aislabys, who had been milking the office until they gave it up as no longer worthwhile, he was a comparatively junior clerk, and had worked under Thomas Empson before replacing him as the deputy registrar in 1710. Jubb was the son of Robert Jubb of York, gentleman, and married in the Minster in 1709, going on to found a church court dynasty, like many others.[141]

When John Aislaby finally resigned in 1714, the desire of the archbishop to improve the efficiency and probity of the court system made Jubb the obvious candidate for the post of registrar. A certain legal standing is shown by his appearance as a notary public in a York cause of 1707, and he was appointed as a proctor in 1714. He

---

[139] Shuler, pp.276-7, 303; E.A.White and G.J.Armytage (eds), *The baptismal, marriage, and burial registers of the Cathedral church of Christ and Blessed Mary the virgin at Durham, 1609-1896*, Harliean Society, 23, (1897), p.113. Burrell senior's will was witnessed by his nephew, notary public. DPRI/1/1709/B11, 27 Oct 1709.

[140] Burrell to Jubb, 17 Dec 1714, doc. **81**. Burrell junior was buried in June 1720. *Durham Cathedral registers, op cit,* p.116.

[141] 'Thomas Jubb, notary, registrar to the Dean and Chapter, son of Robert Jubb, of York, gent. Buried at St. Michael's-le-Belfrey 5 Sept. 1736. His widow Dorothy, was buried there 15 March, 1753. Their youngest son, Henry Jubb, apothecary, was lord mayor of York in 1773.' R.H.Skaife, (ed), *The Register of Marriages in York Minster, illustrated with biographical notices, 1681 to 1762,* (1873), p. 410.

soon proved himself an energetic and efficient administrator, though somewhat pedantic and unpopular in his zeal to protect and claim all the rights of the church.[142] Though he found the registry records to be in a state of chaos on entering his office, his future command of the cases he pursued on behalf of the church show the value he must have set on putting them straight.[143] No-one was going to pull the wool over Jubb's eyes. Thus was the scene set for his long distance attempts to control and steer the work of the Hexham church courts, the fencing this entailed with Ritschel, followed by the more orderly partnership with Andrewes. His long tenure might have come to an end slightly before his death, for notes in the Hexham Correction Court proceedings show his son Robert to have been acting as the registrar by February 1735.[144] Andrewes' letters indicate that he had been suffering from gout since at least 1723.

The Documents

The correspondence is presented in chronological sequence rather than by archival source. The Borthwick correspondence is complemented by a small number of additional letters by George Ritschel found elsewhere. The latter are distinguished from the Borthwick papers in the main body of the text by being given their full archival reference.

1. Borthwick papers

The three bundles of correspondence which make up the bulk of the documents are part of an archive of papers related to the Archbishop's Peculiar Jurisdiction of the Liberty of Hexhamshire and probably survive thanks to Jubb's re-ordering of the Registry after 1710 and subsequent diligence.[145] They are filed in

[142] Till, Study, p.222, BIA CP.H.3687. It is presumably a son of the same name who acted as a prosecution proctor in a 1733 cause. BIA Test.CP.1731/2.

[143] J.S.Purvis, *The archives of York diocesan registry: their provenance and history* (1952), Till, Study, pp.222-232.

[144] BIA Pec.Hex/1.

[145] A summary guide to these and papers relating to other Peculiar jurisdictions, can be downloaded from the Borthwick Institute's website description of its archival holdings at the following address: http://www.york.ac.uk/library/borthwick/catalogues/archival-holdings/. The

chronological order. Other than a single letter from William Carr to Empson in 1700 the main sequence commences with the first letter sent by Peter Burrell senior, during Empson's time as deputy registrar, and presumably retained by Jubb to assist in holding the Hexham surrogates to account. The main body of letters come to an end just three years before Jubb's death.

The letters are mainly concerned with the church court business delegated to Burrell, Ritschel and Andrewes. Alongside the usually colourful commentary on individual cases, gossip from the Peculiar and casual character assassinations, there are more mundane requests for blank licences, accounts for sums owed, claimed and deducted, and other administrative matters. The latter are of value to students of the administration of church business, money transfer and the efficiency of the early 18th century postal system. The last document in the collection is a detailed account of the administration by Mary Lee of the estate of her late husband George Lee, who died without having left a will, and includes his funeral expenses. Copies of other wills are included in support of probate-related correspondence.[146]

In making use of the correspondence it is important to bear in mind its limitations. Coverage through time is uneven. We have nothing between June 1707 and August 1710, although the sequence does re-commence with a summary of court business since the death of the first Peter Burrell in 1708. There is also a gap of nearly two years between the last letter from Ritschel in October 1716 and the first from Andrewes. On the other hand, there is a flurry of letters from Burrell senior in 1705-6 in the wake of his appointment, and many survive from 1713 and 1714 when both Ritschel and Burrell junior were in full flow, and from 1719, the year in which the Laidman was dismissed as the curate of Hexham.

There is no clear seasonal pattern, although it is noticeable that a quarter of Andrewes' letters were written in May alone. This was normally the month of the Visitation Court session, demonstrating

---

full citation for the original documents is York, Borthwick Institute for Archives, Peculiar Jurisdiction, Liberty of Hexhamshire, file 2, (BIA Pec.Hex/2) but to avoid undue cluttering of the text are referred to simply by correspondents, date in this volume, and assigned a unique document number.

[146] Pec.Hex/2 also includes a stray document relating to a tuition bond for one Watkins in Yorkshire in 1722 and a covering letter from a Francis Barroby.

the primary focus of his surviving correspondence on church administration. This was the main purpose of all the communication between Hexham and York, along with the collection of money. There is little observation of events in Hexhamshire which must have generated much local discussion and opinion at the time. There is no mention of Robert Patten's escapades during and after the 1715 rebellion. Likewise, there is nothing from Andrewes on the Jacobite riot in Hexham in September 1718 or about the intimidation of voters during the 1723 election campaign, which led to several complaints to the Quarter Sessions. Perhaps they were not seen as sufficiently rare to merit comment.

The cases which are documented are too few in number to allow any quantitative assessments of the relative importance of the various moral offences or trends over time. Neither do we know whether those which are documented account for all such misdemeanours brought to the officials' attention. The poorest parishioners might have been thought to be beyond redemption, and certainly not worth pursuing for fines or fees. However there is evidence that some campaigns were pursued zealously, at least for short periods of time. Between 1722 and 1725, for example, sixteen presentments were made for fornication. Assuming that illegitimate births were the most secure ground for such allegations, it is curious that the baptism registers of the three parishes note hardly any during this period. However, if the national rate of illegitimacy applied in Hexhamshire at the time, sixteen presentations is a fairly high percentage of the twenty-two that might be expected.[147]

Finally, as with any correspondence, what we have are the views of the writers, justifying their actions, and seeking favours or forgiveness, which we must take care not to mistake for objective accounts. This potentially matters more with the Burrells and Ritschel, with their axes to grind – usually against each other- than with the more urbane and bland Thomas Andrewes, but it does mean the earlier letters offer more entertainment and vivid colour.

---

[147] Presentations from the Visitation and Correction Court causes (BIA Pec.Hex/1), several of which are mentioned in Andrewes' letters. 770 baptisms were registered in Hexham, St. John Lee and Allendale between 1722 and 1725. The national rate of illegitimate births for 1725-49 is given as 2.91% in E.A.Wrigley, R.S.Davies, J.E.Oeppen, R.S.Schofield, *English population history from family reconstitution 1580-1837*, (Cambridge, 1997), Table 6.2, p.219.

Introduction

The other four files in the archive of the Archbishop's Peculiar of Hexham are as follows.

Hex/1 Visitation and Correction Court Proceedings

These include visitation articles, churchwarden presentments, citations, court proceedings, defence and witness statements, commutations, penances and excommunications from 1711 onwards. This is an excellent resource for the further study of Hexhamshire life in the eighteenth century but far too voluminous to reproduce here. An illustrative selection is interleaved chronologically amongst the letters.

Hex/3 Fees

A small number of accounts in varying detail survive for the years 1683, 1696-9, 1701-7, 1719, 1721-2 listing payments due to York for licences, churchwarden dismission fees etc. The 1719 account from Andrewes is included as doc. **110**.

Hex/4 Schools

This includes nominations and letters testimonial for schoolmasters within the Peculiar. It also contains Ritschel's allegations of abuses at the Grammar School, and which can be dated with confidence to January 1714 given the content of his letter to Jubb of 21 January that year. Its content is similar to that given in docs. **5** & **6** of 1699.

Hex/5 Miscellaneous

Various papers dated 1588-1713, including a 1698 legal opinion on a dispute between the minister and the lord of the manor, a 1712 account of church repairs, a 1713 grant from Sir Wm Blackett III to Ritschel of a church pew, and a petition c.1712-3 from St.John Lee regarding churchwardens fees. The building account, pew grant and St. John Lee petition are included in this volume.

Other material within the Peculiar of Hexhamshire papers includes 18 boxes of parish register transcripts [Hex/PRT] for Allendale, West Allen, St Peter's Allenheads, St Mary Bingfield,

Hexham, St John Lee, Ninebanks and Whitley Chapel to the 1840s (though with many gaps in the sequence), and one box of marriage bonds [Hex/MB] covering much the same period as the correspondence (1704-33). The probate records are to be found amongst the records of the various York probate courts.[148]

2. Archbishop of York's papers

The correspondence presented in this volume opens in spectacular fashion with claim and counter-claim in early 1699 about Ritschel's fitness to be Hexham's perpetual curate and Lecturer. They are amongst letters addressed to Archbishop of York John Sharp, now in the ownership of the Society of Antiquaries of Newcastle-upon-Tyne, and held at the Northumberland Archives in Woodhorn.[149] It is not immediately clear how they have come to rest here rather than with many other archiepiscopal papers still in York, but they are part of a larger collection including many papers from Archdeacon of Northumberland John Sharp concerning Hexham parish. Sharp was the grandson of the archbishop, and it is possible that these letters passed to him through his family, and later into the Society of Antiquaries collection.

3. Northumberland Quarter Sessions papers

A small number of extracts are included here from the county Quarter Session records that are directly relevant to the rest of the correspondence. These include a petition from Ritschel to the Quarter Sessions in 1703 regarding the tithes that formed part of his income as Lecturer (NRO QSB 19). There is also a small sequence of letters from Ritschel to an attorney in 1709-10, probably John Ord of Newcastle (c.1657-1721), related to another petition, this time seeking to raise funds to repair St. Andrews church in Hexham (NRO QSB/89 pp. 17-9). The draft petition and formal order of the Quarter Sessions are also given.

---

[148] A guide to which, 'Probate records', can be downloaded from the Borthwick's summary of its archival holdings: http://www.york.ac.uk/library/borthwick/catalogues/archival-holdings/.

[149] NRO SANT/GEN/ECC/3/3.

Conclusion

This collection conjures up an image of black-gowned pedants scribbling at their desks. From within the cloistered precincts of ancient churchyards they directed most of their energy into scoring points and trading waspish insults over obscure and arcane principles of canon law far removed from everyday life. In the scramble for position and fees such smallmindedness is in stark contrast to the majesty of the vast buildings in whose shadow they wrote, in York, in Durham and in Hexham. And yet, these private observations, untrammelled by fears of libel suits, and leavened by touches of humanity and compassion, have left behind intriguing illustrations of the lives and concerns of ordinary people, to stimulate further thinking on northern English society three hundred years ago.

Figure 9: Woman performing penance in church.
(Thomas Bewick; reproduced in Peter Isaac, *William Davison's New Specimen of Cast-Metal Ornaments and Wood Types*, 1990)

2. Additional Biographical Notes

Allgood, Thomas (1646 – 1713) Bailiff of the manor of Hexham 1670-87, & 1690-1713

Thomas was the third son of Lancelot Allgood of Hexham, royalist, minor landowner and bailiff of Hexham manor in 1646.[150] Hearth tax assessments of the 1660s and 1670s show that Thomas was by then living in some style in one of the largest houses in Hexham, probably on the site of the present County Hotel at the east end of Priestpopple.[151] He was an attorney, governor of the town's grammar school and a commissioner for land tax in the 1690s.[152] He first served as bailiff under the Fenwicks, perhaps benefiting from a family connection through his wife, whom he married in 1667. She was Isabel Crow; a Patrick Crow was bailiff until succeeded by Allgood in1670. After a short period in the late 1680s during which Benoni and William Carr occupied the office, Allgood returned within a year of Sir William Blackett's purchase of the manor, and had a lease of the Allendale tithes by 1694.[153] With Blackett's son inheriting the estate at sixteen years of age, it is likely that Allgood's influence within Hexham was thereafter all the stronger. He was at odds with Ritschel since at least the latter's appointment to the lectureship in 1683, if not earlier, and this seems to have been a personal rather than a family feud. His elder brother Major Allgood had written and given the oration at George Ritschel senior's funeral in 1683.[154] His sister-in-law Margaret Allgood left £100 to the poor of Hexham by her will of 1707, the interest of which was to be distributed by the principal inhabitants of the town, with the advice of the minister, ie. Ritschel junior.[155] Ritschel, not an objective

---

150 M.H.Dodds, *History of Northumberland*, Vol XV, Simonburn etc. (1930), pedigree chart opposite p.201.

151 TNA E179/ 158 106 r 5-7 (1665), E179/158/110 Rots 28-9 (1673).

152 See mentions amongst the Letters, *passim*; BIA Pec.Hex/4.

153 NCH IV, p.107.

154 Major Allgood, *A Sermon Preached at the funeral of the Reverend and Learned Mr George Ritschel*, (1684). It was Major Allgood's grandson Lancelot who united the family's estates and built Nunwick Hall following his marriage in 1739 to his distant cousin Jane, grand-daughter of George Allgood, another 17th century Hexham attorney.

155 Ritschel, *An Account of Certain Charities*, (2nd edition, 1780), p.10.

observer, claimed that one of Allgood's own cousins remarked that Thomas had been drunk for forty years.[156]

John Aynsley, (1659-1751) Hexham attorney

Younger son of a minor gentry family at Little Harle Tower in Kirkwhelpington, Aynsley appears to have practised as a lawyer and land agent in the Hexham area for most of his long life. He often acted for Ritschel. Unlike other members of his family there is no record of him being admitted to Oxford, Cambridge or the London Inns of Court. It was alleged he joined the Jacobite rebels at Jedbergh in 1715 before changing his mind and was resented by many thereafter as a 'turncoat'.[157] This appears not to have prevented him being granted powers of attorney by many local Catholic estate owners in 1717 who were required to register their estates under new legislation following the rebellion.[158] Within a few years some forfeited local Catholic property was owned outright by Aynsley. He claimed this to be by fair purchase, as in the case of Bywell property forfeited by John Thornton of Nethwitton in 1716, but the picture is at best confused.[159] It seemed clear enough to Jacobites Edward Charlton and Jasper Gibson, (whose nephew's forfeited estate ended up in Aynsley's hands), who beat him up in a brawl in Hexham in 1718. While hardly conclusive as evidence of sharp practice and of being a turncoat, it is noticeable that he campaigned actively in Hexham for the Tory Forster in the 1710 election, but voted for the Whig Jennison in the 1722 election, and then campaigned amongst Hexham's freeholders for the Whigs in the 1730s.[160] By this time, if not well before, he was connected into the predominantly Whig mercantile community of Tyneside. In 1726 he married, as his third wife, the widowed daughter of Alderman William Ramsay, and thus became brother-in-law of the formidable William Cotesworth of Gateshead Park. Aynsley managed the estates near Haltwhistle

---

[156] Ritschel to Jubb, 28 Sept 1713, doc. **64.**

[157] Gooch, *op cit*, p.132.

[158] *Northumbrian Documents, Seventeenth and Eighteenth Centuries, comprising the register of the estates of Roman Catholics in Northumberland*, Surtees Society, Vol. 132, (1918) , *passim.*

[159] NCH VI, pp.242-3.

[160] *Poll Book*, *op cit*, (1841), pp. 12, 45, 147-70, Andrewes to Jubb, 28 May 1733, doc. **169.**

Cotesworth inherited from Ramsay, [161] and the Derwentwater estates at the time they were granted to the Greenwich Hospital following forfeiture. The Hospital's new commissioners accused him of underhand dealings, and he was subsequently removed.[162] Corfe says Aynesley was a Catholic but his son, also John, was baptised in Hexham church in 1694, he gave silver plate to the church in 1722, does not appear on the list included in this volume of 'reputed papists' in 1733-4, and was buried in the parish church.[163]

Bentham, Rev. Leonard (d.1720) Perpetual Curate of St. John Lee

Bentham was a graduate of Glasgow University, and ordained in York in 1676.[164] As perpetual curate of St. John Lee for forty years from 1680, he was notorious for augmenting his meagre income by undertaking marriages and providing licences on negotiable terms. He died in May 1720, leaving his effects to his two sons Cornelius (later of Chester-le-Street) and William (who was still of Acomb when he died in 1773) and daughters Anne and Isabel.[165]

Blackett, Sir William II (1657-1705) Lord of the manor of Hexham

The first Sir William Blackett (1621-80) established the family's fortune as a Newcastle merchant, coal owner and through his leading role in developing the regional lead industry. Sir William II was his third son, rewarded by his father for his business talent, through bequests of the family's lead mining leases and lands in 1680. Sir William II added the Wallington and Hexhamshire estates, purchased from Sir John Fenwick in 1689 on highly advantageous terms. Taking his place in the Newcastle merchant community as Mayor and MP, he played an active role in resisting the attempts of James II to wrest away the town's prized independence. These formative experiences made him a natural supporter of the succession of William and Mary, and, politically, a Whig.[166] His Newcastle,

---

[161] E.Hughes, *North Country Life*, (1952), pp.122-3.

[162] TNA ADM 66/105. My thanks to Liz Sobell for this reference.

[163] Corfe *Hexham Lives*, op cit, pp.47-8, HPR, NCH III p.175, doc **171.**

[164] BI, Inst. AB 7, Episcopal Act Book.

[165] NCH IV, p.131.

[166] A.W.Purdue, *The Ship that came home*, (2004), pp.35-41. An annuity of £2,000 to Fenwick was part of the purchase price of the Wallington and

London and wider business commitments will have left him little time for direct involvement in Hexham life and government, where he relied primarily on his bailiff Thomas Allgood. That he was prepared to write personally to the archbishop in May 1699 to seek the removal of Ritschel as his Hexham curate, suggests, however, that Blackett shared his at least some of his bailiff's antipathy towards the minister.[167]

Blackett, Sir William III (1690-1728) Lord of the manor of Hexham

Not quite sixteen years old when his father died, the third Sir William, who inherited none of his father and grandfather's business acumen, presumably relied heavily upon Allgood and company in Hexham. Indeed, members of the Allgood family remained Blackett's agents for the rest of his short life, during which his ability to spend on a prodigious scale built up a significant burden of debt for his successors to deal with. In contrast to his father's loyal Whig tendencies, he dallied with Jacobitism sufficiently to concern loyalists in Newcastle in 1715, but ultimately decided not to join the rebels. He was a Tory MP for Newcastle from 1710 until his death, and elected Mayor of Newcastle in 1718 despite the resentment of his former Jacobite friends in the corporation.[168] Attendance at Parliament was not a priority for Blackett compared to lavish parties at Wallington, and his outlook is perhaps captured in Andrewes' aside that 'the present Sr Wm Blacket [is not] a person that would give himself much trouble to assert what is claimed for him.' [169] He was succeeded by his nephew Walter Calverley Blackett, who stabilised and enhanced the family's fortunes over the next fifty years.

Hexhamshire estate. Blackett was amongst the MPs who voted for Fenwick's execution in 1696, thereby bringing these annual payments to an end.

[167] NCH III, p.170.

[168] E. Cruickshank, in R. Sedgwick, (ed) *The History of Parliament: the House of Commons 1715-1754* (1970): available online as http://www.historyofparliamentonline.org/volume/1715-1754/member/ blackett- sir-william-1690-1728 [extracted 30 March 2013].

[169] Andrewes to Jubb, 13 Feb 1721, doc. **119.**

Carr, John (1655-1715) Bailiff of Hexham manor, 1713-15

Carr was a member of the Carr family which was prominent in Hexham during the seventeenth century, providing four of the town's bailiffs. He was probably the son of either Benoni Carr, bailiff in 1687 despite being a Catholic, or Richard Carr, member of the 'Four and Twenty' from the 1650s.[170] According to the hearth tax assessments of the 1660s and 1670s, theirs were amongst the larger houses in the town. Ritschel's correspondence suggests that John Carr and Thomas Allgood conspired together against him from the 1680s. They were joint farmers of the Allendale tithes in 1694, and as steward of the manor Carr was effectively Allgood's deputy. His succession as bailiff on Allgood's death had perhaps been arranged between them and Blackett, much to Ritschel's dismay. 'We have got another drinking Bailiff (old Carr) ... whose examples (& practice, for no businesse must be done without a drink offering) have infected not only the Town but also the neighbouring Countrey.' A year later he had 'now so quite drunk away his limbs that he canot stirr, & as before he would not act so now he canot appear.' [171] Carr was dead little more than a year later.

Empson, Thomas (d.1710) Deputy registrar of Consistory Court, York

As deputy registrar to the absentee John Aislaby, Empson was the recipient of most of the letters from Hexham until his death in 1710.[172] He had been deputy registrar since 1691, while also acting as a proctor in the Exchequer Court. Robert Oates, whose exposure in 1698 for selling excommunication annulments led to Archbishop Sharp's investigation into York courts, claimed that the case against him had been engineered by Empson. They had been feuding over the registrarship of the archdeacon of the East Riding's court. Empson claimed not to pay a rent to Aislaby for the privilege of

---

[170] NCH III, p.65; 'Rossiter database' of Hexham people in the seventeenth century compiled from a variety of sources by Anna Rossiter and now available through the Hexham Local History Society's website: www.hexhamhistorian.org.

[171] Ritschel to Jubb: 28 September 1713, 30th August 1714, doc. **78.**

[172] Admon Thomas Empson notary public 29 Apr 1710, will 11 May 1710: Act Books of the Prerogative Court of York.

being his deputy, taking only the clerks fees, although separately said he saw no harm in the practice.[173]

Graham, Rev. William (1674-1764) Perpetual Curate of Hexham, 1721-1764

The appointment of William Graham as curate of Hexham in 1721 ended four years of turbulence and change after the death of Ritschel, including the short tenure of the scandalous John Laidman. Graham, a member of the landed Graham family of Netherby in Cumberland, was already nearing the age of fifty on his arrival in Hexham, 'a very sober Gent; and very orderly' according to Andrewes. The Lecturer and the new curate, both High Church Tories, seem to have presided over an era of much greater stability in the church in Hexham. William Graham was another of the Hexhamshire curates educated at Glasgow University, where he matriculated in 1702 – already aged nearer thirty than twenty – and graduated in 1711. He was ordained a deacon in Carlisle in 1712 and a priest in 1713, where his Oxford educated namesake Dr. Graham, also of the Netherby family, was dean.[174] With his apparently comfortable family background, late and leisurely progress through university and into the church, it is tempting to conclude that, like Andrewes, he had a private income to supplement the curate's meagre stipend. Certainly he was content to remain in Hexham for over forty years. However, he was eager enough to augment his Hexham income, wresting from John Toppin the curacy of Slaley, just to the south east of Hexham, in 1724 with some assistance from Durham. 'Mr. Toppin, This is to acquaint you that Doctor Sayer, Chancellor to my lord bishop of Durham, has appointed me sole curate of Slealey by vertue of a sequestration under his hand and seal whereby I am entitled to all ye profitts due upon ye place since ye death of ye late incumbent [Wm Richardson, who died in Feb 1724] therefore you need not give yourself any more trouble of coming to Slealey. I am, Sir, Yours, William Graham. If

---

173 Till, Study, p.220; Till, *Church Courts*, p.34; Borthwick Cause Papers CP.H.3687.

174 *Munimenta Alme Universitatis Glasguensis, Volume III, Lists of Members*, (1854), pp.46, 175; S.L.Ollard, P.C.Walker, (eds), *Archbishop Herring's Visitation Returns, 1743, Volume 3*, Yorkshire Arch Society, Record Series, Vol LXXV (1929), p.249. Dr. William Graham, Canon of Durham from 1684, dean of Carlisle from 1686 and of Wells from 1704: Foster, *Alumni Oxoniensis, 1500-1714*, (1891), p.593; NCH III, p.298.

this do not satisfy you I'll show my instrument when you come to Hexham.' [175] The value of the Hexham curacy was also increased in 1728 from the Queen Anne's Bounty fund, following which Graham immediately appointed an assistant curate.[176] He made sure to use his response to Archbishop Herring's visitation questions in 1743 to lament his meagre income and request a further augmentation.[177] Further improvement came from bequests from Sir Walter Blackett in the 1750s and Graham saw out his days in Hexham, by which time the curacy was worth £50 per year.[178]

Laidman, Rev. John, (1680-1745) Perpetual Curate of Hexham, 1717-19

The curate who came to Hexham in 1717 was the son of the Rev. Christopher Laidman of Whickham and later vicar of Woodhorn. John was educated at Sedbergh School and St. John's College Cambridge, gaining his degree in 1702/3. Ordained as a priest in 1707 he was his father's curate at Woodhorn for two years, and then at Mitford near Morpeth in 1711-2. His wife was a Mitford, 'Christian', daughter of 'Christian' Blackett, sister of Sir William Blackett II. Laidman's wife was therefore the cousin of Sir William III, in whose gift was the perpetual curacy of Hexham, to which Laidman was duly presented in October 1717 after a further short appointment as curate at Whalton. The real attraction of Hexham to the restless Laidman was not the poorly paid curacy but the prospect of the lucrative Mercers' Lectureship, it having been granted to the two previous curates, Ritschels senior and junior. According to Thomlinson's diary a month later, however, Laidman was not accepted by many in Hexham, which suggests he became unpopular impressively quickly.[179] His hopes dashed, he spent little time in Hexham thereafter, employing a scarcely literate Scotch curate, according to many of the letters of complaint from 1718-9 given in this volume. The profits of the post were sequestered by the archbishop in June 1719, and Laidman was effectively dismissed for

---

[175] Quoted in NCH VI, p.381. Toppin was later the curate of Allendale. See Introduction, pp.12-3.
[176] NCH III, pp.165-6, 171.
[177] Ollard & Walker, *op cit,* p.249.
[178] Henry Richmond to Sir Walter Blackett, 12 Dec 1764, NRO 672/E/1E/3.
[179] Rev John Thomlinson's Diary, published in Hodgson, *Six North Country Diaries*, *op cit*, p.85.

non-residence. His patron, Blackett, did not challenge the decision. In 1724 Laidman was installed as Rector of Whalton, a living evidently prosperous enough for him to remain there for the rest of his life.[180] His avaricious nature appears to have been borne out by the legal challenge from nephews following the death of Laidman's father in 1727, in which they asserted that he had taken the entire estate of his late father, thereby depriving them of their own share.[181]

Laing, James Curate of Allendale, 1724-1728

He came to Allendale in 1724 from Chollerton parish,[182] where he could have been no more than a curate to the long standing incumbent John Bland. Bland was presented to the Durham church court in 1722 for not paying his curate at Birtley, possibly Laing, perhaps prompting his move to Allendale.[183] Archdeacon of Northumberland Thomas Sharp suspected Laing had no licence, and he refused to show one to Andrewes, busying himself carrying out clandestine marriages. One of these, in 1725, was in Thockrington parish, suggesting Laing worked in partnership with Edward Twedale (see below) in this brisk business.[184] By 1728 he had left Allendale, for Andrewes asked John Toppin for his licence in that year.[185]

Pearson, Rev. Dr. William, (1663- 1716) Chancellor of archdiocese of York, 1712-6

Originally from Orton in Cumberland, he took his degree at Queen's College, Oxford in 1685. If the notice included in Foster's *Alumni Oxoniensis* is to be believed, he began an industrious and impressively geographically widespread career collecting church positions in south Devon, becoming the vicar of Kingston immediately upon graduating. 1690 saw him add the rectories of Cheriton Bishop far across the same county, Aston near

---

[180] J & J.A. Venn, *Alumni Cantabrigienses, Part 1, Vol 3,* (1924), p.34.

[181] Durham University Library, DPRI/3/1727/B186; TNA Chancery Bill of Complaint transcribed in http://www.laidman.org/ps06_ 390.htm. No further reference given.

[182] Andrewes to Jubb, 18 March 1724, doc. **138.**

[183] Shuler, pp. 63, 319.

[184] NCH IV p.396.

[185] Andrewes to Jubb, 5 August 1728, doc. **160.**

Birmingham, and Barton in Nottinghamshire at the same time, as well as becoming a York Cathedral Canon and archdeacon of Nottingham.[186] Even if only the last two posts came into the hands of this William Pearson, it represents impressive advancement for a man not yet thirty years old. He 'traded up' from Barton through two Yorkshire parishes, coming to rest at the rich living of Bolton Priory from 1697, by which time he was also sub-Dean at York. He succeeded to the post of Chancellor following the death of his father-in-law, Henry Watkinson, the previous incumbent, in 1712. As chancellor, a prestigious but not greatly remunerative post as supreme judge in the ecclesiastical courts, he was therefore a churchman with a passing understanding of canon law, rather than a trained lawyer, and was hastily made a doctor of law on his accession, to provide a suitable gloss of professional respectability.[187]

Richardson, Rev. William (poss 1671-1724) Reader and assistant curate at Hexham, 1710-9

Richardson was possibly the son of the Rev John Richardson of Aycliffe near Darlington who was educated at Sedbergh and St. John's College, Cambridge, and ordained at Durham in 1692.[188] From 1710 he was engaged by Ritschel as the 'afternoon preacher' in Hexham, the poorly rewarded post Ritschel had identified to Archbishop Sharp as a suitable beneficiary of the Queen Anne's Bounty in 1703. He served as Ritschel's assistant curate at Hexham from 1712, and was the incumbent at nearby Slaley from the same year. Richardson seems to have been regarded as a dependable dogsbody by both Ritschel and Andrewes, deputed by the latter to issue licences in his absence of several months from late 1718. He was effectively left as acting curate in the town after Laidman's departure and during the sequestration of 1719, but then passed over twice by Blackett when the Hexham curacy became vacant in 1719 and 1721. He died at Slaley in 1724. Patten, the curate of Allendale who joined the Jacobite rebellion and then bought his pardon by turning King's Evidence, suggested in later editions of his history of

---

[186] Foster, *op cit,* Vol III, p.1134.
[187] Skaife, *op cit*, No.153, Till, Study, p.218.
[188] Venn, *op cit,* (1924), p.455.

the rebellion that Richardson had been inclined to the Jacobite cause, but decided to remain in Hexham rather than join the rebels.[189]

Twedale, Edward Curate of St. John Lee, 1720-8

An Edward Twedale was baptised at Tynemouth in 1693. Twedale received deacon's orders from the Bishop of Carlisle in 1718,[190] but appears never to have been ordained a priest, and certainly evaded all attempts by Andrewes to show or obtain a licence. He was minister of Thockrington, a separate peculiar of York, from 1718, and then presented to St.John Lee by Blackett in 1720, to succeed the notorious Bentham. He also obtained the curacy of Corsenside and was Master of Hexham Grammar School. Often castigated by Andrewes for performing clandestine marriages, he was also presented to the court at York for frequently being drunk. He was eventually suspended and removed in 1728.[191]

---

[189] R.Patten, *The history of the rebellion in the year 1715*, (3rd end 1746), p.26.
[190] NCH IV, p.131.
[191] NCH IV, p.134.

3. Editorial conventions

Each document is presented and numbered chronologically, and identified at its head in bold type. Letters are identified by date and the name of the correspondents ('from', then 'to') where known, and other documents by their title or a suitable description if untitled. Dates are given in the title line using the modern calendar, to support the chronological ordering of the material, and all cross-references within supporting text and footnotes use the modern calendar form, as well as the associated document number in bold text. As mentioned in the Introduction, unless the source is otherwise identified immediately below the document title line, the original material is held in BIA Pec.Hex/2.

Within each document, dates and place of writing are entered as and where given. Calendar dating followed the Julian form in England until 1752, with the new calendar year beginning on Lady Day, 25th March. The contemporary short form for the months September to December is given where entered, ie. '7ber' to '10ber/Xber' respectively. The inclusion of the corresponding modern date in the document title line avoids any ambiguity.

Transcription of any addressing or envelope information is included at the foot of the letter. Where editorial notes are needed to distinguish these, and any marginal notes/ additions, from the main body of the text, they are given in italics within square brackets. Each word missing through damage or otherwise obscured is indicated as follows: [...]

Text, spellings, capitalisation, punctuation and grammar have been transcribed as entered in the original document, to remain as faithful to the original as possible. The first sentence of each paragraph has been indented. Many words are abbreviated in the original material, and these are handled as follows.

- Abbreviations are left shortened where the meaning remains clear, because of the abbreviation itself or the context in which it is found (eg. 'which' is left as 'wch' where it is spelt as such in the original, 'about' as 'abt', 'Lord' as 'Ld'). All such abbreviations are included in the glossary. Where the final letter is dropped from words such as licence and variance, the meaning remains clear so these are also given as written.

- Shortened forms of forenames are also left as written. Most are either still familiar or obvious (eg. 'Wm' or 'Elizt'). The more obscure are included in the glossary (eg. 'Xtopher')
- Contemporary abbreviations that have passed into reasonably common historical use eg. 'Admon' rather than 'Letters of Administration' are left unchanged and are documented in the glossary.
- A small number of simple and repetitive abbreviations where the meaning is less immediately obvious have been silently expanded, to avoid cluttering the text:
  - 'Ao' –given as 'Anno' 'hu' –humble
  - 'o.r' – our 'wrin' –wherein
  - 'yr' - your
- The letter thorn, similar to the letter 'y' in the way it was represented in residual usage by the late 17th century, and often therefore confused as the modern 'y', has been silently replaced with its closest modern approximation, 'th'. 'Yt', 'ys', 'ym' and 'ye', are therefore silently expanded to 'That', 'this', 'them' and 'the', respectively. 'The' was never pronounced '*yee*'.
- The use of 'ff', in place of capital F, has been silently changed to 'F'
- The use of 'l' or 'li' following a number has been replaced by '£' before the number
- Square brackets are used to expand less frequent obscure or ambiguous abbreviations.

For ease of reference, obscure terms encountered only once are explained in footnotes to the text rather than in the glossary. Otherwise footnotes are used sparingly, to provide clarification rather than interpretation. They are used to identify people named in the documents for whom further contextual information assists understanding. Any such background is given where such individuals first appear. They were invariably people with influence, position or local power already well known to the correspondents. There is much less that can be added by way of footnotes on ordinary people, who are often the subject of the correspondence, and therefore introduced by the writer. It is hoped that the publication of this material will stimulate further research into their lives.

4. Glossary and commonly used abbreviations within the documents

24ly/ 24ty	Parish vestry, comprising 24 men, hence the common shortened form. In Hexham half were appointed by the town (ie. the manor court) and half by the perpetual curate.
7ber	September
8ber	October
9ber	November
10ber	December
Abt	about
Acct/ acctt	account
Acquittance	Receipt
Adcon	See 'Admon'
Admon	Letters of administration, granted to allow disposal of an estate where no will was made
Agt	Against
Allegacon	Allegation, an unproved assertion
Apparator	Church court official who served citations
App'd	Appeared
Borough (jury)	In the context of Hexham, the sub-court of the Manor of Hexham which oversaw the town, and its jury
Bpp	Bishop
Canon law	Church law, administered through the church courts
cause	Case in the church courts
Ch	Church
Citacon/ citation	Initial summons in a church court cause
Clandestine marriages	Marriages taking place other than in a church. There were clear laws for church weddings: banns to be read or licence obtained, wedding in the church of residence of one of the couple, any aged under 21 to have parental consent. This did not, however, mean verbal promises to marry, ie. engagement followed by consummation, or the public exchange of vows (anywhere) were illegal marriages under ecclesiastical law. This confused situation was taken advantage of by unscrupulous

	clergymen, until it was tidied up by Hardwick's Marriage Act of 1753.
Commutation	In the context of the church court system, a payment of fine as a substitute for doing public penance in Church
Com.on	Commission
Compa	Company
contumacy	Contempt of the church court
Decd	Deceased
Dismission	Usually means the annual discharge of churchwardens from their duties – after they have paid their fees
Ecclicall	Ecclesiastical
Excom	Excommunication – see Introduction pp.16-7
Fornicon/ fornicacon	Fornication
Gt	Great
Guardians	Occasionally used instead of churchwardens in the context of this correspondence
Impropriate	A church or parish where the tithes are in the hands of a layman or non-church body rather than the local minister
Inrry/ invry	Inventory - a list and valuation of the deceased's personal goods and chattles. It excluded real property, which fell outside the jurisdiction of the church courts.
Intestate	Someone dying without leaving a will
Jurisdicon	Jurisdiction, usually the short form for the ecclesiastical jurisdiction of the peculiar
Libel	Declaration drawn up by the plaintiff in a church cause, covering points which the plaintiff's proctor is prepared to prove by the evidence of witnesses.
Lre	Letter
Ma[tie] /Majtie	Majesty
Mark	13s 4d, ie. 2 nobles (see below)
Mencon	mention
Mich	Michaelmas, 29 September
Monicon	See monition
Monition	admonishment or instruction
NewCa:	Newcastle
Noble	6s 8d, ie. 3 nobles = £1

Nuncupative will	A will made by word of mouth, and then written down later by the witnesses. A higher standard of proof was typically required than for wills signed and sealed by the testator
Papt	Papist, Catholic
Pd	paid
Pish	parish
Process	In the context of the operation of the church courts within this correspondence, this was the document containing the citations, presentments or instructions to attend the church court sitting
psecute	prosecute
Prsent/ prsentmts	Present/ presentments
Pson	par
Pt	part
P'tence	pretence
Pticular	particular
Proctor	A church lawyer able to act in legal or financial affairs on behalf of his master and as counsel for a client.
Proxy	Substitute person or authority delegated by document
Reced	received
relac.ons	relations
Rd	received
Sd	said
Sequestration	Taking the profits of a parish/ benefice into the hands of the bishop, or other church superior, during a vacancy caused by death, resignation, unlawful absence or improper conduct of the minister.
Sesse/ cesse	a tax or rate, strictly short for assessment
Spr	spinster
Sr	Sir
Stamps/ stamp duty	The duty imposed on different legal documents including documents used as evidence in courts, grants of probate and letters of administration. Introduced in England in 1694, initially for ten years only, it was intended to pay for the war with

France. Payment was authenticated by stamps on the document, hence the frequent references in the correspondence.

Surrog	Surrogate – deputy/delegate
Thoa	though
Visitacon/ Vis^{on}	Visitation – inspection of an ecclesiastical jurisdiction by a senior church official.
Warr't	warrant
Wch	Which
Wd	would
Wid/ Widd	widow
Wors'p'll	Worshipfull, as in 'right worshipful' Chancellor
Wr	were
Whrof	whereof
Wth	With
Xber	December
Xtopher	Christopher

5. Letters from Hexham

1. 2 Feb 1699 Allgood & Carr [192] to Watkinson

[Papers relating to Mr. Ritschel and to Hexham, Bundle 13: NRO SANT/GEN/ECC/3/3/ 2-9]

Sr

Never any parish in this County has been so used & abused by a Minister as this by Mr George Ritschell who is a very Litigious troublesome man & at variance with most of his Parishioners & now as bad as ever, he is rather worse than Parson Walton[193] he pretends to be your deputy here & upon every frivilous matter Showes & threatens the people to make them appeare before the Chancellor of Yorke telling them that (upon his Letter) he can have Citation or Citations when & for what he pleases. Last Sunday he read & published a Citation in this Church in your name agt John Bell & James Watson to appeare before you at Yorke the Ninth of February Instant to be Sworn & admitted unto & Execute the office of Jurors etc or else to Show some good cause & reason (sine ratione) why the Sentence of Excommunication should not be decreed agt them for their Contumacy in refuseing to be sworn and execute the said office, & writ to them that you ordered the Citation for them to appeare before you. Sr if he be your Deputy as he said he is wee have a Motion among us, that Respondeat Superior[194] he is about bringing up the Oath ex officio again & the High Commission Court which wee thought had been & thinke is taken away by Act of Parliament, Severall of the Substantiall Parishioners here were about petitioning the Arch Bishop and others the Parliament, about this Matter, but wee thought it Convenient first to acquaint you therewith, one of them that is now Cited is one that severall yeares agoe was Church Warden & Cited with the rest to appeare before you at Yorke which

---

[192] Thomas Allgood and John Carr: see ABN.

[193] Almost certainly Revd Thomas Walton, rector of Knarsdale near Alston from 1679-94, who was charged with assault in 1686, escaped from custody at Kirkhaugh in 1690, & found guilty of neglect of duty, fornication, blasphemy and simony at the York consistory court in 1693. J. Hodgson, *History of Northumberland*, Vol III, part II, (1840), p.81, NRO QSB/4, QSO/2, f42r, BIA CP.H.4242.

[194] An employer's legal liability for the actions of an employee, established in English common-law during the seventeenth century.

they did, & although they could not be Charged with any thing in reason to ground a Citation upon but his owne false Suggestion and upon Examination of the matter he himselfe was guilty of what he charged them with, And had & published an Excommunication agt them here within a day or two the Citation was returnable which wee were informed was irreguler, & all the Satisfaction they had or gott for their journey & Expenses was an absolution, he reported it was to noe end or purpose, For them to medle with him in that Court at this rate he may Excommunicate most of the Parishioners & they shall have noe relief or Remedy unless they Petition the Parliament which wee are very unwilling to do, if it can be otherwise ordered, Sir Edward & Sir William Blackett[195] can & perhaps will give a Character of him, that he is a man of a very unquiett temper, Malitious & much addicted to lyeing wee have transgressed upon your patience with our prolixities for which wee crave your pardon & leave to Subscribe our Selves Sir

Your Humble Servants
T. Allgood
Jon. Carr

Hexham Candlemas day 1698

[*Cover:*]
The Right Worshipful Dr Henry Watkinson
Chancellor of York these present

2. 6 February 1699 **Ritschel to Watkinson**
[NRO SANT/GEN/ECC/3/3/ 2-9]

Northumb'd

A Brief Representation of Mr Ritschel of Hexham his grievances. containing Reasons agt Mr Allgoods haveing a new 24ty, & being himselfe one of them, and the occasion of the late differenc etc:

---

[195] Sir Edward Blackett of Newby, 2nd baronet (1649-1718): Purdue, *The Ship That Came Home*, *op cit*, pp.77-84, and his younger brother Sir William: ABN.

Imprimis In the year 1684 he haveing deluded & perswaded a great many here in Town to sign a Scurrillous petition agt me to the Rt Worspll Compa of mercers London (wch diverse of them after retracted when they understood the contents thereof.) being disappointed of his gt design & thereby exasperated.

The year following he sued me in the name of Sr John Fenwick then Ld of the Mannor etc for takeing the lead of the north Quarter of the Church, wch was agreed upon before my father dyed, and a bargain made with the plummer by the Ch Wardens Jurors and 24ty & Mr Allgood being then one of them was present at the bargain and well acquainted with it, wch he after denyd it not being reduced to writeing, but when he perceivd that diverse of them wd swear it, he brought not on that action, yet made me attend wth my wittnesses till the end of the Assizes.

The same year the Ch Wardens sued me at Common Law for six shillings & nine penc arrear of Ch sesse wch one in the Shire left at my house, & wch Shortly after I sent to them the very same mony, but they wd not receive it, & after when I tendred it at a publick meeting, they wd not receive it till they had consulted their Atturney who was Mr Allgood, who if he did not at first advise them to it, yet he did manage that action for them wch upon examination appeard very very vexatious and malitious.

Nor hath he faild ever sinc to give fresh instances of his malice both to myselfe & family thoa he seemd reconcild and all former differences quite forgotten, of wch I could give too many instances.

When I begun to cutt my fathers Epitaph, some haveing informd the Ld of the Mannor that stone belongd to him, who referring it to Mr Allgood & his Steward here to examin that matter & my pretensions to it, thoa they seemd satisfyd with what I alleagd that it was an immemorial burying place belonging to the Ministers of this parish, yet after haveing gott or pretending to have gott a order to discharge the workman he not only threatend to indict all that should be concernd in laying down that Stone, but his passion transported him so farr as to bid the workman deface the inscription, & yet he pretended a gt respect for old Mr Ritschels memory.

My Brother[196] haveing gott A presentation from the University of Cambr.e to the Vicaridge of Bywell St Andrew in this County, by vertue of the late Act etc and a Summons for Madam Thornton (A Popish Patronesse & who had given a presentation to another) to appear at Sessions & take the oaths, when the party made Affidavit that he had Summond her & she had declared that she wd never take them, Mr Allgood being then in Court moved in her behalfe, & thoa he was not concernd in that affair, & pretended at that time great kindnesse for my Brother who had never disoblegd him & the Bench had replyd to what he offerrd, yet he could not forbear after a while to move again, wch being the nicking point in order to her conviction & the obtaining that liveing, I leave it to any to judge the Syncerity of his gt affection he bears to my family.

Anno 94 He made an enquiry to our Burw [borough] Jury in behalfe of the Ld of the Mannor concerning the fees belonging to the Minister Clerk & Sexton. And the last Northumb'd Assizes A Bill of Indictmt being preferrd agt me for takeing 5s for a marriage fee with a licenc, that Bill being found ignoramus

2d Bill was preferrd & Mr Allgoods late Clerk Robinson sent up to bring down the Hexham Jury Book & attest it wch I suppose Robinson thought an unquestionable evidenc; when he told one he had that (meaning that Book) wch wd do Mr Ritschels businesse, that Book or verdict allowing 1s for a marriage wch is our ordinary fee. and takeing no notice of a marriage fee with A Licenc. But the worthy Gentlemen of that grand Inquest percevieing it to be pure malice, rejected that Book & Jurys Verdict in that Case & found that Bill also ignoramus.

I might here add the hard usage I mett wth Anno 94 abt my sesses Mr Allgood being then A Com.r for the land tax. and the next year I was told he endeavoured the like, but it wd be tedious to repeat all instances of this nature, for such hath been his constant practice these 15 years last past, to misrepresent & endeavour to expose Mr Ritschel to the Censure of the world & by all means possible to make him uneasy.

Our late differences were occasioned partly upon account of the poor & p[ar]tly upon acct of the church.

---

[196] Rev. John Ritschel (1662-1705), at Bywell from 1690: NCH VI, p.248.

Some poor haveing gott Orders of Sessions for so much a week towards their reliefe & maintenanc, these orders wr brought to the Ch Wardens, but they were so obstructed in their proceedings that office became an intollerable burden.

And thoa overseers for the poor wr after appointed according to Law, yet that did not prevent or lessen their trouble, the Q[uarter]r Sessions have been pesterd with repeated complaints orders made upon former orders, & warrants after warr'ts to bind them to their good behaviour for not observeing those orders, & Mr Ritschel misrepresented as if he were to blame.

In Octobr 96 Mr Allgood haveing gott a Justice of the Peac's Warr't to carry the Ch Wardens bodys to jail for not paying Barbara Gibson Widd 2s per week according to an order of Sessions; but their names not being specifyd or expressd, the New Ch Wardens who were shortly after admitted were threatened with it, whereupon to prevent further trouble, I calld a meeting of the Ch Wardens Jurors & 24ty, who laid on a sesse for the poor according to the pish Rate or Schedule made by the sworn 24ly for the Town, But assoon as those ChWardens began to collect it, Mr Allgood sent for them, & threatend them, & took their Schedules from them.

And yet at Middsummer Sessions after he did move for a warr't to bind them to their good behaviour for neglecting to pay her, & I being then in Court informd them how it was, that they were not to blame & thoa the Court was then satisfyd, & there was no order made while I was there; yet a while after they were taken by vertue of A warr't & forcd to go down to NewCastle etc.

Never had men such a troublesome Officer for the Ch Wardens must pay the poor & that out from the Ch sesse; & yet people were told & made belive that they needed not pay their Ch sesse & most in Town for sometime refused to pay it; so that they could not gett mony for necessary uses & the parish so totally lost its creditt, that none wd trust them or do any thing for it; unlesse Mr Ritschel would promise to pay them.

Indeed his proceedings in that affair have been so very strange, that one may justly wonder at them & must conclude that there is some extraordinary reason for it,

Wch seems very plain to those who know the whole matter, that Madm Mary Fenwick haveing left £100 to bind poor children apprentices, & Mr Allgood haveing gott that mony into his hands, he knows very well what endeavours Mr Ritschel hath used to have it better settled, thoa hitherto to little purpose.

As to the Church: the Slate Roof thereof was grown so ruinous, that in a short time it wd not have been fitt for divine service, the Ch Wardens Jurors & 24ty had been diverse times calld & viewd it; but took no care to prevent its ruins, or rather wd not meddle with it, for that it was supposed to be so very badd that it could not be repaird without takeing down a great part of it, & there was no mony to putt it up again.

A little before winter Anno 96 when it could not be deferrd any longer, I desired the Ch Wardens to sett on workmen at day tale wages to mend it & prevent its falling, which they excused for that they had no mony to pay them & becaus I wd not do it myselfe, I perswaded 2 of the 24ty to do it; but they left it to me to pay them & take care of that concern.

After they had finishd that work, wch they did much cheaper & better than was expected to the gt satisfaction of all people, I calld a meeting of the Ch Wardens Jurors & 24ty & gave them a note of the parish debts, & the debate was whether to borrow mony or lay on a sesse to pay them; Jno Bell offerd If any wd joyn with him to be bound for the Town for the one halfe, & those in the Shire after agreed to lay on a 12 fold sesse to pay their halfe, & no doubt but all matters wd have been amicably adjusted, if they had not been obstructed.

For Mr Allgood appears now at last & will have a new 24ty & they will do great things for the Church; & sent me a note (& of late I have receivd other two such notes) to read in the Ch to summon the Inhabitants of this Town & Shire to meet and consult with the Bailif of this Liberty abt choosing 24ty etc which I refused to read & to wch I answer

If Mr Allgood had appeard before the Ch was repaird while it lay so long ruinous & no body durst or wd meddle with it it had lookt great indeed in him, but not to do it till it was repaird & there was no occasion shows some other design.

And I think its plain enough to those who know Mr Allgoods temper, his former proceedings, & duely considering them & our present circumstances, that it is not so much out of love to the Ch as out of peak & design, haveing so fair a prospect to create new troubles, as he did Anno 84 & 85 when he gott both the Town & me to great trouble & charge and none but himselfe was gainer by it.

Hexham Febry 6 - 98

[*Cover:*]
For The Rt Worshipful Henry Watkinson
Ld Chancellr of York

3. 13 February 1699 **Ritschel to Watkinson**

[NRO SANT/GEN/ECC/3/3/ 2-9]

Rt Worspll

I have seen a copy of a letter from Mr Allgood & Jno Carr of this Town to your Worsp wherein they accuse me of very ill things I conceive myself obleged to have that matter examind to clear myselfe of those foul aspertions, & I suppose both his Grace my Ld ArchBp & your Worsp expect it from me, yet I conceive it not improper in the mean time to give a particular answer to their letter.

Imprimis I may begin with their own words & retort them upon themselves And never any Minister in this County has been so used & abused by a magistrate as I have been these 15 years by Mr Thomas Allgood who upon every occasion hath shewd his implacable malice both to myselfe & family, as will appear from a full account of my grievances too tedious here to relate.

2ly They accuse me that I am a very Litigious troublesome man & at varianc with most of my pishioners & rather worse than p[ar]son Walton...........I have lookt over the depositions agt Mr Walton & find diverse grosse enormitys proved agt him, and I do challenge them to prove any of them or any such like things agt me. If I were such an one, as Mr Walton, one may justly wonder that Mr Allgood who these 15 years has so diligently watchd my Calling, and yet hath never been able to compasse his mischeivous designs agt me. Should have had patienc so long and suffer me to prceed to such a height of wickednesse, & not have begun sooner with me.

As to my being a very Litigious troublesome man at varianc with most of my pishioners, I thank god I live very quiettly amongst them and hope to do so If Mr Allgood will lett us alone; nor have I ever sued either man or woman either in Town or Shire, except Mr C. & John Story who as they had not been long in my pish so they were then abt to leave it, & it was at our Syde Court where the whole charge is or ought to be but eight penc, & it was for just debt & I gott my mony wch else I had lost.

If it be not so, its matter of fact and matter of Record, and so may easily be provd, and I know none can do it so well as Mr Allgood for that he is Clerk of the Courts, and has also a fee for every writt executed within this Liberty and so can give & I desire that he will give an exact catalogue of those Lawsuits wherein I have been concernd.

3ly I call my selfe your Deputy and threaten people upon every frivolous matter to cite them etc: I think myselfe happy that I have nothing from my pishioners but the Surplice fees, and so have no dealings with them in those concerns wch too often occasion suits at Law; I never had occasion to cite any to your Court upon my own account and then why should I threaten them to do it, If the partys beliveing [...] them declare it, If none such can be found it will appear to be their false suggestion, as also that I call my selfe your Deputy.

yet I am ready to gratify their desire, and give you an account of all that I have done sinc I have been concernd under you in this Jurisdiction when you shall please to appoint the time.

As to the instanc they give that I am Litigious, that Bell & Watson were cited etc its a begging the question; that matter being depending in your Court, when it is ended it will then appear, whether they or I ought to be accounted Litigious.

4ly I am abt bringing up the oath ex Officio again & the high commission Court etc and the fear and apprehension hereof hath putt them upon thoughts to petition the Parliamt.

Here is pure Stuffe, and very like Mr Allgood and their former petition wherein they inserted such improbable things, that they needed no answer, and such scurrillous anonymous papers were then sent agt me to the Rt Worspll Compa of Mercers London, that Sr Benj. Thorowgood who then was Master threatend to clapp up on the bearer, and he after told my Atturney he was sorry that he had not secured him till he made it appear of whom he had those papers etc.

5ly they complain of the usage the Ch Wardens had Anno 84 & that I was guilty of those things for wch they were cited etc. If you Remembr Sr they were cited upon a presentmt (a copy of wch I have yet by me) for not giveing in their presentments, and collecting the Brief for the Repair or Rebuilding the Church at Portsmouth etc and they were to appear as I take it upon the 29th of January but Mr Parker & Mr Holmes who were then my Proctors calld them sooner, and because they did not then appear they moved and gott an Excommunication agt them but when they appeard on the day the Citation was returnable they gott absolution & I hope my Proctors mistake will not be laid to my charge, I believe it was a lucky hitt for them & they gott off the better for it.

And whereas they complain that they gott no satisfaction for their journy and expences, that is a very wide mistake for they placed in their accounts that year £8 13s 0d for Councell fees Draft fees & other fees in Court, (whereas I was informd they pd only a dismission fee) and had besides 40s allowed them for their journy as their accounts will yet testify.

6ly They charge me with pretending to have so gt an interest in your Court that its to no purpose to meddle with me there, and their fears hereof are so great, that if I should excommunicate many of my pishioners, they wd have no relief unlesse they petition the Parliamt.

I deny that ever I reported or spoke a word intimateing any such thing, I perceive Mr Allgood has a mind to petition the Parliamt but I canot tell to what purpose he should trouble that August Assembly, unlesse he do really fear that your Court will not do him justice, Mr Walton found justice in your Court nor do I expect to escape it, if they shall prove their Libellous Letter. Or is Mr Ritschel such an offender that there are no Laws in force will reach him, but they must petition the Parliamt and what if the Parliamt should reject their petition as vexatious in what a sadd case wd they be without any hope of relief.

7ly They pretend that Sr Edw & Sr Wm Blackett can give A Character of me (and God knows its a very black one) that I am a man of a very unquiett temper malitious and much addicted to Lying.

I have been acquainted with Sir Edw abt 15 years and he has been pleasd to give a very favourable Character of me. & I know no reason he has now to do otherwise save that I did not vote for the

Gents he joynd with at our last Election for Kts etc: for my part I shall not desert Mr Forsters interest[197] so long as he is for the Ch interest & the present Govermt for that he appeard so great Anno 88 wch I think ought not to be so soon forgotten by us.

As to the nature of the Character they pretend those two worthy Knights can give of me, I desire they may be interceded with to certify their knowledge of me. whether they do either know or believe me to be such a person as they have described me to be.

So much in answer to their letter, what remains is a humble request, that this matter may be fully examined that the truth here of may appear, and the world may know whether I am guilty or not, of those things whereof they have accused me; which will very much oblige

Rt Worspll
Your Worsps
Most Humble Servt
George Ritschel

Hexham Febry the 13th - 98

[*Cover:*]
To The Rt Worspll Henry Watkinson
Ld Chancellor of Yorke These prsent

4. 13 February 1699 **Ritschel to Watkinson**
[NRO SANT/GEN/ECC/3/3/ 2-9]

Rt Worspll

I Receivd your letter with the copy of Mr Allgood & Jno Carr's and these return humble thanks that you were pleasd to give yourselfe the trouble to lett me know who mine accusers are and what they have agt me, I sent a note to Mr Allgood to desire a sight of your letter to them who said he had it not, immediately I sent to

[197] Sir William Forster of Bamburgh, 1667-1700, & MP for Northumberland from 1689. A staunch High Church Tory who was elected one of the county's MPs in 1698 alongside Sir Edward Blackett, in the election to which Ritschel refers here.

Jno Carr who sd he had it not Mr Allgood shall write to Mr Empson[198] to take counsell how [...] affair, in the mean time I have sent enclosed an Answer to their Letter.

When Sr Wm Blackett was here in Octobr last at our head Court our Jurors etc expected I wd have referrd all matters to him, and the steward of his court, & Sr Wm sent for me in amongst them, but when I perceivd how things wd go, I took my leave & left the Room: I was after told Sr Wm Didd them assoon as I cited them to write to Yorke & fee A Proctor & abide me A tryall & it should not cost them a farthing........And that sometime after He did ask Mr Allgood, If he thought I could be turned out of the Curacy who sd he thought I could & Jno Carr sd also he was of the same opinion wr.upon he sd If it wr possible I should be turnd out, & I will give it to thee Tom, and thou shalt give it to whom thou please. This perhaps may seem strange to those who know not a reason, wch I am very sensible is none other, save my voteing for Mr Forster at our last Election, for its by the Curacy I have A vote.

It has been Mr Allgoods desire & project of a long time to have such A Curate as he can manage at pleasure, & so all the affaires both of the Town & parish, the principle wch some wd go on is that the Ld of the Mannor is Improp[riator] & has an absolute right to the Ch & that his Bailif ought to manage everything under him And being also Parsona Imparsonee, as every Minister may choose his own Curate so he may turn me off at pleasure but I perceive Mr Allgood designs to try another way.

Before I sent for the Citation agt Mrs Raw, I not only sent but spoke to her my selfe & told her sinc she had comitted such an offenc she must make satisfaction & sinc she wd be unwilling to do publick penanc she must give somewhat to some pious use, that it cost her £20 as I was told to lye in at NewCastle If she were willing to give £25 wch I thought moderate enough I should represent the matter to your Worsp; If his Grace were pleasd to accept of it, I had no more to do in that matter, & wd not gett a farthing by it I designed to have sent some to her after she was cited, to have made the like offer, but I hear that Walker to expose me hath told in NewCastle that I demand.d £25 for myselfe; and therefore I shall not concern myselfe any further with her or him but leave them to the Law, or to his Grace & your Worsp. If they appear & submitt & are willing to

[198] Thomas Empson, Deputy Registrar at York; see ABN.

give somewhat & his Grace be pleasd to accept of the commutation, These request it may be applyd either to the use of Whitley Chapple, or to purchase A peic of ground close adjoyning to the South syde of our Ch calld Thomsons backsyde, wch is a place for dunghills and a very great neauseanc, I offerd some years ago to buy it with my own mony & enclose it and convert it to a burying place, but the widdow wd not lett her son to sell it then, but I believe in a while they may be under such circumstances that they may be willing to part with it; wch is all at present save that I am

Rt Worspll Your Worsps Most Humble Servt
George Ritschel

Hexham Febry the 13th 98

[*Cover :*]
To The most Revd Father in God John his Grace Ld Arch Bp of Yorke Primate and Metropolitane of England
These present

5. 4 March 1699 **Ritschel to Sharp**
[NRO SANT/GEN/ECC/3/3/ 2-9]

Most Revd Father in God.

I conceive it my duty being under your Graces Jurisdiction, to give you an account of the State of our Free Grammar School, how our Governors of later years seem to have laid asyde their constitutions, & govern according to pleasure, for they keep no Usher & hire a Master for so much a year, & to take of the odium of turning him off upon every little peak, they made the late Master sign a writing to resign the school upon three months warning, nor did they acquaint him with their Constitutions, and the affaires of the school, nor have they A Table of theBenefactors Names etc and they keep their accounts amongst themselves.

Some years ago I accidentally gott a sight and copy of their Charter & Constitutions (wch has been no small peic of mortification to them) & a while after I spoke to some of them abt reforming some things, wch they seemd willing to do, but when I spoke to Mr Jno Carr who is Sr Willm Blacketts Steward here, he resented it ill, and said wd they be governd by an Arch Bps Constitutions, and before Middsummer last when I read the processe for A Court, I cited John Wilkinson & Robt Bell the late Stewards to bring in their accounts, he could not forbear to speak, & said not to you, and after service was ended he continued in great passion, & reproved me for medling with their School, wd they give an account to the Curate of Hexham, it should cost him £100 etc.

They have also the disposeing of some moneys for the use of the poor, how they manage that affair is known to themselves, yet it seems as if due care has not been taken thereof; for that they have A Rent Charge of £100 from old Sr John Fenwicke, and none of them can remember any demand either of interest or principal, & when they demanded it of the late Sr John after he had sold the estate, his Attorney told me he had pleaded, or wd plead that it was paid. And A Governor confest they had other mony in bad hands, And Madam Mary Fenwick haveing left £100 to the Town to buy somewhat to bind poor children apprentices, Mr Algood our Bailife has gott that mony into his hands. Its true that some few have been bound by him, but I have heard some of the partys complain that they could not gett the mony due upon that account. Haveing trespassed upon your patienc by so many particulars these begg pardon for this trouble & leave to subscrib myself

Your Graces Most humble Servt
George Ritschel

I have sent your Grace herewith A Copy of their Charter & Constitutions as also of Madam Fenwickes Bequest

Hexham March the 4th 98

[*Cover:*]

To The most Revd Father in God John his Grace Ld Arch Bp of Yorke Primate and Metropolitane of England at Bishop Thorpe
to be left with the Postmn of Yorke post pd
These prsent

6. 24 April 1699 **Ritschel to Sharp**

[NRO SANT/GEN/ECC/3/3/ 2-9]

Most Revd Father in God.

I lately gave your Grace an account of the State of our Free School, & I perceive Mr Chancellor acquainted your Grace with A letter from Mr Allgood & Jno Carr Sr Willm Blacketts Bailif & Steward here, wherein they accuse me of diverse things & that of the High Commission Court seems to very improbable that diverse Gentlemen to whom I have shewd the copy of their Letter do laugh at them for it. The occasion is said to be the businesse about our Sydesmen, but there is somewhat at the bottome & the design is, if possible to turn me out of the Curacy.

They have of late made diligent enquiry & drawn up a great many Articles agt me, but finding that they will not do the turn. I am told they design to swear treason agt me, wch seems the more probable for that the like happend here abt 16 years ago. Mr Allgood haveing taken a peak agt Mr Armstrong an Atturney drew up abt 40 Articles agt him in order to make him a Common Barraster, wch being not sufficient to do his businesse One MorraLee A cozen of mr Allgoods did swear Scandalum Magnatum[199] agt Mr Armstronge, that He should speak very ill words agt his late Matie when D of Yorke,[200] & by good luck the words should have been spoken in Company but not a man did hear them besides Morralee who haveing none to joyn with him in his evidenc, Mr Armstronge did overcome that gt difficulty & after upon examination of the matter did clear himselfe of their aspertions to the shame of his accusers, who could not prove one of their Articles thoa they had subpaenad no small number of wittnesses.

If they shall exhibit any Articles agt me these request your Grace wd be pleasd to order me A copy thereof in order to my own defenc & that these matters may be brought to an examination. I am

---

199 To slander or defame the great and powerful, a medieval criminal offence that experienced something of a revival under Charles II and James II.

200 ie. James II, monarch between 1685-8.

sorry that I have given your Grace this trouble, for wch I begg your pardon & leave to subscrib my selfe

Your Graces Most humble servt
George Ritschel

Hexham April the 24th 99

7. 11 March 1700 William Carr [201] to Empson

Sir

Yesterday in our Church at Hexham a Monition was read to admonish all & singular the next of kindred of George Heron late of Hexham & pticularly one Hannah Heron his Widdow & relict to prove the Decds Will or to [*deleted*] take Adcon if he made no Will or to shew Cause why (on Friday next) John Armstrong gent principall Creditor should not take Adcon, I cannot heare of any debt is oweing to the sd Mr Armstrong onely Mr Armstrong speakes of a debt of £15 11s, but no body can tell how created, but the Widd has a mind to oppose the Adcon of Mr Armstrong, One Jasper Hall has a debt due to him of abt 16 or £18, & his wife is a relation to the Decd, upon setting up that, I would have Mr Armstrong to shew what his debt is, but rather than he have the Adcon Mrs Hannah Heron the Widd will take the Adcon or Mr Hall whose wife is of kindred, pray hinder his Adcon & see what this debt is for & let me have an Answer as soon as possibly. Mrs Halls name is Anne the Wife of Jasper Hall.

William Bell of Huntwell in the Parish of Allendale yeomn sayd of Elizabeth the wife of John Dawson of Sheelbanks in the sd Parish of Allendale, within the peculiar Jurisdiction of Hexham & Hexhamshire That the said Elizabeth sayd she would lay a wager that he the said Wm durst not deal with his Dame (meaning Anne the wife of Joshua Watson of Huntwell) which said Wm then served the said Joshua; As her man servant (meaneing one Francis Ritson) had

---

[201] a William Carr of Hexham was agent to Sir Edward Blackett in respect of his lead mining and smelting interests at Fallowfield in Acomb parish in 1704 (NRO ZBL 273/13), possibly the attorney of Hexham christening his children between 1690 and 1695: HPR.

done with her, that he lifted up her Coate & tore her smock (a word used in the North fore a womans shirt) And the sd Wm sayd further that the said Elizabeth would have enticed him to do the same thing to her, ~~by~~ by the reason the speakeing these words great difference hath been since between the sd John Dawson & his wife, if these words be defamatory in the spirituall Court, I desire you send a Citation to me at Hexham in Northumberland I am

Your reall friend & Servt
William Carr

Hexham March the 11th 1699
The words were spoken a litle after Chrismas

[*in a different hand:*] Cit[ati]on sent & Appr given

8. Petition Presented at Morpeth Sessions Easter 1703
[NRO QSB 19]

To the Rt Worspll & Worspll her Ma[ties] Justices of the Peac for the County of Northumberland at the Generall Quarter Sessions of the Peac holden at Morpeth for the sd County

The Humble Petition of George Ritschell Clerk & Lecturer of Hexham in the sd County

Sheweth

That of late years (Sinc the Book of Rates was last Regulated) a deal of the lands in village of Keepwicke & Errington in the Parish of St John Lee in the sd County being laid to grasse the Corn tyths of those places wch belong to your Petitioner as Lecturer of Hexham aforesd are very much lessened in their value, and the Book of Rates being now made the Rule whereby to lay on the Land tax, he is now charged higher for the sd tyths then any other in the sd parish.

That for diverse years dureing the late warr the Lands of Errington being charged double he payd equally with that double according to his proportion of Rent, & sometimes more, but the last year the sd Corn tyths of Keepwicke and Errington being lessend in their value above £20 He paid A sixt part more then the double charged upon the Lands of Keepwicke & double the double charged upon the Lands of Errington out of wch the sd tyths issued, thoa he had taken what oaths the Governmt required.

And therefore haveing now made A discovery of the Oakwood Coalpitt in the sd Parish of St John Lees, that Its Lett for 12 years for £30 a year and is not charged in the Book of Rates nor hath ever been charged to the Land tax He appeals to the Rt Worspll Bench & prays Reliefe herein that the sd Coalpit may for the future be charged in the Book of Rates & towards the Land tax, & he may be abated so much as will bring the sd tyths to a due proportion with the Rest of the sd parish & the Lands out of wch they do issue.

And as in Duty bound your Petitioner shall ever prayse

[*entered in a different hand:*]

Keepwicke	7s	8d	……	£120	Pr Ann
the tyths	1	6	……	£8	[*unclear: written over*]
Errington	10	0	……	£200	
Tyths	2	6	……	£12	

9. 6 March 1704 **Ritschel to Sharp**

[NRO SANT/GEN/ECC/3/3/ 2-9]

Most Revd Father in God Hexham March the 6th 1703

The good successe I met with in setting up Whitley Chapple in Hexhamshire & the good effects thereof made me promote the like at Beltingham in the parish of Haltwhistle (thoa not in this Jurisdiction) upon the like occasion for that our presbyterians were setling a meeting etc. And of late we have got an afternoon Lecturer here, wch proves extreamly usefull, especially sinc our Dissenters got their new meeting house & their preacher only expounds at forenoon & preaches at afternoon................I have sent enclosed an acctt of several Impropriate Churches etc. And these humbly Request your grace wd be pleased to favour us with your assistanc that those in your Jurisdiction here vizt Allendale & St John Lees Whitley Chapple & Hexham afternoon Lecturer may be made partakers of her Maties Royall bounty expressed in her late gracious Message to the House of Commons etc

I have sent the same acctt & wrote to the same purpose to Sr Francis Blake & Mr Stote our Representatives for this County[202] & conceive it has as much to plead in its behalfe as any other; as the largenesse of some of our parishes & the poverty of the people so that they are not able to raise any considerable contributions. If all in the enclosed list canot be provided for at present these may assure your Grace that Shotley & Corsensyde & those in this Jursdiction stand in most need. I could write a great deal upon this subject & occasion but wd not seem tedious. If your Grace desire any further acctt or satisfaction, or it be needfull for us to addresse etc: If you please to order any to signify your pleasure herein it shall be readily obeyed.

The kind reception the motion I made some years ago abt Whitley Chapple found with your Grace, makes me hope this will not be ill taken, & that your Graces Candor will accept of my good intentions herein, & my zeal for the Church obtain pardon for this trouble. So that I shall only need to begg leave to subscrib myselfe the Churches &

Your Graces Mt Humbly Devoted Servt
George Ritschell

[*enclosure:*]
10. 2 March 1704 **Ritschel to Sharp**
[NRO SANT/GEN/ECC/3/3/ 2-9]

An Account of the present State of the Severall Impropriate Churches & Chapples in Tindale Ward in the County of Northumberland

The richly endowed Abbey of Hexham being invested in the Crown by the Act of Dissolution that Illustrious Princesse Queen Elizt of blessed memory by her Letters Patents bearing date the 12th day of April in the 21st year of her Reign did give the same with its Appurtenances to Sr Xtopher Hatton Kt etc Reserveing a certain yearly fee of £91 10s 5d out of the severall Impropriated tyths, £58

[202] The Whig Sir Francis Blake (1638-1718) of Ford Castle, MP for Northumberland from 1701: B.D.Henning (ed), *The House of Commons 1660-90*, (1983), p.665; Bertram Stote (1674-1707) of Jesmond Hall, MP for Northumberland 1702-5, a Tory: E.Cruickshank, S. Handley & D. Hayton, *The House of Commons 1690-1715*, (2002), p.583.

7s 9d pt thereof to be pd to the Respective Curates of the Impropriated Churchs & Chapples vizt Hexham St John Lees etc the Remainder to herselfe & Successors.

Imprimis The Curate of the large & popolous parish of Hexham has only £13 6s 8d per annum pd out of the sd fee farm Rents. Mr Richard Fishbourn Citizen and Mercer of London by his Last Will haveing left mony to augment such small liveings certain corn tyths were purchased with a part thereof for the maintenanc of a preaching Minister or Lecturer at Hexham who being now the Curate also he doth not stand in need at present, but when they shall happen to be separated the sd Curate will be a fitt object of Royall bounty, the fees being so extreamly small.

There is in Hexham Shire A certain Chapple Calld Whitley Chapple wch had been totally ruined but abt 55 years ago a small thing was erected there to teach a petty school in. Anno 94 the Quakers from severall parts came thither to preach & make proselytes & had done much mischiefe if it had not been prevented by repairing & augmenting the sd Chapple & haveing a preaching Minister etc.

The Curate of Slealy at present preaches there every 14night, but the people are so very poor, that their contributions raise little above £9 per annum thoa that part of this Shire be above 9 Northren Miles in length & there were above 700 Souls on that syde Anno 95. Its said that there were some Lands formerly belonging to the sd Chapple wch are now in the possession of Laymen.

2d Allendale a large & popolous parish containing the South West part of this County has two Chapples calld East & West Allen Chapple both in repair. The Curate of Allendale doth service there once a month. He has A salary of £8 per annum reserved out of the the sd fee farm Rents and some tyths etc the whole is now between £20 & £25 per annum & the present Curate is very poor.

3d St John Lees A Large parish has two Chapples vizt St Marys Bingfield & St Oswald both totally ruined. Yet the Curate of St John Lees doth receive the respective salarys reserved out of the said fee farm Rents for the Curates of the sd Chapples all three make £18 per annum

4th Shotley a large parish, contains the South East pt of this County the Impropriation belonged to Blanchland Abbey, the

Minister of Edmond Byars in the County of Durham doth service there every 20 days for wch he has A salary of 20 nobles.

5th Slealy a small parish some wd have it to have been a Chapple belonging to Bywell St Andrew Church. The Curate has a salary of 20 nobles reserved out of the sd fee farm Rents. Of later years Mr John Shaftoe Vicar of Neather Warden by his last Will left £10 per annum for an augmentation to the sd Salary.

6th High up South West Tyne is Lamley a very small parish formerly a pt & parcell of the Monastery of Hexham, the parson of Knaresdale doth serve the Cure there, for wch he has some small gratification, it might conveniently be united to Knaresdale parish.

7th Lower down in West Tyne in the parish of Haltwhistle is Bellingham Chapple supplyd of late with a preaching Minister upon a like occasion as Whitley Chapple & proves of great use & advantage to that part of the Countrey wch is very popolous, and farr distant from the parish Church, the Schoolmr of Heydonbridge now preaches there every 14night the contributions are small.

8th In Reedwater is Corsensyde a small parish, & a very poor Countrey syde the Curate has only 20 nobles per annum & the present Curate is very poor.

9th Thockerington a little small parish, is an Impropriation & a prebend belonging to Yorke. I have known the whole lett for £24 per annum & will not exceed £30, out of wch there is £10 per annum reserved for A Curate £5 Reserved Rent for the Prebendary who has & may dispose of the rest at pleasure for 21 years. The Vicar of Chollerton doth supply that Cure at present.

10 Ovingham a large wide parish an Impropriation worth £400 per annum the Impropriator allows £26 per annum besides the fees to the present Curate.

In the last place I wd seriously recommend our late afternoon Lecturer here at Hexham our people being so very poor & their contributions so very small that they will not raise above £20 per annum and wch is worse they begin allready and are like to fail; Sinc the present Curate desires nothing for himselfe he hopes some notice will be taken of this poor Lecturer, and is confident if this matter were fairly represented, & her Matie understood the necessity & usefullnesse both of the sd Lecturer & a preaching Minister at Whitley Chapple; & how much the Crown formerly got by Hexham

Abbey & how little it left to this large & popolous parish, She wd think them both proper objects of her Royall bounty.

Hexham in Northumberland.

These are to certify all whom it may concern that this is a true & impartiall acctt of the premises. In Witnesse whereof I have hereunto sett my hand this 2d day of March Anno Dni 1703

George Ritschell Minister of
Hexham aforesd

[*Cover:*]
To The Most Revd Father in God John his Grace Ld Arch Bpp of Yorke at the Parliament London These present

11. 5 July 1705 **Burrell to Empson**

Kinde Sir,

This morneing our good friend Mr Rowell was taken up dead by a fall from his horse att Sunderland bridge, two miles from this place, Soe that you att present want an Agent for business in Hexhamshire, If you and your friend concerned in the Exchequer[203] think me A fitt person to serve you there, I am and shall be ready soe to doe, who with due respects & service to you presents

Sr, Your assured humble Servt
P.Burrell

Durham 6th of July 1705

Pray let me know vizt what Day the returne of the Mandate for the Convocation must be sent you, it has hitherto been neglected & it shall be sent accordingly.

[203] ie. York Exchequer Court.

12. 11 July 1705 **Burrell to Empson**

Kinde Sir,

I thank you for your civill Lettr & shall be ready to serve the Gentlemen you mention if they please to depute me as their Agent att Hexham, to whome pray give my most humble Service tho' unknowne. Inclosed you have the Convocacon Process[204] & the returne, Pray let me know if my Lord of Durham's Proxy be att prsent expected & you'l much oblige

your assured humble Servt
P. Burrell

Durham 11th July 1705

13. 6 August 1705 **Burrell to Empson**

Kinde Sr,

I heartily begg your pardon for the trouble I have given you about Hexhamshire business, where you tell me I may now safely act, If you think A formall deputacon needless, then Surely I should have A Note undr the hands of your two Registrs whose names you doe not mention, pray be pleas'd to give my humble service to them both & if they'l please to trust me with blanck Licences & bonds of their severall sorts I shall account for them as they are used, & I desire they'l give me A particular of the fees that they expect I shall be accountable for & the Person to whome I must account & send business. Pray let me know when my Lord of Durham's Proxy ought to be with you. I am

Sr Your obliegеd humble Servt
P. Burrell

6 Augt 1705

[204] Burrell appears to mean a diocesan order normally issued prior to a visitation, requiring attendance by the clergy and churchwardens, possibly to give him the authority to act in Hexhamshire.

Mr Hilton is patentee in the place of Mr Newhouse & Mr Smith is endeaving to succeed Mr Rowell - but cannot as yet p[re]vaile with our grt Chapter [205]

Writt of the absence

[*Cover:*] For Mr Tho: Empson of Yorke These post pd

14. 20 September 1705 **Burrell to Empson**

Kinde Sr

The last Moneth by the Stage-Coach I sent you my Lord of Durham's proxy for the Convocacon & desired A Line of your receiveing it, but as yet none is come, pray when att leisure let me hear from you, for my Lord designes for the South fourteen dayes hence. I desire you'l speake to Mr White your Printer to print me A dozen Bonds & Licences for Marriage of your forme for Hexham as alsoe A dozen Bonds for Citacons Adcons and the like number for Wills, upon Stampt paper or parchmt as with you is used & upon receipt of them with his Bill the Charge shall be paid to Mr Croft the CoachMaster & as I like them shall send shall send for More.

Pray let me know what the two gent that came from London to view offices as to the useing of Stamps did with you, & what objectons they made, as alsoe whether you use Stamps att the begining of A Cause or the Proxy upon Stamps serves. I heartily begg your pardon for this trouble who with due respects & service rests

Sr Your oblieged humble Servt
P. Burrell

20th Sept 1705

[205] John Smith, seeking the Durham registrar position made vacant by the death of Rowell, evidently seeking favour from the Dean and Chapter. The other Durham registrar, Gabriel Newhouse, also died in July 1705: Shuler p.288.

15. 5 October 1705 **Burrell to Empson**

Kinde Sr

I reced the Stamps wth your Bill wch comes to £5 0s 6d by the bearer you'l receive £5 for Mr White has charged too high for printing & for halfe A Quire of paper more then there is for the Licences & the bonds for Licences are but halfe sheets - Pray take his acquittance, for the use of

Sr Your assured humble Servt
P. Burrell

5th Oct 1705

16. 20 October 1705 **Burrell to Empson**

Kinde Sr

Upon Wednesday the last of this Moneth I designe to have A Courte att Hexham & shall give you A particular of what business happens, if you'l give any direccons they shall be observ'd. Dr Morton Arch-deacon of Northumbland is & for some time by past has been from home & his proxy & that for the Clergy within his Archdeaconry are lockt up & cannot be come att, pray let me know when of necessity you muste have them & they shall certainely be sent to you by

Sr Your oblieged humble Serv't
P. Burrell

Durham 20th Octr 1705

17. 13 November 1705 **Burrell to Empson**

Kinde Sr

I was att Hexham the last of October when I took security for thre Wills & one Adcon & gott the old & new Churchwardens of Hexham, Allandale, St Johnlees & St Oswalds sworne. You herewith have the fower bonds & the Originall wills & Invryes as alsoe the same ingrossed & I desire you'l send the Adcon & Probats undr seale with an account not onely what I must pay you for them but likewise for the Churchwardens & it shall be imediately sent you. Mr Ritschell tells me that by your direccons he has six shillings & eight pence for every Probate Adcon Tuicon[206] & Licence wch I scarce beleive, if it be true twill not be worth my time to attend his Worshpp, I told him ten groates might seem sufficient considering he has noe trouble, wee never allow anything in that kinde here, pray let me have your direccons herein, as alsoe if you think fitt Mr Skepper's[207] to whome pray give my humble service. As it was the first time of my goeing to Hexham I gave Mr Ritschell twenty shillings, but can if you please have a bettr & more easy & serviceable com[missa]r[y] for nothing. His brother's Invry & Letter to Mr Skepper he desired might be herewith sent wch pray ordr to be deliverd. I perceive he has (since he knew I had orders from you) been doeing business without my knowledge which for the future I hope you will not suffer. I got the ten Licence bonds herewith sent but noe Moneys from him, he promissed to bring it to Durham ere long & then the fees for them shall be return'd to you. He made A great complaint of Mr Bentham Curate of St John lees irregular Marryages undr prtence of haveing licence & severall other Misdemeanrs but soe soon as they two whisper'd together I heard noe more of the matter, nor of A great Criminall one Lambert in Allandale that he complains off. He's soe forward & dexterous in business that as he thinks he needs noe assistance. Mr Ritschell gave me 21s 6d to send Mr Skepper for the Adcon of his brothr John Ritschells goods & to save A second trouble I here send you that & five pound more wch pray place to account till I hear furthr from you, Who with due respects & Service rests

Sr your oblieg'd humble Serv't
P. Burrell

Durham 13th Nov 1705

[206] Tuition bond: taken out by those nominated by will, or appointed by the probate court, to administer a decaseed's estate to ensure the education and maintenance of minors until they came of age.

[207] Clerk in the York registry office who handled the accounts. Probably the Moses Skepper, who died in York in 1713, apparently confirmed by docs **60**, **61** below.

If there be ani appeal admitted on the behalfe of the Churchwardens of Easington agt Christopher Ste ... [*surname obscured*] that you are desired to appear for Hendry pray give A line in answer.

18. 8 December 1705 **Burrell to Empson**

Kinde Sr Durham 8th Dec 1705

Yours came safe wth the Seales inclosed for wch I thank you, but must not think of giveing a second trouble if Mr Skepper (to whome pray give my service) insist upon haveing what's charg'd in his Bill you sent me, considering what I paid Mr Ritschell (to wch you gave noe answer) I am a looser by goeing to Hexham. Under writt you have what Mr Rowell last answered & even out of that he pd I finde he had halfe of the Registers fees allow'd for his trouble as Mr Mawd can tell you & as Mr Rowells Notes mentions the 13 June 1704 the Registers Note came to £3 0s 6d & out of it he had £1 12s 9d allow'd. If it will give content that business be paid for as formerly I shall be ready to answer expectacon. Mr Ritschell was expected here yesterday but neither he nor his money are come as yet. soe soon as I receive it you may rely of hearing from

Sr your oblieged humble Serv't P. Burrell

13 June 1704	£	s	d
Testm Henry Fenwick I. ult £40 [208]	1	4	0
Testm Jos.Bell I. ult £20		19	10
Tuicon James Bell		12	8
Adcon Lawrence Dickenson I. ult £40	1	5	8
Adcon Elizabeth Fairless infra £20 [209]		10	10
Adcon Jo. I. infra £5		2	10
etc			

[208] Inventory value above £40.
[209] Less than £20.

19. 10 February 1706 **Burrell to Empson**

Sr Durham the 10th Feb 1705

The last Post I had A Lre of request from Mr John Bland (who the Inhabitants of Hexham have those for their afternoon Preacher) to have A Licence to preach as their Lectrer. Pray let me know if you can save him A York Journey, but if you cannot doe that I desire you'l get him leave to continue preaching 'till the weather & wayes Doe mend & be pleasd to let me hear what Testimonial & Certificate will be expected by him. If this may be done by Com.on pray send one Directed to our Surrog Mr Abraham Yapp A.M & Mr Wm.Stainforth A.M: jonm. & divm.[210] & I will see you paid. I was in hopes ere this to have heard from you that the Acct. wth Mr Skepper had been assertain'd upon the old foundacon Mr Rowell had of wch I gave you A particular in my last. Pray be soe kinde as all leisure give me A line what you have done & likewise what I must doe wth Mr Ritschell abt the allowance he demands. He has not pd one farthing, but has had 4 Licences since - soe soon as he payes, you may expect to hear from

Sr Your oblieged humble Servt
P.Burrell

20. 28 February 1706 **Burrell to Empson**

Sr, I heartily begg your pardon for the trouble I have given you abt Mr Skeppers Acct. It's now assertaine'd, Soe that I request you'l please to pay his Bill out of the money sent allowing £2 10s 6d disburst by his Order.

Pray att your leisure let me know, what I am to answer for Licences, Churchwardens fees dismissions, pennances etc I have not reced one farthing for any of the particulars you mencon save Churchwardens fees, wch you had an account of in November last. Soe soon as Mr Ritschell makes payment, you may expect to hear from me. I shall get you a Certificate for Mr Bland I have by your Coach sent you what Juniper Berries I could get & am

---

[210] Jointly and severally. A.M. is MA, Master of Arts.

Your assured humble
Serv't P. Burrell

Durham 28th Feb 1705

[*Cover:*]
For Mr Empson att his Office in the Minster-yard Yorke
These with a Bundle

21. 5 April 1706 **Burrell to Empson**

Kind Sr

Inclosed you have as desired a close Copy of Mr John Clavering's will the charge of it wth stamps & Postage will be 6s 6d. I gave you an account in November last that I reced for the Churchwardens of Hexham, Allendale, St Johnlees & St Oswalds but nothing for Bingfield nor as yett anything for Licences from Mr Ritschell who tells me he's useing all possible care to get you money, soe soon as it comes you shall hear from

Sr Your most humble Serv't
P. Burrell

Durham 5th Apr 1706

pray send Mr Skeppers acct.

22. 22 May 1706 **Burrell to Empson**

Kinde Sir

This day Mr. Ritschell paid for the ten Licences I sent you bonds for Soe that if you'l let me have your Charge for them as alsoe for the Churchwardens fees of Hexham, Allandale, St Johnlees & St Oswalds wch I gave you formerly an Acct. was what I have reced, I shall take care to answer as you'l direct. Bingfield Churchwardens did not pay, I Designe for Hexham the 5th of June but by reason of the scarcity of Money in the North am in noe prospect of much business. In the meane time pray let me have your Note what I owe as alsoe what you charge for dismissions etc as I formerly requested of you.

The parish of Thockrington is neglected wholly, noe business of Ecclicall Cognizance being done there by any; If you'l give Directions I shall take care that the Churchwardens fees & such other matters as shall happen be returnd to you. In the meane time with due respects & Service I rest

Sr Your oblieged humble Servt
P.Burrell

Durham 22nd May 1706

23. 12 June 1706 **Burrell to Empson**

Kind Sr

Herewith I send you what was done att Hexham Courte & two Licence Bonds, pray give my service to Mr Skepper & desire him to send me three probate.s & an Adcon as the bonds here sent requires, with his Bill & the money shall by the next weeks coach be return'd him. I reced fees for Hexham, Allandale, St John Lees & Bingfield Churchwardens, but not one farthing for dismissions If you'l send me your bill I shall not faile to returne you money to satisfie it. Rich'd Lambert for fornicacon should be prosecuted, he despises what can be done att Hexham agt him & offers himselfe ready to receive aerticles. Mr Ritschell tells me that he has good proof agt him if you think fitt to psecute him. Pray desire Mr Skepper to charge in his bill what he must have for a search he made for Mr Ritschell.

With due respects & service, I rest

Sr Your oblieged humble Servt
P. Burrell

12th June 1706

pray send the acquit[ance] you had from Mr Skepper.

24. 27 June 1706 **Ritschell to Empson**

Dear Sr Hexham June the 27th 1706

I gott not yours of the 22nd instant till yesterday for our post goes but twice a week to NewCa:. In Answer to wch Mr Wise was Minister of Allandale in this Jurisdiction, wch is a Curacy worth between £20 & £25 per ann.

I granted 4 Licences for marriage & returned for every one of them 19s 4d: vizt 13s 4d for the Licenc & 6s for the stamps, wch is as much as I ever knew taken upon that acct.

Richard Lambert is not of this pish but of Catton Lee in the pish of Allandale & is the same person I formerly wrote abt; & I am apt to beleive wd have submitted to our Court If he had not been dissueaded by an Atturney here in Town, the womans name had the child to him is Mary Forster she was then his Housekeeper.

There is one John Buckton of Allandale A B'smith guilty of the same offenc with one Jane Raven; He sent to me before our last Court that he wd come & compound this matter If I wd be easy other wise he wd leave the Countrey, but I have not sinc heard any further from him – perhaps he has mett with different advice.

And one Wm Reed. A Phisician in Allandale & Elizt Roddam were presented for the sd offenc of fornication but did not appear at our last Court; If Mr Chancellor think fitt to send processe agt any of them I shall afford my best assistanc.

Sr Its a good day & I am forced to begg leave of Compa to write thus much & therefore hope youl' excuse my adding any more; save to begg the favour to give my servic with due respects to Mr Chancellor; & that my Mother & Sister joyn with me in our services to you & Mr Brathwait.

I am in hast Dr Sr
Your Most Humble & devoted Servt
George Ritschell

25. 23 September 1706 **Ritschel to Empson**

Dear Sr Hexham 7ber 23d 1706

I sent an answr to yours of the 22nd of June, & have not sinc recd any from you or Mr Chancellor. I was informd that Jno Carr of this Town designd to make a complaint agt me to his Worsp and I wrote to him, that If he did it by word of mouth, he wd desire him to put it in writeing & (If in writeing) order me a copy thereof, that I might give an answer thereto in my own defenc; If you have heard or know any thing of this matter, these begg the favour of you to give me an account thereof wch I shall take as a particular obligation. Be pleasd to give my servic with due respects to Mr Chancellor. My Mother & Sister Remember them to you I am

Dr Sr your affect & oblegd humble servt
George Ritschell

26. 10 December 1706 **Burrell to Empson**

Sr

You had an appeal admitted the last week in a Cause here depending betwixt Wilkinson & Errington for proveing the Will of Tho: Browne in Solemne forme Sentence for the validity of the Will was read the 22nd of November & by reason Mr Tho: Errington the Executor is a papist, the Testators relacons will not allow him to be qualified to be an Executor tho' not convicted. Mr Errington desires you'l eithr appear or cause an appearance to be made for him on Thursday next & he'l take care to content you. Pray remember att your Leisure to let me know how the acct stands between you, Mrs Rowell & me that the same may be discharg'd. And for Mr Erringtons satisfaccon I desire you'l give me a Line that you have had this from

Sr your oblieged humble serv't
P.Burrell

Durham 10th of Dec 1706

27. 27 December 1706 **Burrell to Empson**

Kinde Sr

Your Acct came safe for wch I thank you. I have not reced A farthing from Bingfield wch made me omitt it There has not been a dismission since I was concern'd , tho severall have been Cited, such things are conceal'd & kept from me Sr I sent you first 10 bonds & two times after two Apeice & shall send you the names of all the fourteen as they stand in my Acct if they'l be serviceable to you. You make noe mencon of the Money I sent you in November 1705 : how much remaines in your hands, nor doe you take notice of the Copy of Mr Claverings will & Codicill, be pleased to place them to acct & let me know the ballance & it shall be sent you by the Coach or as you'l direct. I desire you' give my Service to Mr Mawd[211] & request him to give an Acct what business he had in the Jurisdiccon belonging to this Courte since the death of Mr Newhouse[212] wch was the 26th of July 1705. If he'l pay you any money pray receive it into your acct. I writt to him some time agoe but got noe answer I was att Hexham the 29: Oct last but lost my labr meeting with no business, tho' timely notice was given Wishing you a pleasant Xtmas & a good new yeare. I rest

Sr your most humble Serv't
P. Burrell

Durham 27th Dec 1706

28. 23 January 1706 **Burrell to Empson**

Sr

Your acquitance had of Mr Skepper is for £3 10s 6d the remaindr of the five pounds formerly sent is £1 9s 6d wch wth 6s 6d for the copys sent will be £1 16s 0d & inclosed you have £5 17s 2d

---

[211] William Mawd, proctor and deputy registrar of the Exchequer Court in York, which included probate work: Till, Study, pp. 191-2.

[212] Gabriel Newhouse *op cit* was evidently acting surrogate in Hexham for York Exchequer Court business.

wch makes up the Ballance of the Accts in the inclosed Notes, under which pray let me have your receipt -- Mr Mawd has not (as Mr Smith tells me) accounted or paid a farthing to him for any business done within the Jurisdiccon belonging to the Bpps Chancellr & Register. Pray doe as much as give my service to him & desire he'l gratifie me with a Line in answer to a Letter I sent him 3:Monethes agoe. Pray tell Mr Skepper (wth my humble service) that his direccons shall not be neglected. I begg your pardon for the trouble here sent upon you & with cordiall respects & service doe rest

Sr your oblieg'd humble Serv't
P. Burrell

Durham 23th Janry 1706

29. 23 June 1707 **Burrell to Empson**

Kinde Sr

On Wednesday last I was att Hexham where the Churchwardens of Hexham, Allandaile & St John Lees were sworne & paid their fees & for their Registrs but att Bingfield & St Oswalds they have noe Churchwardens nor was anything reced for them, the Minister there Mr Bentham is an ill man & severall Complaints are made agt him for dishonest & idle dealings, he reports that you have tollerated him to grant Licences wch I hope is not true, for he shifts not to marry without Licence. Pray for the credit of the Courte doe not trust him with any Licences for his charactr deserves noe such trust. You here have Eight Licence Bonds, Six of wch I had this day from Mr Ritschell If you please to make up your Bill Mr Skepper will pay you, I have herewth sent him money & with due respects & Service doe rest

Sr your oblieged humble Serv't
P. Burrell

Durham
23th June 1707

Pray tell Mr Webster[213] that there's noe hopes of geting any money of Mr Hanby but I have got a note from Mr Croswell for the paymt of his bill & soe soon as I receive the money he shall hear from me

30. 1704 to 1707 **Abstract of Letters**

[*Apparently in the hand of Thomas Jubb; possibly prepared after he entered the Registrar's office in 1710*]

An Abstract of Mr Ritchells Letters to Mr Chancellor & Mr Empson concerning Hexham in the Severall yeares following.

Chancellors Letters

1704 9ber 9th	Mr Ritchell sent a Moyety of Mr Herons Commutation to Mr Empson wch with the Fees was £8 1s 8 as appears by Mr Ritchells Letter

Mr Empsons Letters

1705 20th Sept, 5th Oct	It appears by Mr Burrells letters that he had Licences etc printed at York and sent by the Coachman to whom he paid Ready Money ~~and~~ for Stamps & printing & by his Lr dat 28 Febr 1705 I prceive he answers all Fees as well dismissions & Penances etc but its not apparent what allowed him
1706 22 May	Mr Burrell desires to have orders and Authority to dispatch business within Tockerington parish Qr where Tockerington is
27th June	Mr Ritchell says he answered 13s 4d for every m[atrim]oniall Licence besides Stamps. Qr where the Fornicators if psecuted are obliged to appear if at York?
Mr Burrells Lr 23 June 1707	Bentham Minister at Bingfeild & Allandale an Ill man & Notorious for Cland[estine] Marriages. Qr if the pishioners may not lay an assessmt without the four & twenty

[213] Proctor at York: Till, Study, pp.191-7.

31. 5 November 1709 **Ritschel to Ord**
[NRO QSB/89/p.17/17]

Sr Hexham Nov 5th 1709

As to the charge of repairing our Church If we compare it with others of late in the like case. I find the Charge to repair Ely Cathedral (wch was occasioned only by a unexpected breach in the North Cross Isle) £2800. Chester Cathedral £7000. St Germans Ch £4000. Wye Church £3000. St Gyles in Shewsbury £4426. Beverley £3500 St Mary Rad Cliffe £4410 and am apt to beleive some of them were not in so gt decay as Hexham & perhaps could get workmen to certify as great a sum, wch they might easily do with a reserve (as I doubt is too Common in those cases) vizt to take down & rebuild our Steeple & the roofe on the North & South Quarters & make them angular as at first etc. But I conceive such a charge might do us more prejudice nigher home than it wd do us service in Yorkeshire & further off & therefore canot approve of it;……..I pretend to know the State of our Church better then any body else haveing made it my businesse for above 15 years last past upon any great rain when the wind did vary to search and discover the defects thereof. & by a computation I find that there is at least twice as much to do, to finish the repairs thereof, & put it in a right condition as has been of later years done unto it by wch computation our charge should amount to abt £2400. But it canot be denyed that this parish has been sadly abused & imposed upon by knavish workmen & the managmt of our Grandees, we pay dear & have it ill done, at an unproper season as I have often complaind to little purpose. & told them I could do them more reall service with halfe the mony, for that its not done effectually

Sr

The charge to finish the repairs of our Church according to the best computation I can make to do it effectually & as it ought to be doth amount to the sum of twelve hundred pounds and upwards. I did allways look upon it as a material Article & did & wd have put it in our last petition, after that Art. Vizt

And it being a very large & antient fabrick built above 1000d years ago is now through the injurys of time & weather grown so very ruinous that they are no longer able to support the same without some publick assistanc joynd with their own endeavors, the charge to repair the sd Church by a moderate computaton amounting to the summ of £1200 & upwards etc

This Court being satisfyed of the trueth of the premises, & it being matter of trouble & griefe to us to think upon the ruin of so stately and beautifull a fabrick etc but I wholy referr these to your own discretion & am

Sr Your very Humble Servt
George Ritschel

[*Cover:*] For Mr John Ord, atturney at Law at his house in Newcastle These

32. 2 February 1710 **Ritschel to Ord**

[NRO QSB/89/p.17/33]

Sr Hexham Febry 2d 1709

Mr Aynsley[214] shewd me the representation of our Church wherein we find diverse mistakes, & besides you have forgot 2 material Articles vizt. To insert the charge the parish has been at to repair our church wch exceeds what I have observed in any of our late Ch Briefes.........2ly to go abt from house to house wch I proposed to my Ld ArchBp & Mr Chancellor doth account it the most probable & effectual way........& therefore have sent back the former, & made a new draught as like a Briefe as we could, as we desire it may be, & therefore I took diverse Briefes & laid before me, & what is not matter of fact you may find in one Briefe or another.

We conceive it most proper to go upon the foundation laid at Hexham sessions. as I remember you told me you made an order upon the Grand Jurys Representation: If not pray omit that clause,.........& we think it proper to tell the reason why we did not proceed for a Briefe, you will find the same in Market Rayson. Mr Aynsley gives his service to you. he is gone to Morpeth else wd have joynd wth me in this, he see & approved of the enclosed draught & we desire you will be pleasd to correct mistakes If there be any, &

[214] John Aynesley; see entry in ABN.

alter what doth not please. but hope you will find so little to do in it that it will not give you much trouble & therefore request youl be pleasd to dispatch that matter assoon as possibly you can; & pardon this new trouble from

Sr your very Humble servt
George Ritschel

33. 5 October 1709 Draft petition to Quarter Sessions
[*but presumably prepared later following correspondence from Ritschel to Ord given in doc. 32 above.*
NRO QSB/89/p.17/30]

Northumbr// To the Worspll her Majestyes Justices of the Peace for the County of Northumberland att the Generall Quarter Sessions of the Peace holden for the Said County att Alnewicke the Fifth Day of October 1709:

The humble Petition of the Minister Church Wardens and Inhabitants of the Town and parish of Hexham in the Said County

Humbly Sheweth

That att the last Generall Quarter Sessions of the Peace holden att Hexham for this County the Thirteenth Day of J[uly] last upon application made to that Court all the Justices then prsent accompannied by the Gentlemen of the Grand Jury were pleased to goe and view that part of the Said parish Church repaired by the parishioners of the Said Parish which appeared to them to be very ruinous and in great decay and att the end of that Sessions the Said Grand Jury did by way of Presentment recommend the Same to the Said Justices and desired that they would be pleased to Certifye the Truth thereof to her Majesty in order to obtaine her gracious Letters Patents for a Brief to repaire the Same But your Petitioners being Sure Informed that Collections by way of Brief of late fall Short of the partys expectation, to avoid the Charge thereof Your Petitioners are advised rather to obtain a Recomendation from your Worshipps of the ruinous State of the Said Church to the Lord Arch Bishopp of Yorke and the other Bishopps of that Province; for that his Grace haveing been acquainted therewith is very favourably inclined thereunto

Your Petitioners therefore humbly pray your Worshipps to Certifye and recommend the ruinous State of the Said Church and your Petitioners Inability to repaire the same att their own proper Charge without Some publick assistance Joynd with their own endeavours to the Most Revd Father in God the Lord Arch Bishopp of Yorke and the Right Reverend the Lord Bishopp of Durham the Lord Bishopp of Chester and the Lord Bishopp of Carlisle That they would be pleased to grant your Petitioners their Licence and order to be read in the respective parish Churches and Chappells in the respective Diocesses on Sundays and other Festivalls to aske collect and receive the Charitable Benevolence and Contributions of well disposed people towards the repaire of the Said Church And that their Lordshipps would be pleased to recommend the Same to all the Ministers and Curates in their respective Diocesses to exhort and Stirr Upp their respective Congregations to contribute cheerfully and Liberally to Soe good and pious a worke and that they and their Church Wardens may be further assistant to your Petitioners in going about from house to house upon the week days to aske Such contributions as aforesaid and take the names in writeing of all Such who Shall Contribute thereunto and indorse the Summe collected by them on the back thereof in words att length and Subscribe the Same with their proper hands together with the Name of the place where & the time when collected and pay the Same onely to Such person and persons as Shall be Nominated and Deputed to receive the Same under the hands and Seales of Five or more of the Trustees hereafter Named And that your Worshipps would be pleased to Nominate and Appoynt Sir John Delavall Barrt Sir Thomas Loraine Barrt Sir Wm Blackett Barrt[215] Sir John Clavering Barrt Thomas Forster Esquire Wm Loraine Esquire John Ogle Esquire Gawin Aynsley Esquire Robert Lisle Esquire John Bacon Esquire John Coatsworth Esquire Roger Wilson Esquire William Ramsay Esquire Thomas Blenkinsopp Esquire The Mayour of Newcastle for the time being Nicholas Ridley Esquire Tho: Bewick Esquire Mr John Wilkinson Mr Tho: Allgood The Reverend Mr Geo: Ritschell Mr John Ord Mr Jo: Armestrong Mr Jo: Mowbray Mr John Aynsley Mr George Mowbray & Mr Robert Coatsforth to be Trustees and Receivers of the moneys collected on this behalfe and have the Management of the Said repairs and that nothing be done therein without the advice

[215] Sir William Blackett III; see ABN.

and consent of the Major part, att least of Five or more of them, one where of to be a Justice of the Peace

And your Petitioners as in Duty bound Shall ever pray etc

34. 5 October 1709 **Brief from Quarter Sessions**

[*Also presumably prepared later following QS endorsement of draft petition given in doc. 33 above.*
NRO QSB/89/p.17/34]

Northumbr// Att the Generall Quarter Sessions of the Peace held att Alnwick in the County of Northumberland for the County aforesaid the Fifth day of October in the Eighth yeare of the Reigne of our Soveraigne Lady Queen Ann by the grace of God of Great Brittain France and Ireland Defender of the Faith &c Before John Ogle Thomas Collingwood Francis Forster William Taylor and Thomas Burrell Esqs and others her Majties Justices of the peace for the said County:

To all Christian people to whom these presents shall come greeting Whereas this Court as well by the View of severall of her Majties Justices of the Peace now present in Court as by the view of Gawin Aynsley Robert Lawson John Baron and John Cotesworth Esqs Justices of the peace for the said County and of the Grand Jury att the last Quarter Sessions of the peace held for the said County att Hexham upon the Thirteenth day of July last past as otherwise is credibly informed That the parish Church of Hexham built upwards of one Thousand Yeares since formerly a Cathedrall dureing the continuance of the Bishoppe of Hexham and as the part now standing (being onely the East part from the Great Cross Ile) shews it has been a magnificent Structure and a true Testimony of the zeall of primitive Christianity but now by the length of Time is become so ruinous that the parishioners are not able to repair the same without the Contributions of others and part of one of the Isles in the Month of June last haveing fallen down in the time of Divine Service and the remaining parts being so very Ruinous the parishioners cannot assemble in the said Church but in great Consternation and fear And being further Informed that to preserve so much of the said Church standing as will be Convenient for Celebrating Divine Service the charge will amount to Twelve hundred pounds and upwards It is thereupon by this Court for the help and assistance of the said parishioners recomended to the Right Reverend the Lord Arch

Bishopp of York the Right Honourable and Right Reverend the Lord Bishopp of Durham the Right Reverend the Lord Bishopp of Carlisle and the Right Reverend the Lord Bishopp of Chester to grant unto the said parishioners their licence and order to be read in their respective Churches and Chappells in their Respective Diocesses on the Lords day and to Exhort all Ministers and Curates in their sermons on such days to stirr up their severall parishioners to Extend their Charity towards so pious and Christian a Worke and that they and their Churchwardens may be in the most effectuall way be assistant in Collecting and receiveing the said Charity and to Indorse the same on the back of some Authentick Copy of the said Licence or order and to pay the same Collected to such persons as shall be authorized under the hands and seales of any of the Trustees for the said parishioners to be named and also indorsed upon the said Authenticke Copy of the said order or Licence Given under the seale of the said Court of Sessions the day and yeare first above written:

[*in a different hand:*]
Ex. p Tho: Ord C I E Par

35. 13 August 1710 **Burrell jnr to Jubb**

Sir,

Yours I reced and am glad to hear you succede honest Mr Empson. As for ~~when~~ the business I undertook for him was sweareing the Churchwardens & granting Licences which he allowed me 3s 4d for every instrument. I never goe to Hexham but once a yeare & god willing designe to be there att michaelmas next I accounted with Mr Empson about a moneth before his death & have an acquittance from him. What licences has been granted since his death I shall give you acct but att present cannot by reason I deliver them to Mr Ritschell minister there blank for which he acct to me once a yeare if ther's occasion for it sooner I write to Mr Ritschell & you shall be satisfied therein if ther's any thing I can serve you in here shall be very ready and am in haste

Sir your very humble servant
Peter Burrell

Durham Augt 13th 1710

Last yeare there was but 9 in that peculiar granted; I reced a lre from Mr Shaw[216] wherein he mencioned that he succeeded his unckle with that same quer you mencion.

36. 1708-10 **Abstract of Court Business**
[*in Ritschel's hand*]

An Acct of Businesse done in the peculiar of Hexham sins Mr Peter Burrell senr his last Court the 31: of May 1708 till of last Court kept there the 20th of November 1710

Marriage Licences granted 1708
July the 4th To Henry Ramsey Maulster & Elenor Grery Wid.
9'ber 20th Willm Johnson tan[ne]r & Barb.Leadbitter spr
X'ber 7 John Bell Glovr & Elizt.Robinson spr
10 John Aidon Glovr & Ann Pattison spr
27 Matthew Atkinson Carpentr & Isabell Rowcastle spr
Janry 29 Tho.Tulip of Acomb taylr & Elizt.Dinning spr

Anno 1709
May 10 Robt.Forster of Eshells & Margt.Baxter spr
18 Robt.Stainby of Allanheads & Ann Richardson spr
29 Jno.Buckton of Broadgatehead & Mary Thirllwall spr
July 6 Jeremy Hill weavr & Hannah Lowthian spr
Octobr 28 Xtopher Simpson of the Lee & Susan Smith spr
X'ber 13 George White of Humshaugh & M.. Elizt.Teasdale spr
Janry 24 John Green of Keenlysydehill & Elizt. Whitfield spr

Anno 1710
June 13th James Broadwood of Burntongues & Elizt.Johnson spr
29 James Atkinson of Kirkheaton & Ann Heron spr
Novem13th Mich. Weldon of Little Whittington Gent. & Elizt. Robson spr
All the Bonds Returned to York by Mr Burrell

Anno 1708
7'ber 28th Admon of the goods of Mr Joseph Gill of Hexham granted to Mr Humphrey Gill his son

---

[216] Probably refers to John Shaw, proctor at York. See doc **128** below.

Octobr 1 Admon of the goods of Mr Xtopher Lowdin of Allenheads granted to Jos.Langhorn of Penrith Cb & Willm.Mowbray of the Inner Temple Gen.
9'ber 9th Proved the Last Will of Willm.Pearson of Hexham Spittle Gen.
Janry 18th The Last Will of Thos.Richardson of Frosthall

Anno 1709

May 24th Proved the last Will of James Kennett of the Holehouse Gen.
June 7th It. The last Will of Robt.Farbridge of Ashabank
It. at the Court the 28th of June 1709

Proved the last Will of John Whitfield of Scots Meadows
Itm. of Jos.Salmon of Hexham tannr

June 29th Granted Admon of the goods of Carlton Hebden of Wall Gen. to Elizt.Hebden his wid.
Decembr Granted Admon of the goods of Mrs Mary Allgood of Hexham spr to her Broth James Allgood Clerk Rector of Ingram.

Anno Dni 1710

April 25th Granted Admon of the goods of Francis Sheild of the Burnfoot to his son Francis.
June 16 Prov'd the last Will of Tho. Smith of Thockerington.
July 29th Granted Admon of the goods of Tho.Simpson of Dotland B[lack]smith to Jane his wid.
Octobr 5th Granted Admon of the goods of Edw.Goelightly of Grundridge to ~~Elizt Heron~~ Mary Heron of Castlemains as principal creditrix by vertue of a Decree of the Court of Yorke

Itm Admon of the goods of William Thirllwall of Newbigin Esq to Mr John Shaftoe of Hexham as principal Creditor by vertue of a Decree of the Court of York

Octobr 10th Granted Admon of the goods of Peter Thirllwall of Grundridge to his son John Thirllwall
Oct 28 Proved the last Will of Willm. Richardson of Harsley senr
at last Court 9'ber 20th

Proved the last Will of Willm.Ritson of Allandale
Itm Granted Admon of the goods of John Thompson of Hexham Butchr to Jane wife of John Bell, his Daughter.

37. 11 January 1711 **Ritschel to Jubb**

Sr Hexham Janry 11th 1710

One of our Carryrs brought me your lre dated 31 Xber wch he sd was given him at NewCa: by A Berwick Carryr, the post goes twice a week from here to NewCastle wch I take to be a more certain way. In answer to yours Be pleasd to give my humble service to Mr Chancellor I thank him for his care of our Church, but have not any such moneys in my hand nor did ever receive any but what I acquainted his Worsp therewith. I beleive some might have been got at Court 1709 If her Majtie had not pardoned them, two were cited at our last Court the 20th 9ber Jos. Cook of this town Glovr who deneys the fact & one Jno Dawson of Allandale, I gave him 14 days to consider of it wr he wd submit to what I proposed, & I wd acquaint Mr Chancellor with it or he wd contest it, I have not recd an answer & wrote to him last Tuesday for it.

Enclosed you have an acctt of business as desired I designd to have wrote to you & Mr Skepper after our Xmas entertainments were over, If possible to retreive the businesse of this peculiar wch is like to dwindle away to nothing, Mr Burrell when last here sd he wd come again no more, wrupon a certain Atturney or Sollicitor here in town, then in Compa told me after that he wd accept of it, I should be unwilling to do anything wch might not look like fair dealing, but If Mr Burrell decline it, shall propose such terms as I take wd be for the interest of your Court & the ease of the Countrey, Pray give my service to Mr Skepper, I have not Recd the businesse dispatched at our last Court If they be in his hand I desire he will send them the first opportunity, for that the partys concernd have been at me for their seals; I have wrote to Mr Burrell this post abt them.

Sr these congratulate you succeeding My Dear old friend Mr Empson in the Regists Office I conceive it very proper to settle a correspondence between us, & you may shortly expect to hear further from me Be pleasd to give my service to Mr Brathwait & Mr Shaw, wishing you all health & a happy new year I am

Sr your Humble Servt
George Ritschel

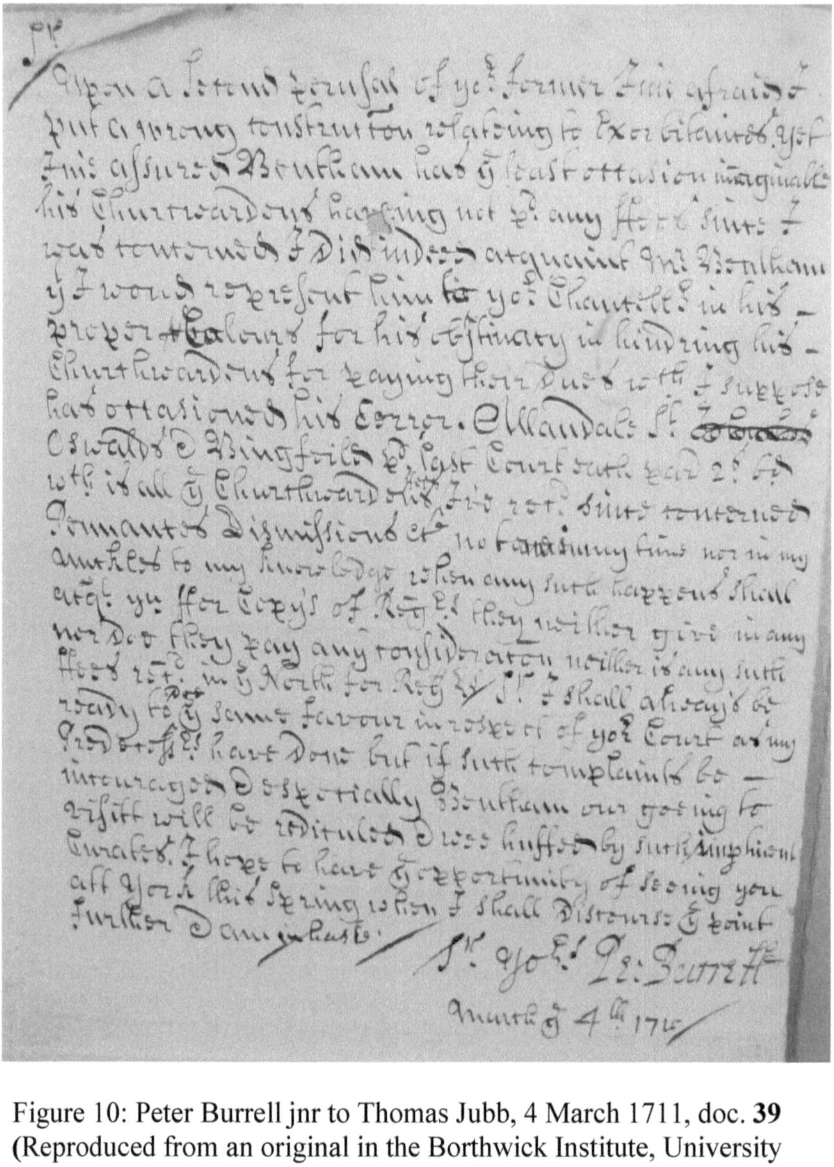

Figure 10: Peter Burrell jnr to Thomas Jubb, 4 March 1711, doc. **39** (Reproduced from an original in the Borthwick Institute, University of York, Pec.Hex/2)

38. 11 February 1711 **Burrell jnr to Jubb**

Sir, Durham Feb 11th 1710

The money I desired Mr Skepper to pay you was for 7 licences (viz) 10s each 3s4d I have for writeing Licence Bond stamps etc As for taking exorbitant fees of St John Lees parish is very false they haveing never pd any fees since I was concerned but by Mr Rowells & my unckles accounts they have always answered both at Easter and Mich: Mr Bentham[217] as I'me credibly informed is both Reg & Chancellor & likewise very guilty of clandestine marriages both for people in our jurisdiction & elsewhere in serio I beleive denys noe body. Exorbitances never was my business if it's practicable in Yorkshire very much ridiculed att Durham what Mr Ritschell has done I cannot answer for only I know there's noe good understanding betwixt him & Bentham who is really scandalous according to informations. Sir I don't get my charges by goeing to Hexham if it's doeing you no service nor profitt to Sir

Yours whilst Pr.Bur.

Sir,

If theres any mistake I beleive its betwixt the Churchwardens & Apparitor for Proclamations & prayer Books Churchwardens fees is pd according to the pleasure of the minister sometimes nothing wch I've seen frequently before I was concerned. My Lord of Durhams App[arator] has supplyed them with Books as occasion happened but since the yeare 1708 has not reced any consideration for soe doeing pray my service to Mr Skepper & desire him to make a returne of the business sent him along with the Bonds from

yours P.B.

39. 4 March 1711 **Burrell jnr to Jubb**

Sir,

Upon a second perusal of your former Ime afraid I put a wrong construction relating to Exorbitances. Yet Ime assured Bentham has the least occasion imaginable his Churchwardens

---

[217] Leonard Bentham, curate of St. John Lee; see entry in ABN.

having not pd any fees since I was concerned I did indeed acquaint Mr Bentham that I would represent him to your Chancellr in his proper colours for his obstinacy in hindring his Churchwardens for paying their dues wch I suppose has occasioned his letter. Allandale St ~~John Lee~~ [*erased*] Oswalds & Bingfeild pd last Court each par[ish] 2s6d which is all the Churchwardens fees I've reced since concerned Pennances Dismissions etc not in my time nor in my unckles to my knowledge when any such happens shall acq[uain]t you For copys of Reg[ister]s they neither give in any nor doe they pay any consideration neither is any such fees recd in the North for Reg[ister]s. Sir I shall always be ready to do the same favour in respect of your Court as my predecessors have done but if such complaints be incouraged & especially Bentham our goeing to visitt will be rediculed & wee huffed by such implient curates. I hope to have the opportunity of seeing you att York this spring when I shall discourse the point further & am in haste

Sir Yours Pr.Burrell

March the 4th 1710

40. 13 April 1711 **Ritschel to Jubb**

Sir, Hexham April the 13th 1711

I receivd a lre from Mr. Peter Burrell of Durham wherein he tells me, that he had one from you in which you acquaint him that Mr. Bentham had complained to you, that either he or myselfe had taken exorbitant fees of him and says, that sinc he was concernd, (to his knowledge) he never paid him any, & consequently the charge doth lye against myselfe to which I answer 1 that Mr Bentham never paid me any fees but for his marriage licence viz. 4d for your Court & Mr Rowell, nor did I ask or he offer me anything for my trouble, 2ly what fees have been paid by Exchequer or Adm[inistere]d in that parish were ascertained by Mr.Rowell & Mr. Burrell nor did I take any more, … 3ly When Mr.Burrell came first here upon the 28th June 1709 we had a great flood and our boats would not go, so that none of St. John Lee parish appeared at Court save the old & new Chapelwardnes for St.Oswalds who came about by Corbridge, and Mr.Burrell having not settled matters with Mr.Skepper, desired me to receive the fees from the Ch.Wardens (which I never had done before) & pay off the Bill where he lodged & we had adjourned the Court, which I did & receivd of the Chapel Wardens aforesaid of each halfe a crown, but because that chapel is gone to ruin, and they collect no sesse nor have any allowance for their trouble Ive fixt the fees at 1s 3d a piece. No Ch.Wardens app'd at that Court & Mr.Burrell left me a note of fees to receive of each parish 14s 0d vizt 2s 6d for Easter & 5s 6d for Mich Vizitaton, their usuall fees in the Diocesse of Durham. Mr. Bentham came along with his Church Wardens the 12th of July after, & Mr. Rowell one of them (with whom I had a contest in your Court) would not pay any fees for Mich. Vizitaton because we had none, & thereupon I respited that matter till Mr.Burrell came again, & they paid no fees till our last Court upon the 20th of November when not only Mr.Rowell but John Errington of Beaufront Esq.[218] app'd in behalfe of the Countrey; the matter was debated in another room. I told Mr.Errington that for my own part I had no benefit by those fees, had served this Jurisdiction about 27 years & never took a farthing of any Ch.Wardens upon that account thoa Mr. Empson had assured me I might insist upon a fee, & perhaps whoever did succeed me would not do so, and left it to them and Mr. Burrell who came to a temper, and he abated them but how much I know not.

If this be what Mr.Bentham means it doth not at all affect myselfe, nor do I know of any thing else, If you please to send me a copy of his letter I doubt not to give you a satisfactory answer.

Sir its my opinion that those who would accuse others should take care that themselves be not guilty of the same or greater offences and one might wonder at Mr. Benthams confidenc herein who not only raised his own fees in that parish sinc he came But has played so many scandalous tricks to get & extort money from people to the prejudice of our Courts. I doubt upon enquiry you wd find new matter agt him sinc he was last admonished & her Maj^{y}'s pardon otherwise I was fully resolved to have preferred a Bill of Indictmt agt him at our Qr Sessions for takeing 20s for a prtendd licence for marriage. I was told he did endeavour to obtain a faculty to grant such licences, which was denyed; However an ignorant person in his parish not long sinc (as I am told) did positively affirm that he had power to marry any without either licenc or Banns but enough of him at present.

---

[218] Catholic landowner (c. 1656-1713): Gooch, *op cit*, p.54.

Sir the state of this Jurisdiction at present is not good, it has soe declined ever sinc the Revolution & Indulgenc, before which time we kept Court twice a year, offenders were presented app'd at Court submitted & paid dismission fees, but now they regard us no more than we do the thunder of the Vatican. And here be pleased to take notice that sinc I have been concerned there was never anything paid (to my knowledge) for comutation of penance in St.John Lee parish nor in Allandale but what the Rascal Yarrow our Apparator's son got of Buckton & his father told me that himselfe got 20s of one after a pardon. There have been diverse such offendrs on that Syde & If Lambert had been prosecuted its not improbable that some would have submitted, but he escapeing as he did, they have learned to send some Attorney to appear for them, deny the fact & bid us defiance.

One Jos. Cook of this town glover and one Dawson of Allendale were cited at our last Court for fornication. I expected they would have submitted & wrote to Dawson who seemd inclined and promised to come to me when he came to town abt Candlemas but I have not sinc seen or heard from him. I suppose they have advice to the contrary, they know what we can do, & unlesse your Court would second us & take notice of those who will not submit at this Court, I know not to what purpose we should cite any more of the like offenders. I am

Sir. Your Humble servant
George Ritschel

41. 24 May 1711 **Ritschel to Jubb**

Sr, Hexham 24th of May 1711

I Received yours of the 21st of April, wd have answerd ere now, but that I deferrd writeing till I should receive back again the businesse I then sent to Mr Skepper wch I expected the sooner for that I desired him to hasten; Pray tell him that I have not yet received those wills under seal nor any lre from him, that he wd hasten them if yet in his hands & let me know Mr Chancellors pleasure abt Dixon (& I shall send him that Will with 2 Admons) for that the Ex[ecuto]rs are very impatient to have it proved.

I wrote to Dawson who came hither the other day & submitted & gave me a note to pay twenty Nobles at Martinmas next for Commutation of his penanc & Fees, he was unwilling to exceed £5 & considering his Estate & family I think it high enough, Pray give my service to Mr Chancellor & acquaint him herewith & I shall observe his directions herein.

Joseph Cook a glover here A Papist hath a Freehold hous or Burgage, sinc his wife dyed has led an idle lewed course of life & is at some times not right in his head, for wch reason some wd disswade me from meddleing any further with him. But he is so notorious haveing been guilty of the same Crime before her Majties pardon & hath now as its sd his housekeepr with child etc that it were a shame to passe him by. but the other evening the Bailiffes took him to carry him to our County Jail for Debt, wch is the fittest place for him & I think best for us to let him alone till his return; Mr Benthams pretended Licences were before her Majties pardon If any thing happens at or before our next Court I shall give you an acctt therof & am in the mean time

Sr your Humble Servt
George Ritschel

Be pleasd to give my service to Mr Skepper & If he be unwell or from home, take care to send me those wills under seal for such delay will doubtlesse lessen the interest of this Jurisdiction

42. September 1711 **Visitation Articles**

[BIA Pec.Hex/1]

[*in George Ritschel's hand*]
A true presentment or Answer to the Book of Art[icles] made by the churchwardens of Hexham at Michaelmas Visitation 1711

Tit. i
Art: i. Our parish Church being an old decayed Cathedral, is now grown very ruinous & out of repair especially the Roofe of the South Quarter & of the North & South Isles, the Steeple also and Bells and windows
Art: - ii iii iv & v. We have a font of stone & all things convenient for divine Service and all the other things required save that of late our Registers are only in paper

Tit. ii
Art: i. Our Ch[urch]yard is well fenced, but not so decently kept as it ought to be, diverse encroach[en]ts have been made into it before our remembrance, and diverse windows and doors before or about the late Revolution
Art: - ii & iii Our Minister's house is in good repair and we have A terrier of the tyths &c belonging to him, and nothing to present concerning them.

Tit. iii
Art: i. Our Minister is licensed by the Bpp &c
Art - ii He is constantly Resident
Art – iii He doth use the form of words prescribed by the Book of Comon Prayer &c
Art iv He doth celebrate the H[oly] Sacrament of the Ld's Supper so often as every one may receive thrice a year
Art v He doth Catechise &c but we have not had an Episcopal Confirmation since our Remembrance
Art vi. He doth not neglect to visit the sick &c
Art vii He hath not marryed any we know of contrary to the Canons
Art viii He doth declare the Severall Holydays &c
Art ix He is a man of sober studious peacable – and exemplary life
And we know nothing to present concerning him

Tit. iv
Art: i. Our parishioners demean themselves reverently &c
Art ii. We present Henry Collison of Hexham Butchr & Margt Wood of the same spr
Itm Thomas Elliot of Gilligate Cordwainer & Jane Chain of the same wid. for single adultery
William Ellis Cordwainer & Margt Todd spr, Thomas Stokoe Glovr & Mary Simmons spr
[*line obscured*] Nicholas Dixon Taylor & Diana Eliot spr for fornication
John Armstrong de Intack & Margaret Nicholson for cohabiting as man & wife.
Art iii. We present the severall & respective persons in the Schedule herunto annexed for not paying their respective proportions of Ch. sesse vizt.

Itm John Gibson of Hexham Curryer & John Bell of Gilligate Glover son of Wm Bell Butcher for not paying the Minister & Clerk their accustomed fees

Art iv There be a great many Legacys left to our poor But the Minister & Ch.Wardens being not concernd in the Managemt and distribution of diverse of them we canot give a true account thereof. But those wherein the Minister & Ch.Wardens are concernd have not been misspent or Embezelled.

Art v There be diverse who come very seldome to our Church but do not wholy Exempt themselves

Art vi, We have A publick meeting house and an Assembly of Dissenters & believe they are duely qualified &c

Art vii There be diverse in our parish above the age of 16 who come to church but not to the H. Comunion &c

Art viii & ix We have Nothing to present &c

Tit. v

Art i:ii We have a parish Clerk duely qualified He is of an honest life & conversation He is Chosen by the Minister & doth perform his duty but his wages are not duely paid him

Art iii. We have also a Sexton; & his wages are not paid him for two years ending at Easter last past

Tit. vi

Art i We have a Master of the Free grammar School. He is licensed by the Bishop & doth teach his Schollars the Church Catechism &c

We have also diverse petty schoolm[aster]s & believe that none of them except Abram Teasdale J- Broadwood & Cutht Stokeld have a Licence to teach

Art ii We have a Free grammar School founded by Q: Elizt of Blessed memory & ordered by 12 Governrs & Also ordered according to the Constitutions of the sd School.

Art iii Mr. Edw: Charlton Mr. Cuth Lambert & Mr. John Elliot practice Physick & Surgery & we believe have Licence, But do not know that any of our Midwives have any Licence

Tit vii

Art i Our Ch: Wardens are chosen the one halfe by the Minister the other by the parish courts or 24ly

Art ii iii They provide bread & wine & we know nothing to present concerning them

Jon Liddell Wm Leadbitter Cuth Heron Edward Kell
[*each sign*]

43. 29 November 1711 **Ritschel to Jubb**

Mr Jubb, Hexham Novemb 29th 1711

We had a Court here on Monday last Mr Burrell designs to write to you next week If he be not prevented, Its with great regret I write to Mr Chancellor because of his age, but canot well avoid it at present, be pleasd to give the enclosed with my humble service to him, & let me know his Worsps answer & directions abt our Fornicators.

Sr In persuance of your lre dated 21 April 1711, These may inform you that there is a Comon fame of Willm Elliot of this town Weavr & Alice Hedley of unlawful dealings between them & that they have both the French disease; He was appointed a ChWarden this year but has got another to serve for him I sent for & spoke to him abt it, He was obstinate & wd spend the last groat he had: I told him he might expect to be prosecuted; Its not a groundlesse report so much appears by their looks & other ways, that has quite ruined his businesse & few care to be anyways concernd with him so that he is designing to let his houses & go into the Countrey.

There was a like fame of one Cotesworth joynr and a widdow in Allandale, who laid an information before Justice Wilson for haveing the Carnal knowledge of her body or to that effect, he brought me a Certificate from Mr Wilson, that upon examination that Information was found groundlesse........but the Minister of Allandale tells me that report was true, and has promised to bring the woman hither before xmas and give me satisfaction therein wch If he do you shall here further from me abt it & Elliot;

I wrote to Mr Shaw last monday to get Thomasen Price put off till next terme; Pray give my service to him and tell him that Simon Armstronge has espoused her Cause agt Elliot & his son shee borne, he has employd an Atturney here, I desired he might be continued Proctor in that Cause. Be pleasd to cutt off and give the enclosed to Mr Skepper I am

Sr Your humble Servt
George Ritschel

[*annotated by Thomas Jubb on back of letter:*]
by Mr Chancellors Letter of this Same date he Mentions beside, Dawson of Allandale Thomas Elliot of Hexham Cordwainer 20 Nobles Comutation
Nicholas Dixon Taylor........£2 13s 4d
Mr L.M. a Young Gentleman 8. 0. 0
that desire to Comute.

44. 29 November 1711 **Ritschel to Watkinson**[219]

Rt Worspll Hexham Novem 29th 1711

I Received a lre from Mr Jubb your Registrar dated 31 Dec 1710 by your order desireing to know if I had any Comutations in my hand, I had none at that time nor ever did nor shall receive any before I acquaint your Worsp herewith.

We assure ourselves that his Grace my Ld ArchBpp and your Worsp have still at heart the ruinous state of our Church, and never had sinc my remembrance such an opportunity to do us a particular favour this way, for besides Dawson of Allandale Tho. Elliot of Hexham Cordwainer, being guilty of the same crime came to my house & submitted. I told him he must pay 20 Nobles wch made him uneasy. Nicholas Dixon Taylr has given a note to pay £2 13s 4d at Easter or Whitsontyde If your Worsp shall approve thereof. And a young Gent A Sollicitor who is not willing to have it noysed abroad, Whom therefore I shall call Mr L.M: I told him he must pay £8 0s 0d wch he was very unwilling to do; Dawson has notified he came here last monday & wd have borrowd the mony & pd If I did insist upon it, but was very urgent, that Allandale alone might have the benefit of it, till I convinced him of the great necessitys of our Church; Every of them will expect at least desire an abatemt, & our very aged sexton who is also apparator, must of necessity have some small pt thereof to support himselfe & wife, he has acted as Sexton here abt 70 years, & has assignd all his wages for the paymt of a debt for wch

[219] Dr. Henry Watkinson, Chancellor of York 1673-1713. See Introduction pp. 18, 25.

he was bound, & haveing nothing but his fees to live upon is sometimes under very great hardships.

If his Grace shall be pleasd to permit it to be applyd to the use of our Church I shall make the best I can of it and take care it be effectually applyed to that purpose, and to make it more effectuall, shall call our 24ty & make this proposal......that if they will lay on a sesse of £30 to be added to it, I will advance and lend them as much money (without Interest) as will rebuild the roofe of the North & North East Isles .....wch is such a proposal as they will doubtlesse comply with, unlesse the old Spirit of contradiction be still too predominant, & If it be I hope your Worsp will be pleasd to make use of your authority to compell them to reason......The Trustees of Sr Willm Blackett did rebuild what was beat down by the fall of the battlemt on the other syde; but there was some pt next adjoyning to be done by the parish wch if it had not been done wd certainly have proved very prejudicial to that syde of our Church; wch wd have been unfit for divine service in bad weather, I calld the 24ty a few of them app'd & viewd it, but took no further notice as soon as Mr Aynsley & I got the Recomendaton from our Quarter Sessions (for none besides were concernd in it) I set on Workmen & did that & some other little things abt the Church; & paid them out of my own pocket expecting to have been repaid out of that Collection not doubting of the successe thereof, ... I have advanced abt £10 upon & to very good ends & purposes, upon the head of such comutations.......and shall be willing to postpone them till another opportunity provided so great a peic of service may be done to our Church. And therefore these humble request your Worsp wd be pleasd to give my duty to his Grace & acquaint him herewith, and use your interest with his Grace wd he pleasd to permit that the said Comutations, and what more can be got upon that account may be applyed to the repairs of our Church; My Sister gives her humble service to your Worsp and your good Lady. I am in syncerity

Your Worsps Most Humble & devoted Servt
George Ritschel

45. 27 December 1711 **Burrell jnr to Jubb**

Sir,

Ive inclosed you 10: L[icence] Bonds & 2:Prsentmts wch are the first I ever had & I desire you'l send Process agt the persons prsented. Also I desire you'l send a citaton agt the Churchwardens of St Jo Lee for not paying their fees haveing not pd any this two yeares by past nor has Bingfeild Churchwardens pd any; yet that impudent fellow Bentham came & sitt downe to Dinner called for the best of liquors & Ime assured put me to 4s 6d charges, when he had done sharpt out of the company without takeing any notice not soe much as thanks soe that I think it's very reasonable the Churchwardens should be obliged to do their duty as the rest does otherwise t'will be a matter of ill consequence. Sir, I have ordered Mr Skepper to pay you £5 for the 10: Licences soe that I have but 3s 4d for writeing & trusting stamps for a yeare wch I hope you'l consider Mr Ritschell haveing 6s 5d clear money does not any way contribute to the charge of a dinner wch lyes all upon me & my allowance will not answer and att Visitacons its expected by the Gent. there the same entertainmt as formerly. I have an informacon that there are some Comutacons wch Mr Ritschell has made in Hexhamshire but he gave me an acct that he had intimated the same to you by Lre if he has not I would have you give him a Line without takeing notice of me in the matter.

I am Sir Your very humble servant
P Burrell

Durham Dec 27th 1711

46. 24 January 1712 **Ritschel to Jubb**

Sr Hexham Jany the 24th 1711

I wrote to you the 29th of 9ber. wch I suppose you Received & have not sinc heard either from you or Mr Skepper or Mr Burrell Mr Paton Minister of Allandale[220] according to promise, sent Margaret Richardson of the Crosse House in Allandale Widdow,

[220] See Introduction, p.4.

here on xtmas Eve who saith (& that she will swear it) that one Summer Evening John Cotesworth of Hexham joynr called at her house etc and did diverse times strive with all his power and might to have the carnal knowledge of her body, that at last she was so much out of breath with striveing with him & got such a grievous stroke upon her breast (whether accidentally or design odly she cannot tell) that his member did touch her naked thigh out of wch issued a deal of corrupt matter wch run down upon her skin whrby & the sd stroke she lay a long time in a very sadd & miserable condition, & that he has quite ruined her both as to her reputation & way of living wch was by drawing & retailing of ale & Beer etc I am told that the night before he lay at Tho. Whites in Allandale Town, Whites Wife laid a pair of clean sheets on the bed but the next day when she came to make the bedd, or take them off again, found them so stained that she was extreamly troubled & showed them to Mr Reed a Phisitian who said it was the effects of the Fr[ench] pox.[221] She wd needs have brunt the sd sheets but that her husband prevaild with her that good washing wd make them serviceable without danger.

I sent one afterwards to Alice Hedley of Hexham Wid. who confest that the sd Cotesworth for abt 3 years last past had been endeavoring to be base with her, (He is also a maulster & she was often concernd for him abt it) and that in April or May last he had the Carnal knowledge of her body; whrby & sinc wch time she hath been grievously afflicted wth sores &Ulcers hath been under the Dr & Surgeons hands & is not yet perfectly cured.

Its reported & believed here that Cotesworth gave them to Hedley, that Hedley gave them to William Elliot of Hexham Weavr her LandLd for she lived in a pt of his house; that Elliot gave them to his Wife, who was with child wch child dyed of Ulcers & Sores when abt 2 months old, but Hedley will not confesse any thing of Elliot; so that we have only an evil fame of him. I sent for Cotesworth abt 10 days ago told him that both Richardson & Hedley had Confest advised him to submit & bid him consider of it & give me his answer, but have not sinc heard from him. He alleages that his distemper was only the effect of the Measles & that Hedley had confest that what ill or harme She gott of any was by a kisse of an

[221] Syphilis; named the ‘French pox’ in England after an outbreak amongst French soldiers in the late 15th century. In France it was known as the ‘English disease’.

Officer at the Bull Inn here in Town, & expects that Mr Elliot of this place his Dr & Surgeon will helpe to bring him off /turn over

He spoke to me one day abt Willm Elliot his Friend and told me he had no such distemper. I only smiled at him & thought it not fit to enter upon a discourse wth him upon that subject, being very confident that whatever he may say to helpe to keep his patients from being prosecuted, when he comes to be examined he will swear the trueth. I told Coatsworth It was no matter what his distemper was sinc they had both (vizt Richardson & Hedley) confest etc

Sr Notwithstanding the ill state of Hexham Church, It being a shame such offenders should go unpunished, I had rather the Comutation money should be applyed to the prosecuteing of them, especially Cotesworth, the matter being so plain agt him, & I am apt to believe the chiefe reason why he does not submit is that he expects no body will trouble themselves to do it,

We are here in hopes of a peac & some expect a general pardon Be pleasd Sr to give my humble service to Mr Chancellor & acquaint him with the promises I desire his Worsp wd be pleasd to give me an order to receive the Comutation money of Dawson Tho. Elliot etc least the hopes of a pardon may make some of them retract; I hope his Worsp will be pleasd to order a prosecution agt Cotesworth & If he be so foolhardy as to contest that matter, to see you here at Hexham, Where I should be very glad to see, These Wish you a happy new year I am

Sr your very Humble Servt
George Ritschel

Pray show Mr Skepper & Mr Shaw what follows & relates to them

Mr Skepper

Be pleasd to give Widdow Fairlambs lres of Admon granted at our last Court, to Thomasin Price of Acomb who designs to be at Yorke on the last of this month to give her answer to a libell etc the poor Wid hath sent diverse times for them for that Sr Wm B- Steward will not pay what was due to her husband till she has got them I wish you a happy new year & am

Sr Your Humble Servt
George Ritschel

47. 25 February 1712 **Ritschel to Jubb**

Sr Hexham Feby 25th 1711

Yours of the 14th I Reced the 16th Inst, & deferrd an answer till I could speak wth the Criminals abt their Comutations I wrote to Dawson but do not expect an answer till to morrow. Mr L.M. is unwilling to pay £8 0s 0d, or wd have time he designs to be shortly at Nuby[222] at Sr Edw. Blacketts & If time permit to see & discourse you abt it Tho. Elliot seems positive not to pay so much as 20 nobles I shall speak to some Friend of his to perswade him & Dixon is not to pay till Easter or Whitsuntyde Diana Elliot in St Jno Lee prsentmts I take to be the same person he was concernd with.

Collison & Wood, Ellis & Todd, Stokoe & Summers Smith & Johnson were all presented for fornication, Smith was a souldier quartered here Stokoe is gone into her Majties service, & Ellis If I be not mistaken. & as for Collison he is so deep in debt that he canot continue long in the Countrey or out of jail. Armstronge & Nicholson were clandestinely marryed If marryed at all, for wch they were cited the court before but did not appear, they have nothing & no true settlemt here so that I conceive it best not to take any further notice of them. Gibson & Bell are Dissentrs & our Fees being small I am not willing to put them to any further trouble or charge than to cite them at our next court when I suppose they will pay them.

As to Answer to Title 4 Art. 3rd [223] that schedule was for those who should not pay their Ch sesse, but none was made for that those in Hexhamshire have no money nor will have any till Duxfield pay.

As to Art. 7. you must know Sr that not halfe the people in this pt of the world who come to Church, come the H. Comunion, in former times before our late unhappy Civill Warrs, as I find by our Registrs there was always above a thousand comunicated at Easter, but now we have not halfe the number thoa our Congregations be more numerous, & if we should compell them to it, I doubt might thin our congregations & not augment the number of Comunicants so that I do not conceive it worth our time to cite any save John

---

[222] ie. Newby Hall, Yorkshire.

[223] Visitation articles, Title 4, 3rd Article, (see doc. **42**) which contains no names other than the Gibson or Bell referred to by Ritschel here.

Cotesworth & William Elliott agt whom we have only Comon fame. As to Mr Burrell he takes the same Fees here as in the Diocese of Durham vizt. 8s 6d at Easter & 5s 6d at Mich. vizitaton. St John Lee has two Chapells vizt St Oswald & Bingfield each pay 2s 6d there has not been any dismission Fee pd by any cited to our Court for diverse years & sinc he pays for the dinner it wd not be worth his time unlesse he had some benefit by Mr fs businesse. At a Court at Corbridge he produced & read pt of a lre from him wherein were containd the terms he offerred for transmitting the same (wch I do not remember exactly) for wch he thought he was well rewarded for that he had nothing to do but to take them from me at Corbridge Court & transmitt them.

I can transmitt them to York: either by post or NewCastle Stage Coach, as easily & at the same charge as to Durham, wch is but an unnecessary trouble to send them to him, but this Jurisdiction is so small, that neither Mr Burrell nor any from Durham wd trouble themselves with it, without some benefit by Mr Skeppers businesse & therefore I wish he wd let me know (as I once desired him) how much he expects for every probate & Admon & what he will abate in Case of poverty wch too frequently happens; that I might know better how to make Mr Burrell suitable encouragemt & not seem hard upon the poor.

I had a lre from him the other day wherein he desires me to send him the names of St John Lee ChWardens for that you designd to cite them to Yorke to pay their Fees there; wch I conceive wd be somewhat severe; but if upon such processe they come hither & submitt & pay whats reasonable & the charge of the processe, it may do well and teach both them & others a better temper for the future, & pray let me know what Fees to take of them if they submit, their names are vizt. John Lee senr Robert Thompson Alexander Maughen & George Angus old ChWardens of St Jno Lees, for Bingfield George Wilkinson, New ChWardens for St John Lees John Lee junr & George Angus the other two are not in the processe.

Be pleased to give my humble service with due respects to Mr Chancellor & show whats on the other Syde[224] to Mr Skepper. I am

Sr Your very humble Servt
George Ritschel

[224] This must refer to one of the first four paragraphs of the letter.

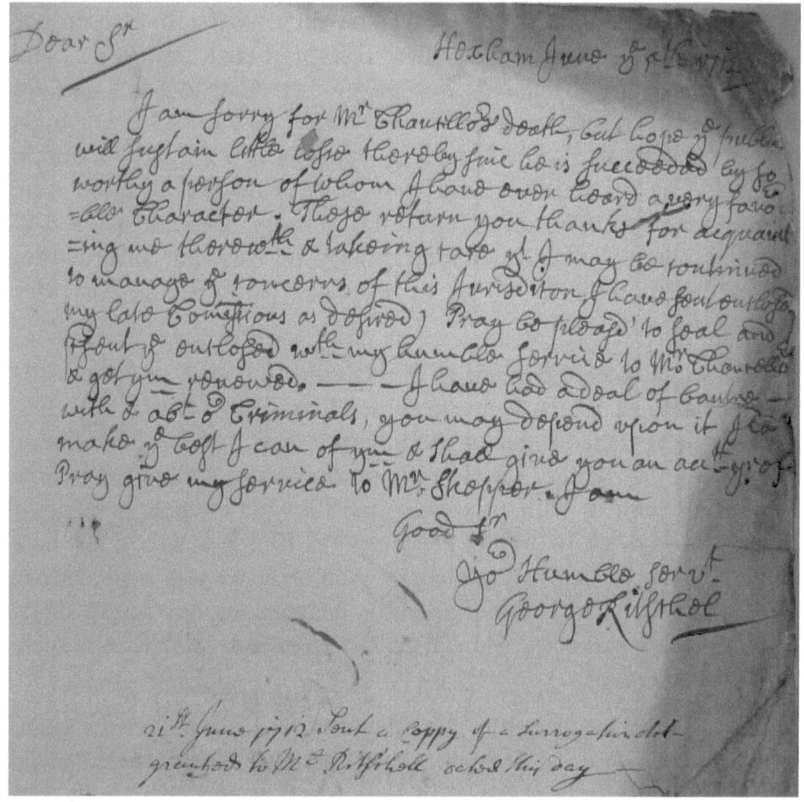

Dear Sr

Hexham June ye 5th 1712

I am sorry for Mr Chancellor's death, but hope ye publick will sustain little losse thereby since he is succeeded by so worthy a person of whom I have ever heard a very favourable Character. These return you thanks for acquainting me therewth & takeing care yt I may be continued to manage ye concerns of this Jurisdicton I have sent enclosed my late Commissions as desired) Pray be pleased to seal and send ye enclosed wth my humble service to Mr Chancellor & get ym renewed. —— I have had a deal of bother with ye set o Criminals, you may depend upon it I'le make ye best I can of ym & shall give you an acct thereof. Pray give my service to Mr Shepper. I am

Good Sr

Yor Humble servt.

George Ritschel

21st June 1712 Sent a Coppy of a Surrogation [illegible] granted to Mr Ritschell [illegible] this day

Figure 11: George Ritschel to Thomas Jubb, 5 June 1712, doc. **48** (Reproduced from an original in the Borthwick Institute, University of York, Pec.Hex/2)

48. 5 June 1712 **Ritschel to Jubb**

Dear Sr Hexham June the 5th 1712

I am sorry for Mr Chancellor's death, but hope the public will sustain little losse thereby sinc he is succeeded by so worthy a person of whom I have over heard a very favourable Character. These return you thanks for acquainting me therewith & takeing care that I may be continued to manage the concerns of this Jurisdicon. I have sent enclosd my late Comissions as desired, Pray be pleasd to seal and present the enclosed with my humble service to Mr Chancellor and get them renewed. I have had a deal of bantre with & abt our Criminals, you may depend upon it Ile [I'll] make the best I can of them & shall give you an acctt thereof Pray give my service to Mr Skepper. I am

Good Sr Your Humble Servt
George Ritschel

[*In Jubb's hand:*]
21st June 1712 Sent a Coppy of a Surrogation granted to Mr Ritschel dated this day

49. 23 June 1712 **Ritschel to Jubb**

Kind Sr Hexham June the 23rd 1712

Inclosed you have the Citaton As to the Criminals Tho. Elliot & Dixon (who comitted the fornication wth Diana Elliot) submitted & Compounded sometime ago, Stokoe & Smith are abroad in her Majties service I cited Collison & Ellis who are both very poor & have submitted to your Court; a friend did endeavour to perswade Ellis If he could procure 20s to pay your Court Fees, hopeing you wd be favourable to him wch he was willing to do. Collison has been a very wicked lewd fellow, his LandLd Mr Heron who stands engaged for abt £60 for him lately put him in jail here, & the last week took him out again & has gott him up again & engaged £11 for him upon his promise of amendmt, & upon Condition to send him imediately to jail again if or when ever he shall be drunk, wch I conceive may be as probable a means to reform him as any we can use. I could wish he might be severly punished; If his circumstances wd permit & conceive If I can perswade Mr Heron to pay 20s for your Court Fees (for he is not worth a groat himselfe being £150 in debt,) & Ellis to do the like & both of them to do their penanc in my house before two Ch Wardens; will be the best we can make of them least If we strain it too farr we make nothing at all; & believe me Sr Wt.ever yourselfe or any may think I could not possibly make any more of the other Criminals who have Comuted. I suppose Armstronge & Nicholson were marryed by a buckle beggar they have now turnd beggars themselves so that we must passe them by as such. I sent to Gibson his wife presently brought our Fees, & wth some ado I got a shilling for you to pay for the stamp of the Citaton, Bell is a poor man & wd have pd pt of the fees, wch we must be content to want, rather than cite him.for that people here ab[ou]ts wd exclaim & reflect both on your Court & my selfe If I should do it.

St John Lee ChWardens & Wilkinson are Cited. Jno Lee was wth me & Submitted rather than contest anything. He is a Credible [...]-tial person & one of their 24ly & tells me that of late years they [...] not had or laid on any sesse for their Ch but wts done abt it is pd out of the poor sesse & they wd Make the ChWardens to pay the Fees out of their own pockette, as they do in St Oswald & Bingfield Chapelry, where they have or Collect no such sesse for those Chapels are both ruined.

I wrote to Mr Bentham & desired him to give his 24ly notice to meet & adjust & regulate that matter, & Lee to assist in it. We are to have a Court here on Wednesday next after wch I suppose Mr Burrell will give you a more satisfactory answer abt them. Be pleased to seal & present the enclosed wth my humble service to Mr Chancellor. I am

Dr Sr Your Humble Servt
George Ritschel

50. After **25 June 1712** **Petition of the Minister, Churchwardens and Four & Twenty of St John Lees**

[BIA Pec.Hex/5]

Comitu Northumbe
To the Reverend Doctor Pearson[225] Doctor of Laws & Chancellor of the Ecclall Court of Yorke.

The Humble petition of the Minister Church Wardens Overseers of the poor & Four & Twenty of the parish of St John Lees in Com. prd. May it please your Worshipp :

We the Minister Church Wardens Overseers of the poor & Four & Twenty of the said parish part of the peculiar Jurisdiction of Hexham within the Diocess of Yorke humbly shew unto your Worshipp that Mr George Ritchell Minister of Hexham aforesaid & surrogatt unto your Worshipp of the Ecclesiastical Court there held together with Mr Peter Burrell Officiall of the said Court some time heretofore haveing refused to receive for Admission and dismission from the Church Wardens of this parish the Fees formerly paid (tho imposed upon in the same) but insisting upon more & larger then your petitioners are informed ever were paid your petitioners (by John Errington Esq., the Cheife of Beaufront & one of the parishioners abovesaid) did address Doctor Watkinson late Chancellor therein humbly praying his Worshipp's Finall determination and Judgement in the same & what order his Worshipp was pleased to make in the same for the quiett regulation & Government of our Church & parish affaires we were ready to obey & stand to notwithstanding any complaint to the contrary but heard of noe Order his Worshipp made in the same save that he was pleased to say that such Officers as were imployed for holding Courts under him had certaine Allowances for their service from himselfe & knew not of any Fees were due from our Churchwardens upon which your petitioners did acquiess without giveing his Worshipp any further trouble. But now soe it is the said Doctor Watkinson being dead the said Mr Ritchell & Mr Burrell hath taken advantage of the same & combineing together to perplex your petitioners & the rest of the parishioners being all concerned either mediately or imediately & to putt us to unnecessary charge & trouble

[225] See ABN.

have brought, along with the process for calling the last Court which was held the 25th day of June last [1712], a Citation set the 26th of the same & as your petitioners veryly beleive by tampering with one of the churchwardens the said Ritchell has prevailed upon him to pay 2s:6d: towards the Fees & to amuse & afright the other to comply with their unreasonable demands has caused the said Citation to be published against them for the Nonpayment of their Fees & pretends he has returned the same into the Eccesiastical Court att Yorke & your petitioners expecting noe Favour from the said Mr Ritchell & Mr Burrell but that they will take all Advantages possible against the churchwardens for their non Appearance personally in the Consistory att Yorke according to the returne of the said Citation (tho the same as your petitioners hope to make appeare is very irregular being brought in Doctor Watkinsons name) (who att that time was dead) thought it very convenient to prevent charges & soe have prevailed upon the Bearer Mr. Bentham our Minister to waite upon your Worshipp with this our petition on purpose &

Therefore Humbly pray your Worshipps Favourable clemency & serious consideration of the premisses & that your Worshipp will please to make an Order & settlement in the premisses which we will be very ready to obey soe that the said Mr Ritchell & Mr Burrell's proceedings on the said Citation be discharged & your petitioners as duty bound shall ever pray etc.

These are the Names of the Four and Twenty belonging to the Parish of St. John Lees within mentioned. [*all sign:*]

John Hemsley John Lee William Lee Thomas Hutchinson John Armstrong George Angus John Lee Christopher Dobson Edward Nicholson Thomas Hemsley William Smith Nicholas Maughan John Pattison George Charlton Edward Foster Robt. Smith Jon. Hudspeth Nicholas Rowell Wm. Dixon Jon. Hutchinson John Errington Simon Armstrong H. Rowell Thomas Bell

51. 24 July 1712 **Ritschel to Jubb**

Sr Hexham July 24th 1712

I Recd yours of the 12th Inst, In answer to wch I told Elliot at first that he must pay 20 nobles for Comutaton of penanc[e], expecting his circumstances had been better then they are, wch he did not nor wd consent to do, When he came at Easter to adjust that matter, he brought only 40s & protested it was all the money he had or could gett, and being under some trouble of mind, was like to have made some desperate resolutions, as to leave the Town & his family etc whrupon I was forced to give him comfortable words & promisd to write to your Court to accept of it, & because he went away in some discontent & a very nigh neighbour of his a few days before had laid violent hands upon himselfe, It put both his Bro in Law who came along with him & myselfe in such a concern for him, that I sent presently after him & his wife I believe procured the other 20s, otherwise for my own pt he might have gone Free, rather then I wd have exposed him to any temptation. Dawson complaind very sore for paying so much, & sd a Friend of his who had served my Ld Bpp of D[urham] a gt many years, had calld him a great many fools & blockheads for giveing a note to pay it, & that he wd have brought him off much cheaper,

Mr L. M. was very unwilling to sign a note to pay £8 he took journey next day for London I was very urgent with him to call at Yorke & try If he could get any pt of it abated, I showed them your lre abt the Fees, but to no purpose, so that If Mr Chancellor think fitt to insist upon them they must be deducted out of the Comutations, the women are always included. Hen. Collison hath nothing (Margt. Wood went out of the Countrey shortly after she was delivered) & Mr Heron will not pay a farthing for him upon that acctt for that he is & like to be so gt a looser by him that not long sinc he did supply his family & fathers too wth bread, & knows not how soon they may stand in need of his Charity. I sent to Willm Ellis who was from home & I suppose will submit. As to Mary Summers etc I conceive its not worth our time to enquire after such vagring Scots Spinn[ster] husseys our Justices of the Peac are abt setting up a hous of Correction in this County, the Grand Jury at the last Quarter Sessions did recomend Hexham as a proper place. If it take effect may save us the trouble for the future.

I wrote to John Lee, who sent me word that he was busy leading his hay but wd submitt & pay his proportion rather then contest any thing for the Pish at his own proper charge I perceive that the rest of them being but poor, do not design to trouble themselves abt it; I suppose Mr Burrell ere this hath given you an acctt of that Pish at our last vizitation.

Sr I Received your Lre of the 21 June, wth the Substitution & upon our Court day the 25th at Dinner. Mr Burrell came hither from Durham that morning & went to Corbridge that evening so that I had not time to write, He could not tell me your engrossing Fees, so I gave him 5s; 1s for the Stamp & 1s for Gibson, & am still indebted to you for your trouble & care therein for wch I heartily thank you, & sinc I take no Fees or have no benefit by keeping the vizitation Courts & of late have had so much trouble about them I conceive as he Concluded I may do you as much service another way, I desired him to give you an acctt hereof & am apt to believe the reason why he did it not then that he got not home from Corbridge till late on thursday night & Mr Skepper took journey soon next morning.

In Feby 1708 I made an acctt of all the money received for Comutation of penanc for 25 years vizt from St Andrew day 1683 When my father dyed till St Andrew day 1708; & do not find that ever your Court Recd any Fees save once, sinc wch time I have advanced & laid out upon the head & in expectation of such

	£	s	d
Comutations vizt abt Hexham Church	10	14	4
An Apprentice Fee for Jos Walton Orphan 40s & Cloaths for him 20s	3	0	0
Itm abt Whitley Chapel	3	15	8
Given our very aged Sexton & App[arator] halfe of Tho Elliots	1	1	0
Itm to J K for prswadeing Alice Hedley to Confesse J Cotesworth		5	0
Itm After to Alice Hedley When Cotesworth wd not do anything for her & she was like to starve		5	0
Ditto To Margt Richardson When she came hither & made her Confession she haveing nothing to carry her home		2	6
	19	12	6

Now the Whole Comutations If or When pd amount to 19 – 13 - 4 so that If they were all in my hands there wd remain but 10d for my other small expences; But Nich. Dixon the poor little Taylor will expect something vizt 3s 4d again, & our aged sexton & App[arator] should have at least 10s more, & who hath allways except that once Recd what should have been pd as Court Fees.

I must here remark that neither Hexham Church nor Whitley Chapel wd have been fit for divine service in bad weather without the sd repaires, that there be some places in the roofe of our Church wch ought to be mended this summer, to put of till they can be rebuilt, to preserve the timbar & prevent future damage. This Countrey is very poor at present by reason of the gt decay of the lead trade & want of a pay, so that the Church sesse for the year 1710 is not yet Collected in the Shire, nor will be till Duxfield pay & The Town will not lay on any more, till that in the Shire is Collected & payd, so that nothing will be done to our Church unlesse I do advance & lay out the money; our Clerk & Sexton want their wages for the two last years wch I have advancd & laid out for them upon the head of the aforesd sesse, & In hopes my project or some other to repair our Church will take effect. I lately bought ten tun of choise timbar for that its a penny worth & such like for that use. after a short time will not be got hereabouts for money, so that at present I am above Fourty pounds out of pockett. upon acctt of our pish for wch I expect no Interest & shall be unwilling to lay out any more before I am cleared off the old Score upon the head of Comutations, wch I wholy submitt to Mr Chancellors pleasure. Be pleased to give my humble service to him & acquaint him with the premises. Pray give my Service to Mr Skepper I desired Mr Burrell to pray him to take out Excomunicatons agt those who did not appr to prove the Wills etc Mr Burrell seemd to grant that our Courts canot compell any man to prove a Will, If so It wd seem hard to ~~compell~~ excomunicate such for not doing it, & I wd not proceed any further agt them. Pray give my service to Mr Shaw & tell him I Recd his last lre abt Thomasin Price, but canot at present give him a satisfactory answer

I am Sr Your very Humble Servt
George Ritschel

52. 9 November 1712 Jackson to Ritschel

Sir

Yours I have Just now received wherein you say you writt to Mr Chancellor & sent him my Note Upon my acct. as well as Upon anothers, You may beleive me Sr that £8 Ill never pay for I find it altogether an Imposicon Upon us for wch reason my friend has Imployed a fitt person in that Court to make an end of it, tho I must prsume to tell you that noe man ought nor dare in Law receive money Upon that acct. but since it is not Mr Ritschell business hopes He'l still continue his friendshippe &c

Your Friend
Jo Jackson

Hexham 13th 9'ber 1712

53. 13 November 1712 Ritschel to Pearson

Revd Sr Hexham Novr 13th 1712

These return my thankfullness for your very kind letter. I writ to Mr Jackson & have sent enclosed his answer, he being a Gent, of an Estate. so civily used in this matter haveing wrote that note himselfe & promised upon honour to pay it at St. Luke Fair I did not expect he wd have made any such objections otherwise should have taken a bond of him. If he escape as perhaps he expects to do I doubt it will be to little purpose to trouble you with any more such criminals who will be sure to hear of it. I sent our App[arator] to Mch. Dixon who could not meet with him.

The abuse of our Church by pidgeons was certainly very scandalous & in a great measure to be attributed to Mr John Carr Sr Wm Blacketts Steward here who pretends they are the Lds pidgeons (& we may mend our Ch windows) so that none must or dare) to meddle with them. I never do use or carry a gun else wd have done it myselfe, but got a Gentlewomans little son who is an artist at it, & has killd some & driven the most of them back again to their own coat, so that our Church in that respect is much better at present then

I have sometimes known it. I wish it could be kept decent & clean as it ought to be, but that wch I have most at heart is to preserve the roofe & thereby the fabrick that it may be capable to be repaired, when we shall be able to do it, I shall do somewhat at present if the season permit, & design God willing in the spring to gett afoot my old project to do it by subscriptions, wch if it do not succeed, I must begg your Worsps advice in that matter; as to some other project; & remain

Your Worsps Mt Humble Servt
George Ritschel

[*Cover:*]
To The Revd & Worsp[fu]ll Mr William Pearson Archdeacon of Not[t]ingham & Chancellor of York at his Hous in York
These present post pd

54. 9 February 1713 **Burrell jnr to Jubb**

Sir, I sent my Clerk to Mr Mascall[226] wth your [letter] who told him that care should be taken for your speedy paymt & he would imediately write to Mr Brathwaite abt it. You write for Prsentmts the last Vis^on^ at Hexham wch Mr Ritschell has (if any) tho' I beleive there was none given in; Nor was there any Vis^on^ Mich: last att Easter before was not one penny reced. but of Allandale 5s 6d soe that you may consider what I had for my trouble when I pd for the Entertainmt wch came to 37s I hear Mr Ritschell has made severall Comutacons but never takes any notice but tells me he acquaints your Mr Chancellr therewith, one lately made with a young attorney who imediately after he pd his money comenced his Action agt him but what issue its brought to I cannot instance, Your best way att the next Vis^on^ will be to call 'em to York for its really a very unprofitable post. I am

Sir your humble servt
Pr: Burrell

Durham Feb 9th 1712

---

[226] Presumably Francis Mascall of Durham, attorney, 1662-1725: J.C.Hodgson (ed): *North Country Diaries, Second series*, Surtees Society, Vol 124, (1915), p.92.

55. 16 February 1713 **Ritschel to Pearson**

Rt Worspll Hexham Febry 16th 1712

According to your order I receivd £8 of Mr Jackson (& have given Nich Dixon till Whitsontyde to pay his, at what time he expects a pay at Fallowfield lead Works.) before wch time he canot possibly pay it) and have sent his Grace a Certificate, wch I conceive very proper for my own justification, for that at last Corbridge Court they told me, it was a Comon report through all Durham that I was goeing to be sued for money wch I had receivd. when they understood how it was, were very well pleased, and lately at a Christening dinner here Mr Jackson could not forbear to make reflections, I thank god I am above them & am sorry he should so much expose himselfe.

This had come sooner, but that I hoped to have sent herewth an Account I am publishing of our Charitys on this syde the Countrey, in wch is an Art[icle] in favor of Hexham Church, I set the period at Xtmas, but the weather proveing so badd and other things hindering, got not to NewCa: till last week; and sinc it cannot be done within my limited time, will be forced to give your Worsp a further trouble.

Sr I heartily thank you for this application of that money, that is for paying me off that old debt, wch I have wanted about three years, & If I had not disbursed it god knows in what a sad condition our Church wd now have been in, for we can get no Ch sesse for want of a pay at Duxfield, and no body troubles his head abt it; I am ashamed to tell it, we did not observe the last fasting day for that my Ld of Durhams App[arator] who sends the Books & Proclamations, wd not send us any, for that our ChWardens had not pd him; I pd him off when he was last here, & he hath promised, that for the future we shall not want any thing of that nature upon my promise to pay him, so sad is our case; I have been forced to lend our Clerk & Sexton abt £12 upon the head of their wages till god send better times & more plenty of money among us; Being now cleard off my old arrears I shall god willing begin again, and your Worsp may depend upon it. that nothing shall be omitted for the interest of our Church that lyes in the power of

Your Worsps Mt Humble & obleged servt, George Ritschel

56. 13 February 1713 **Hexham Church Repairs**

[BIA Pec.Hex/5]

To The Most Reverend Father in God John his Grace by Divine providence Lord ArchBishop of Yorke Primate of England and Metropolitane.

We whose names are hereunto Subscribed, being Churchwardens of the Towne & parrish of Hexham in the County of Northumberland and Diocesce of Yorke. In persuance of Mr Chancellrs order To Mr George Ritschel our Minister, to Receive Eight Pounds of Mr John Jackson & two pounds thirteen shillings and fourpence of Nichollas Dixon Taylor. & apply and dispose of the same Towardes the repaire of our Church, Doe hereby Certifie your Grace. That we have Examined the s[ai]d Mr Ritschels accounts, Whereby it appears unto us, That he hath Actually & bone fide Disbursed ten pounds thirteen shillings And fourpence, vizt In filling up the two great Cracks or breaches on the North Side of the steeple, in rebuilding a part of the Roofe of the south Isle next to that which was beat downe by The fall of the Battlement the 15th of May 1709, Building up the wall at the East end of the North & south Isles, Mending the Windowes on the South and West side and other Needfull things about our Church, soe that he hath not any of the sd moneys in his hands, nor hath disbursed any of it for his owne Proper use, In Witness whereof he have hereunto set our hands this 13 day of February in the yeare of our Lord 1712.

[*in Ritschel's hand:*]
I do also certify & attest the trueth hereof as witness my hand ..
George Ritschel Minister of Hexham

churchwardens [*each sign*]
Jo. Hearon Edward Kell George Farlamb Thomas Huback

57. 30 March 1713 **Ritschell to Jubb**

Sir Hexham March 30 1713

I thank you for your last in putting me in mind of Mr.Chancellor and thoa I did not forget it, I have ordered Mr. White the Printer at NewCa: to lend you herewith twenty copys of my Acct of our Charitys and of your gift; and desire you to seal and present the gilt copy with the enclosed letter with my duty to his Grace. If he be at home. If not to give it with the other for Mr.Chancellor, with one of your copys and so many of the rest as he shall think fit to dispose of, reserving one of you to your selfes I have also sent you two poor admons believe me they are very poor ones and must pass as such or not at all, I am in hast

Sir,
Your humble Servt
George Ritschell

I have sent a pt of my Project to repair of our Church.

[*Cover:*]
For Mr.Thomas Jubb. at the Registers Office nigh of Minster in York.
To be left with Mr.John White of NewCa: and sent by the Stage Coach. with a Bundle. With care

58. 13 April 1713 **Ritschel to Jubb**

Kind Sr Hexham April the 13th 1713

I have yours & Mr Smyth's of the 6th Inst. & since Mr Burrell desires to be eased of the trouble of keeping Court here (for I know of little other trouble he had in the managemt of this Jurisdiction) I have spoke to Mr Thomas Baxter, A Solicitor here in Town, He keeps our post house, & we used to adjourn & keep our Courts at his house, and because he & those of his profession have 10s a day for sitting Comissions in Chancery etc I proposed to give him 20s a year for keeping Court twice a year vizt. acting as Register that while, & I wd adjourn the Court from the Church to my house to save expences, & wd treat my Brethren etc as I found occasion; & he should Frank all Court businesse between here & NewCastle, wch he was willing to accept of, & I conceive may do very well If those in St John lee parish do not create us any trouble about their Church Wardens Fees, wch I shall endeavour to prevent, if possible, by soft & easy means. If this please; I desire Mr Smyth will send a note or table of your Fees, of wch there must of necessity be an abatemt in Cases of poverty wch too often happens for that this syde of Tyne is reduced to great poverty by reason of the decay of the lead trade, & I shall answer all such fees and return them, as we shall agree upon, for I do not always receive them when I dispatch the businesse, George Thirlewall being here in Town this day attending a funeral from Grandridge I got him & two of his Neighbours who have made an Inventory etc the Decd was a Batchelour, who was unfortunately killed, at a late fox hunting, creeping under the rock where the fox was to encourage the terryer; a great stone sunk down upon him.

Sr I should be glad to see you at Hexham, but as our business will not encourage I doubt it wd not be worth your time unlessse you have a mind to see this Countrey; We have at present a very sharpe season, & a deep snow in the moors, & I perswade myselfe if you had been this forenoon upon Harwood moor[227] you wd not desire to see it again in such weather.

Sr I thank you for you care in what I sent last. Be pleasd to give my humble service to Mr Chancellor, after I have heard from him, you may expect to hear further from me turn over

Pray give my service to Mr Smyth who I suppose doth manage the office at present, I hope we shall settle the affaires of this Jurisdicon to the advantage both of your Court & the Countrey, I am

Sr Your Humble servt
George Ritschel

59. 18 May 1713 **Ritschel to Jubb**

Sr Hexham May the 18th 1713

I have not Recd any acct from Mr Chancellor abt our Church, nr any from you since the 6th of April to wch I sent an answer the 13th at this rate both our Church & this Jurisdicton are like to go to confusion I have been ill served with Stamps since our last Court or rather not at all, the last year was very remarkable here for a multitude of weddings, & at last Court I had marryed four Couple only takeing the partys bound & Sworn etc for want of

---

[227] above 1,200 ft in attitude, 8 miles south of Hexham.

Blanck Licences, wch I filled up assoon as I got them & now I am got to the same length again. I sent several times to Mr Burrell, for such Blank Licences & some Will Bonds; but he never did send any and when I was last at Durham told me he had none etc.

And therefore these desire you to send me by the first opportunity four Blank Licences for marryage, I design God willing to be at NewCastle this week, & to fix a Correspondence with your Stage Coach man, abt transmitting business's, & shall send you some Wills, & enclosed a guinea for the sd 4 Blank Licences or the stamps thereof, wch I shall deduct from Mr Burrell when I acct with him. I also desire you to send me some Will and Admon Bonds & some Blank Licences for marriage and Bonds & that for the future I may not want any of them, especially Blank Licences. for that I conceive its not consistent with my reputation or Interest, to grant any Licence, or marry any unlesse at the same time I have such Blank to fill up before marriage; for that the Officers belonging to the Stamp Office are sometimes Comeing hither & I may be liable to a reproofe if not some trouble & reflections; I shall as often as there shall be occasion account with you for the sd Bonds & Licences.

This had come some time ago but that I deferrd writeing in Expectation of an answer to that of the 13th April, & to have Recd an acct of his Graces & Mr Chancellors pleasure concerning our Church, till wch time we know not how to proceed in that affair.

Some of my Books wch Mr White send hither, were so ill stitched that I was forced to get them done, over again. & some of them imperfect. I had the same complaint from my Friend at London of those he sent thither, & doubt those you have are like them And therefore these request you will be pleasd to peruse them & those you find imperfect return them to Mr White, & those wch are ill stitched get them done over again & right done by some Bookbinder with you & place it to my acct. Be pleased to give my Humble Service to Mr Chancellor. I am

Sr Yours etc George Ritschel

60. 30 May 1713 **Burrell jnr to Jubb**

Sr

I sent once more to Mr Mascall who desires your Bill & promises to pay the money to your order. My adviseing you to call the Churchwardens to York is to make 'em sensible of their Contempt otherwise there will be noe occasion to attend the Vis^{on}; Att Easter Anno 1712 not one Churchwarden appear'd but Allendale & if you intend a Vis^{on} this year you must actually send Citations agt them all Mr Ritschells wanting Licences is occasion'd by himselfe he promiseing to be att the expence of disburseing money for the Stamps wch he's not done therefore I think its reasonable he shou'd be att the outlay pvided I write 'em he haveing soe good allowance declare as 6s 5d & I've but 3s 4d paying all charges & Mr Ritschell will not grant any unless they marry with him wch is a treble advantage soe that he takes their Bond & Marry's without a Licence & when I goe there I supply the defects; tho' all the Clergy in the peculiar is disturb'd & really hinders the Churchwardens to attend the Vis^{on} You mention halfe of the Fees is expected as to the Guards[228] wch Mr Empson made me a Complemt of but very small but if I must pay them shall be very willing not haveing reced a 3d part of the fees due the 3 Chappells never pay's more than 2s 6d p Annum wch I never reced of them but one Vis^{on} In case you'l propose any method whereby I may have my expences & a small consideration for my Journey shall be willing to give my assistance if not I hope you'l not take it ill I doe assure you I never [*crossed out*] had soe much as pd my expences since concerned my Unkle Burrell & Mr Rowell as I've been informed by Mr Ritschell had alway's a Fee allow'd before Dismissons upon Comutatons wch I never had & likewise their charges pd thereout; I reced but of one Parish Anno 1710: & one Chappell) Anno 1711: of 2:) Anno 1712 of 1:) soe that you may compute the Dividend I desire you'l let me know who succeeded Mr Skepper in the peculiar of Hexham. Im'e a goeing to keep Court at Corbridge where I suppose Mr Ritschell will be who generally comes & takes a dinner wth us & shall settle the matter as to Licences & likewise as to the Vis^{on} wch I shall acquaint you with I am

Sr your assured humble Servt
Pe: Burrell May the 30th 1713

[228] the churchwardens.

61. 11 June 1713 **Jubb to Burrell jnr**

Sr York 11th June 1713

I Accknowledge my Hearty thanks Due for the trouble You have had upon Mr Mascall his account, of whom I Desire You will Receive the Summ of three pounds Eleaven Shillings, remaineing Due to Me for the Transmission in his Cause, and Your Receipt shall be his Discharge, which when received You may please to Remitt to Me the next time You Send any Mony to Mr Wm Mawde[229] who succeds Mr Skepper. The Said Transmission Contain'd 480 Folio's, which att two pence each, amounts to Four pounds Over and above Eleaven Shillings for the Seal of Court and the Notariall Certificate and Queens Duty thereupon, but I Received twenty Shill[ing]s in part upon Service of the Memorial transmittence. The Best Method I Can att present think of for the more Effectual Regulation of the peculiar Juron of Hexham, being You have no Seal by You (I presume) for that peculiar, will be for Me to send Mr Ritschell Blank Licences from hence under the Seal of this Court and Signed by the Chancellor (as all the Licences are that are Dispatched by our Surrogate) out of which You Shall have Your Former Allowance of 8s 1d Each Licence. And as for the Church and Chappell wardens, either You or I Shall Send a process Yearly against them to appear att the Visitation and if they Neglect either to appear, pay their Useual Fees (of which You are Better Judge than I) or Don't give their Answers to the Book of Articles (which I Suppose You take Care to Deliver them Yearly) Decree them to be Excommunicated. And as for the Delinquents I would have them Cited to appear the next Visitation after they are presented, and then proceeded agt or Dismiss them as the Law Requires, which may Easily be Done if You will but give Me an Account of what has been Done or Omitted after Your Return from the Said Visitation. And if You will take the trouble to Inform Me of the Names of the Chwardens of the Severall places that Did not appear, Did not pay their Fees or Neglected to Make presentments the Last Visitation, and Fix the time when You propose to keep the next Visitation Court there, I will Send You a p[ro]cess for them to appear, and in Case they Don't then appear and Submitt thereto, paying also Five Shillings for a Dismission Fee, You may prceed to Exco[mmuni]cate them, and this You may Do

[229] See also Introduction, p.25.

without Calling them to York or Suffering the Visitations to be rendred Ineffectuall or his Grace's Jurisdiction to be trampled upon. As to the Fees You must Receive I Cannot (as I have said before) Inform You, but I find that Chwardens for these Severall places Following were sworn and pd Fees (vizt) Hexham, Allandale, St Jno Lees, St Oswald & Bingfield, And for these five its very plain by all the Accounts of that peculiar I have by Me (vizt For the Years 1683, 1696, 1701, 1702, 1704, 1705, & 1706) that Your predecessors accounted Yearly for Each place to the Chancellor One Shilling & to the Register 1s 6d, for the Chwardens Fees & for Copyes of the Five Registers 5s and had allowed for their taking halfe of the Registers Fees (Vizt) Nine pence for the Fees of Chwardens of Each Church or Chappell & Six pence Each Register. Indeed by Some of the Said Accompts itt appears that the Said Jurisdiction was Visited and the Chwardens paid Fees twice Every Year as above menconed but as they Don't appear to have been answered more than once (Saveing in the Year 1683 when they were answered twice for Allendale) I shall not Expect it oft[e]ner, Notwithstanding You take the Fees as formerly twice in Every Year, and this I hope You will Comply with & Lett Me have Your thoughts herein. When any Commutation shall be made for the Future I shall expect to have Fees answered & halfe of Such Fees Due to the Register Shall be accounted for to You, but as yet I reced no Fees att all but they as well as the Commutation Money have been allowed Mr Ritschell towards the Defraying Some Disbursements upon the Church of Hexham wch he has been att I am

Sr Yours
Tho Jubb

62. 23 June 1713 **Burrell jnr to Jubb**

Sir,

Yours I recd and intend to persue the methods you propose. Munday the 20th day of July I propose to be att Hexham in order to attend the Vis^{on} and woud have you send me A blank Process agt the Churchwardens under the Chanc[ello]rs hand and seale. The names of the Churchwardens I cannot acquaint you with by reason none appeared Anno 1712: save Allandale but will send the Process to Mr Ritschell & hele insert them; As to the Licences I think it very proper wee shoud have [th]em under the Chanc[ello]rs hand & seale wch I also desire you'l send wth the Process & books of Artickles : Pray acquaint Mr Mawde of my goeing to Hexham & in case he expects I shoud serve him there let me hear from him by way of Tolleracon that I may be impowerd by him to Act Im'e in hopes of getting Mr Mascalls money this Weeke he haveing made a faithfull promise to

Sir Your humble Servt
Pr: Burrell

Durham June the 23[d] 1713

63. 25 June 1713 **Ritschel to Jubb**

Sr Hexham June the 25th 1713

I suppose you Received the Wills I sent you by your Stage Coach wch I expected back again under Seal on Tuesday last, & that you are sensible the affaires of this Jurisdiction are out of order as well as our Church, our ChurchWardens are very impatient to be dismissed & unwilling to officiate any longer, & I promised them to write to you the last week upon that subject. & since you have signifyed your inclination & desire I conceive it very proper that you pay us a vizit & keep a Court here. assoon as conveniently you can, in order to settle these affaires & that you may be able to give Mr Chancellor an acct of the State here of wch wd be too tedious to write, The Gen[ll] Quarter Sessions of the Peace for this County will be holden here the 15th 16th & 17th of the next month, wch time wd be improper for you to be here, I conceive you may set out from York on Monday morning & be at Hexham next day at noon or in the evening, & on Wednesday keep Court here, & go see St John les. Bingfield & St Oswald Chapels; & If the weather be favourable on thursday go see Allandale. & come back to Hexham in the evening; & may return back again to York on fryday & Saturday unlesse you have a mind to go abt by NewCa: & Durham If your businesse will permit you (I hope your journey will be no Small diversion in the Summer season) Pray send us Process for a Court some time before, & Be pleasd to alight & lodge at my house, wch will not only save charges but afford us a better opportunity to discourse matters, Be pleasd to give my humble Service to Mr Chancellour. Hopeing shortly to see you here I shall add no more save that I am

Sr Your Humble Servt
George Ritschel

64. 28 September 1713 **Ritschel to Jubb**

Sr Hexham 28th 7'ber 1713

I Recd yours of the 25th of June & shortly after one from Mr Burrell we put off the visitation for diverse reasons (yesterday I Recd that Process) & design to keep it the 4th of 9ber, I shall insert the Names of our ChWardens & Criminals etc and observe the other pticulars of your lre, but pray send me by the first opportunity some books of Articles etc whrwith we have been so ill served or rather not at all of late years of wch our ChWardens have justly complaind.

The project abt our Church is not like to take effect at present for that we have got an[othe]r drinking Bailiff (old Carr) considering his temper his former conduct & behaviour & present course of life etc I conceive it wd be to no purpose to attempt any thing of that nature, a certain person some years ago gave this Character of our late Bailiff in Compa of diverse Gentn that he knew a man (nameing his Cousen Tom. Allgood) who had been drunk fourty years, I am sure Carr hath as well deserved that Character for above 20 years last past, nor do I expect he will ever forfeit it; whose examples (& practice, for no businesse must be done without a drink offering) have infected not only the Town but also the neighbouring Countrey.

Be pleased to give my humble service to Mr Chancellor & tell him that I have done and am doeing a great deal to the roofe of our Ch so that I hope it shall not fall in my time, but being obleged by Article with our 24ty not to meddle wth the repaires of the Ch I know not how to come by my money, unlesse he be pleasd, the next Comutatons be applyed to that use.

I lately published & returnd a Monicon for the next of kin to Mr John Heron etc He had not long since a bastard Child & if he had lived a while longer might have pd a good sum upon the 5th of Augt he did bequeath £5 to helpe to repair our Ch at what time he was abt to make a new will, but the party who had his will in keeping being out of town, & he who was to draw it wanting a certain settlemt of his Estate, & his memory not serveing exactly as to that matter, it went off However I made a M[em]dum vizt

Hexham in Northumber

Memorandm. That this evening being Wednesday evening the 5th day of Augt 1713 Mr John Heron of the New Hall in Hexham aforesd did give five pounds to helpe to repair the Church of Hexham aforesd & ordered it to be put in his will, which I am ready to depose upon oath. As witness my hand George Ritschel

Pray give my service, & show this to Mr Mawde, & let me know w[hethe]r it be of any force, so as it may be annexed to his will in the nature of a Codicil, when they come to prove it or it may be put (& to put it) into a form that may make it effectual.

I lately employed one in NewCa: & sent one on purpose into Cumberld to enquire abt two bastard Children, but have not yet got the satisfaction desired.

As to the Copies of our Charities I sent you, the design was not so much in hopes of subscriptions, as since men are so much led by example, if some of them might induce some of your wealthy Citizens to follow Mr Fishborns example in favour of the poor Clergy of your City, If you think they may be serviceable to that end. Be pleasd to keep & dispose of them to the best advantage If not Pray send them back again by your Stage Coach, with some Books of Articles of visitation etc for that Mr White hath disposed of all his Copies, & there be a great many here in this Countrey who have not seen any of them. Pray give my Service to Mr Shaw I have not now time to write to him & Mr Mawde & direct your Books of Articles to be left with Mr Andrew Kennedy at the White hart in NewCa: (Whr your Stage Coach lodgeth) with whom I have fixed a Correspondence to transmit any thing to you, it being a needlesse trouble to do it first to Durham. I am

Sr, Your very humble Servt
George Ritschel

65. 5 October 1713 **Ritschel to Jubb**

Mr Jubb. Hexham 5th Octobr 1713

I wrote to you the 28th of 7ber for some books of Articles of Visitation I have yet some of those printed at York by Stephen Bulkley 1679 wch I conceive not very proper since the revolution yet have had no other but two I found amongst my Brothers papers printed since for the Diocess of Durham wch I have kept & our ChWardens have made their answer by them.

In former time the ChWardens of every parish had such book given them every Court. for want whereof they have complaind of late years, & it wd seem hard to require them to give an answer to what they had not, & particularly George Wilkinson who is only a poor miller, Bingfield Chapel & St Oswalds both entirely ruined, (& perhaps seldome comes to St John lee Ch & did not hear of our Court, at least was never admitted Chapel warden & I am confident is altogether a stranger to such book of Articles.

I also desired your advice & assistance & Mr Mawde's as to Mr John Herons bequest to our Church, wch was after this manner at the request of some friends & relations I went with them to the bedsyde & told him they desired he wd be pleasd to alter his will & appoint other guardians for his Children for that he & their mother haveing so many relations, they had reason to take it ill that he should leave them to strangers, wch he consented to do; whrupon they & the party who was to ~~alter the will~~ draw another will, went into the next room to examin some deeds & there was a woman left in the room & I desired her to go out (for that I had no mind she should hear it, & least I might have occasion to mention the bastard child) & going to the bedsyde sd

Sr I desire you will be pleasd to give five pounds to help to repair our Church, & I promise you I will take care it be faithfully applyd, He spake somewhat abt a Briefe & after consented, saying well well, whrupon I asked him, Will you please to give it now in money (knowing that he had abt £150) or that it be set down in the Will He replyed, Let it be put in the Will, whrupon I went presently into the next room & acquainted them therewith, Mr Herons Will was proved here on Wednesday last, When I told the Ex[ecutor]s, that I had given you an acct hereof (& designed to swear it at our next Court) & expected the favour of your Court herein it being for so charitable a use, they seemd content to do what your Court should please to order in that matter. Be pleasd to favour me with your sentimts & assistance, if it do affect or can be put into a form or method wch may affect his will whereby you will very much oblege

Sr your humble Servt
George Ritschel

Pray give my Service to Mr Mawde

For Mr Thomas Jubb

66. 26 October 1713 **Ritschel to unknown**

Dear Sr Hexham Octobr 26th 1713

I Received yours of the 13th Inst wth 14 Copies of my Charitye (& These return you hearty thanks for your care & trouble therein) as also the Booke of Articles, & sent one of them to Allendale & another to St John Lees.

I know that you can act as Proctor in Testamentary Causes but our people here comonly go first to an Atturney of wch we have here no want) & I knew not of Herons till the monition was brought to me, & besides Mr Shaw upon Mr Empsons death did step in & hath secured to himselfe most of the businesse of this Jurisdicon (vizt. hath obleged & engaged the several Atturneys here) & what I have had with him of late, was to helpe him to some small sume due to Mr Empson, & to adjust accounts with Mr Skepper who did charge me with 15 Wills & Admons done before our last Court for wch I have Mr Burrells discharge, & one done since our last Court, wch was done by him at Durham & I nevr see that Will, only did Certify a Codicil, for that he fears she canot charge it to Mr Burrell. But when anything of that nature happens wherein I am consulted, you may depend upon it I shall direct them to Mr Jubb.

Sr Be pleasd to give my humble Services to Mr Chancellor I have inserted the Names of our ChWardens Sydesmen & Criminals in the Process, & you may believe it has & will be no small trouble to our App[arator]s son (for he is nigh 100 years old & could do nothing herein) to Cite so many Considring the Countrey.

M^s^ Mary Carnaby Spr (a popish Gentlewoman here in Town) who went from hence to NewCa: bigg with Child as was reported, is come back again, & doth not deney that she had a child; but hath made a resolution that she will not Confesse the father. ----One Mr J--- W--- an a Cumberland Gent. who doth lodge at her Mothers house was supposed to be the man, & our ChWardens yesterday 14night when they did meet to make & did make up their Prsentmt and answr to the Book of Articles, without any Scrouple did prsent him & her for fornication, they are both Cited, He desired to speak with me, did deny that he was the Father, & wd gladly know how he might Compel her to confesse who was the father for that he wd not lye undr the Scandall. I told him he might Consult some Civilian, I should not be inquisitive after that matter, If he or whoever was the father wd make any proposals I should acquaint my Ld ArchBp or Mr Chancellor thrwith, & did believe his name might be Concealed;

Yesterday after evening service I went to See a Gent here in Town where happened to be diverse others, one of them hinted at it a certain Justice of Peace answered I wd be sued for what I had done, I replyed I was not to be affrighted from my duty; this afternoon one told me that she had Cleard Mr J... W....n & that her Mother & she designd to be with me, who came after it was dark, & said she had cleared the aforesd Gent who had Feed one to appear for him, that she was not obleged to Confesse who was the Father, I supposed it was by (& desired to see the Affidavt she had made, before the aforesd Justice of the Peace, wch she sd she had not; I told her these matters did not properly belong to Justices of the Peace & perhaps his Grace might take it ill that he should meddle in it, If she had or wd voluntarily purge herselfe by oath before me (wch I did not nor wd desire her to do unlesse she wd voluntarily offer herselfe) prhaps it wd give more satisfaction. She replyed she wd not give any further satisfaction then she had done (that she had nothing to give us) I told her I desired nothing of her & advised her to get some Friend to get it off at York, she begun to be angry & sd I needed not to have taken notice of her & had a mind to reflect & so we parted. I had almost forgot to tell you, how she wd leave the Countrey - whrupon I read to her a pt of your lre dated the 25th of June Concerning such Criminals, that you wd send Excom after them that people may see that fleeing the Countrey will not excuse thm.

Sr We have a great many Rakes here in Town & you may believe me that they are not my friends, & by prosecuteing some, I expose myselfe to the indignation of all the rest for that it may happen to be their Case who will all be ready upon occasion to do me a prejudice. I do not fear nor shall I regard their Censure & Clamors, but am very unwilling to expose myselfe to any trouble at Law, & therefore begg your advice & directions in the prsent Case. our post goes but twice a week to NewCa: If you can conveniently pray let me have it by fryday post, otherwise I shall not receive till Wednesday upon the Court day - I conceive as not impropr that you acquaint Mr Chancellor herewith & I shall observe his ordrs & directions herein. It grows late & I am in hast of the post

Good Sr
Your very humble servt George Ritschel

67. 6 November 1713 **Burrell jnr to Jubb**

Sir,

Wednesday last I was doeing your business att Hexham - But to noe purpose only Ive recd your fees for 7: Licences. The Churchwardens of Allandale appeared & pd their fees as usual, but if I had not a true interest in their Minister that he's soe officious as to take care of them they woud be like the rest already complaining that noe body pays but themselves. Hexham Guardians has pd nothing this 3:yeares & when I spoke to Mr Ritschell he tells me they are still poor, Yet Ime of opinion in case he had 6s 8d as he has out of other instrumts he woud not abate the least penny; St Jo. Lees, St O[swald]: & Bingfeild has pd nothing Bentham & Mr Ritschell being att difference I doe suppose Bentham is the hindrance. I shall send or bring you Hexha Prsentmts being for London very shortly & will wait of you either goeing or comeing with an acct of who is Cited but not one appeared save one which appeared & submitted to Mr Ritschell I Did not see him nor would Mr Ritschell let me Know how he had submitted but said he woud give an acct to York I suppose the man is poor & I think his name is Gibson. I shall att meeting discourse further upon these matters & am

Sir Your very humble servt
Pr: Burrell

Novr 6th 1713

I hear by some Attorney's & other people that there are severall Comutaons made tho' Mr Ritschell tells me he does nothing without your [Chancellor's] order

68. 19 November 1713 **Ritschel to Pearson**

Rt Worspll Hexham Novembr 19th 1713

I have given Mr Register an acct of our late visitacon here the 4th Inst. & desired him to acquaint your Worsp with what is material. Inclosed is a Copie of Sr Wm.Blacketts grant etc one in Town here designed to have beggd that very place of him to build a pew upon (& had bespoke some materials) wch could not have been done without prejudice to the Minister & perhaps might have created some trouble if I had not prevented it by getting a grant of it before him. These begg the favour of your Worsp to grant me leave to take in & ad to it so much of the Isle adjoyning as shall be found needfull to make it a convenient pew or a gallery.I do not design to do it imediately for what I bestow upon our Church shall rather be upon the roofe to preserve the Fabrick. I have done a great deal to it this summr in hopes of some Criminal money wch is not like to answr expectation. I have not seen Sr Wm.Blackett since he came last into the North, he was not at NewCa: when I was there upon the 8th of September & I after sent my papr abt the Wall enclosd' in a letter by our post, wch he signd very readily. I believe he wd do for our Church if there were no false brethren to obstruct it; I went to see my Ld Derwentwater, who took me asyde & did ask me if I wd any thing upon the subject of our Charities (wch I had sent him) I told him I came only to wait upon & dine with his Ldsp I believe his Ldsp wd act honorably herein & thought I came on purpose abt it, the late Mayour of NewCa: intimated their good inclination, to give £50 out of their hutch, But Bacchus, the old faction, & spirit of opposition are still so prdominant that I conceive it not propr at prsent to attempt anything of that nature; I hope I shall see Mr Jubb at Hexham next visitation, that he may give your Worsp a particular acct of the State of our Church & this Jurisdiction wch wd be tedious to write. I am in Syncerity

Your Worsps Most humble Servt George Ritschel

69. 8 September 1713 **Blackett to Ritschel**
[BIA Pec.Hex/5]

[*copy in Ritschel's hand:*]
Know all men by these presents that I have given and granted and doe hereby give and grant unto George Ritschel of Hexham in the county of Northumberland clerk (present Lecturer of Hexham afores[d]) full power licence and authority to take down the wall on the Back of the pulpit between the 2nd and 3rd pillars on the north side of Hexham Quire, to make the pulpit larger (it being so strait and mean) and make a stair to it out of the north Ile (this being so very bad) to give more light to the pulpit, and that part of the church in lieu of what hath been obstructed of late on the other side), and to build and erect a pew upon the remainder for himself and successors, provided he convert his own pew to the use of the publick, vizt do make it a common pew for weomen when they come to be churched, and the infant children of those, who have noe pews, when they come to be Baptized. In wittness whereof I have hereunto set my hand this 8th day of September 1713

Wm Blackett [III]

70. 21 December 1713 **Burrell jnr to Jubb**

Sir, I have by Mr Croft sent you 9:L[icence]:Bonds wth £4 10s for the Fees As alsoe Hexham Prsentmt & the Process. None of the Churchwardens pd anything save Ellandale wch I hope you'l omit in order to defray my expences. I desire you'l give a Line wth an Acquittance upon Receipt hereof to

Your humble servt
Pr: Burrell Durham Xbr 21st 1713

71. 21 January 1714 **Ritschell to Jubb**

Sr Hexham Janry 21st 1713/4

I received yours dated the 12th of Xber with 4 Blanck Licenses & 4 Bonds & one enclosed from Mr Mawde wth Sheilds Admon. These are upon acct of the Governrs & Stewards of our Free School the abuses of wch are so great that I conceive they justly deserve to be reformd & redressed they are of a long continuance since those dismal times of anarchy & confusion, when there was neither King nor Bishop here in England & for some years no Minister here at Hexham in the time of the great Rebellion, the then Governrs had a favourable opportunity to take the whole affair of the school into their hands & manage it at pleasure, and their succescors have since the Restauration followed their example

It is now at least 20 years since I accidentally got a sight & copie of their Charter & Constitutions. wch hath been no small peice of mortification to them,) sometime after I discoursed diverse of the Governrs abt that matter who seemd willing to reform [*word rubbed out*] abuses according to their Statutes, but when I spoke to Mr John Carr our prsent Bailiffe he replyed wd they be governed by an ArchBishops constitutions & sometime after when I cited the then Stewards to appr at Court here & give in their accts etc he could not forbear to speak in Church upon my nameing of them, before I had done with the Process, & after sermon was ended continued in great passion, wd they give an account to the Curates of Hexham it should cost him £100 first, an Attorney here in town haveing seen their Charter & constitutions was of opinion that if he wd spend £100, (wch I am very confident he will never do) they could not avoid it, When I first shewd them to Mr Rowell of Durham then Register for this Jurisdicon, he was confident that if my Ld. ArchBpe did see or know of the Charter and Constitutions he wd certainly Cite up those Governrs. abt 15 years ago I sent his Grace a Copie thereof with a Complaint agt them I have been told that his Grace wrote to them & sent them a Copie of my letter; & I suppose they made plausible allegations & Fair promises to reform abuses, but I have not as yet observed any thing of it; his Grace had then a pticular reason not to proceed any further in that affair for that they did solicit his Grace to call in my Licence & turn me out of the Curacy, & the matter at last seemd to drop on both sydes. But now I conceive I have a favorable opportunity in diverse respects, occasioned partly by our late visitation wch if it had not been singular or they had taken it to be so had never given themselves the trouble to appr or make any apology & therefore I desire that matter may be brought judicially before Mr Chancellor to whom I conceive it doth proprly belong, & that Mr Burrell did not either undrstand or considr it aright, when he sd in Court it did not belong to us it must be tryed at Comon Law; I prsume I have a good cause (& may promise myselfe succesce) if it be rightly managed, but want to be informed how to begin & proceed herein, whether by Libell or Allegacon as I have hinted and since it must be tryed in a Court whrof yourselfe are Registed if you canot act yourselfe I desire Mr Shaw may be concernd as Proctor, & that you & he will take Dr Ward or some Advocates opinion in the matter how to begin & proceed therein.

I have sent you enclosed my charges agt them, wch I suppose will serve to frame either a Libell or Allegation,) & that I need not add any more, yet there is one point I wd gladly have determined vizt. since the Revenues of the sd school are all in money by their Statute, that no Lease shall be made granted & seald, do not import as much as that no Bond for any of the school money shall be Executed, without the privity and prsence of the schoolmr but if the school were setled upon the old foundation & the Master had the keeping of one of the keys & were admitted into the mystery, this wd partly fall in of Course.

My Account of our Charities doth contain the sum & substance of their Charter & those statutes wch relate to the matter in hand, If it now be needfull (as I suppose it will be if that matter happen to be scanndl) I shall send you a Copie thereof; After a certain Dissenter here in town had read my Acct he gave his sentimt of it that it wd displease some persons meaning our Governrs, for that it made a discovery of their school; I am apt to believe they will not be pleasd with this proceeding, but I shall not regard their displeasure provided I gain the point, I do not prtend to make Libells or Allegations or give directions in such an affair, yet with submission conceive : that there must be two either Libells or Allegations, viz. one agt all the Governrs for subverting the Constitution & not obsereing the Statutes of their school. & the other agt Robson & Leadbitter the late Stewards, by way of Appeal to Mr Chancellor for his opinion & sense of that Statute; that the matter is distinct & they canot both be tryed by the same Libell or Allegacon, & if so I conceive it more propr to begin & meddle only with the sd Stewards; & put in the Libell or appeal so much as is propr of my charge agt the Governrs, that this affair may occasion you a journey to Hexham & such a journey may be very serviceable to adjust the whole matter relateing to our school; Be pleased to give my humble service to Mr Chancellr & if you think fit you may acquaint him herewith, I conceive its not so propr for me to do it for that he is to be Judge in the case.

Pray deliver the enclosed to Mr Mawde with the several Wills & bonds & the Inventory mentioned therein, & let me have the Citation agt Robson and Leadbitter assoon as conveniently you can; with my advocates opinion & your own upon this affair, by post, I expected ere this to have Receivd the business dispatcht at our last Court, & to have wrote you upon the subject of your last lre wch conteining subject matter enough for another letter. I shall add no more at p[res]ent but deferr that till another opportunity. Wishing you a happy new year I am

Sr Your humble Serv't
George Ritschel

72. 28 January 1714 **Ritschell to Jubb**

Sr, Hexham Janry 28th 1713

The last week I sent you a packet by your Stage Coach wch being then at York as our Post tells me it will not return back again thither before Saturday next when I suppose you will receive this. [...]ately see a Durham Gent here who told me Mr Burrell had not & wd not take jurney for London as he expected when here but I suppose he sent you the Processe with Hexham prsentmts & the Apparators Certificate of those he had Cited. I was then of opinion that Allendale & St John Lee Churchwardens wd not make any prsentmt or answer to your Book of Articles & must beg leave to tell you that with submission. I do not like it so well at that used in the Diocesse of Durham, & if we should observe what relates to Dissenters, they wd all conclude that I stood in need to let blood or designd to raise a persecution agt them I have had thoughts of late years to compose a Book of Articles (out of those several forms I have) adapted prticularly to this Jurisdicon to have it corrected & approved by Mr Chancellor & printed by Mr White of NewCastle & more especially for Bingfield & St.Oswalds Chapel propose no more questions then are propr for those places & leave a space between, whereon to insert a Categorical answer. As to Mr Bentham & our Criminals, if you have thoughts to see Hexham in the Spring I conceive it best to let them alone till next Court. I have been a long time concerned for this Jurisdicon, & have a great desire to put everything into ordr & that we may all come to such a temper & termes that it may be more easy for the future. I conceive the greatest difficulty will be with St.John lees abt the Churchwardens fees (& thrfore I wd not take notice of Mr Bentham till that matter is adjusted) for of what shall be done if it be a favr to them will be a prsident to Hexham & Allendale. I have thoughts of being in Durham before Easter & shall pay a visit to Mrs Rowell, & if she have shall endeavr to get the Court Rolls & paprs of her husband relateing to this Jurisdicon while he was Register, wch I conceive may be of good use to us. I canot charge my memory what fees he took of the respective Ch: wardens, wch amounted much abt the same we demand at prsent, otherwise be sure Hexham & Allendale wd have desired an abatemt. If you can put me in a way how to look on Mr Warburton again I shall do what I can in that matter. The Register of this Jurisdicon never used to grant marriage Licences.

Sr

The subject of what I sent you last week is chiefely upon our Freeschool upon better considration I conceive it my duty to acquaint Mr Chancellor with my design therein, & thrfore these desire you to cut off & seal & prsent the enclosed wth my humble service to him. I conceive it needlesse to add any more upon that subject before I know your sentimts of that matter & have directions [...] proceed therein. I am

Sr your humble serv't
George Ritschell

73. 29 January 1714 **Ritschel to Pearson**

Rt. Worsp[ll], Hexham Janry 29th 1713

These are to informe you that the Governors of our Freeschool of a long time have not & at prsent do not observe their Constitutions, whereby the Stewards are to prsent their accounts every year to the Comissary of HexhamShire at his next Court after the feast of St.Michael. & how prudently the same was provided & how needfull it may be to prserve the revenues of the School (wch are all in money I leave it to your Worsp to judge. I Cited them the last Court they apprd but by putting as I conceive a wrong construction upon that Statute evaded the force & intent thereof. And since the exposition of all & every of Statutes and ordinances of the sd School as often as any doubt shall arise thereupon is to be referred to the judgment of the Ld ArchBishop of York for the time being or his Chancellor, I thought fit to appeale to your Worsp for your judgmt therein, and have wrote to Mr Jubb that matter may be brought judicially before you, & so conceive it not propr for me to say any more upon it save to request your Worsp wd be pleasd to give yourselfe the trouble to hear & determine that matter & reform the several abuses of our School according to their Charter & Constitutions. I foresee I shall be misreprsented by our Governors as litigious & troublesome, but my design being so just, will be a sufficient apology, I have a great desire to reform what else is amisse in this Jurisdicon & put all things ordr & if possible to keep & leave them so, wch I hope to effect by your Worsps assistance. Mr Jubb hath acquainted me with your favourable inclinations as to the pew I wrote abt for wch these return my thankfullness. I heartily wish you a happy new year, & am in syncerity

Your Worsps Most humble serv't
George Ritschell

74. 1st April 1714 **Ritschel to Jubb**

Sr Hexham 1 April 1714

The reason of my so long silence has been the death of our late worthy ArchBp[230] wch loss I hope will be made good by so worthy a successor. If as I suppose you continue your resolutions to keep a visitation Court at Hexham there be some points wherein I desire to be informd & to acquaint you with viz.

Whether we shall do it Ecclesiatim, St.John Lees stands over agt Hexham on the Northsyde of Tyne & we may easily do both the same day & go the next day to Allendale. If the severall partys are to be Cited personally as the last Court that we may have the Process in convenient time before, I suppose leaving a note at the house will serve if any of them be from home,

Itm Whether the Curates of Allendale & St.John lees ought to take Licence If not I conceive it will be to no purpose to mention it to them

---

[230] Archbishop John Sharp, who died 2nd Feb 1714.

Itm Since Hexham & Allendale Schoolmasters may be compelld to take Licence, that you wd be pleased to bring your Register Book along wth you (as Mr Empson did Anno 1705) to save the trouble of going to York to subscribe

I conceive it was best to take no notice of our Criminals till next Court. Mrs Mary Carnaby lives here in Town as brisk as ever, If she must be Cited personally I shall take care she be the first that is Cited, least upon notice of a Court she withdraw. Ann Bell of Hexham spr (a rich mans daughter who Comitted fornication with John Gibson, I am told is removed to Durham. She was not cited the last Court. I believe her Father & Brother had rather compound that matter then have her exposed by being cited publickly: thoe the last year they did sufficently expose both themselves & her.

The ChurchWardens of Thockerington (abt seven Miles North of Hexham) did formerly appr at our Courts (so that I took it for a percell or member of this Peculiar)[231] & its great pitty if they now have any, but that they should appear somewhere. If you think fit to speak to Mr Micklethwait abt it be pleasd to give my service to him, & if he shall think fit to annex it to Hexham Jurisdicon as it was in my Fathers time I shall be ready to serve him therin.

We have had very fine weather of late & the ways are very good, but I suppose you do not design to see Hexham till abt Whitsontyde after you have done all your visitations at Home, & I wd have Robson & Leadbitter late Stewards of our Freeschool first cited, in hopes that your comeing to Hexham will save them the trouble of goeing to York, for that I wd put you to as little trouble & charge as possible to prevent their being too angry. Be pleased to Comunicate to Mr Shaw what I wrote to you upon that subject, with my services to him.

I expected to have been at Durham the begining of Lent about a certain businesse wch went off otherwaye. Itm the 22d of March but was prevented, and to have got a sight of Mr Rowells Court Rolls for the Jurisdicon, haveing of late been makeing an Account of the prsent state & businesse done within this Peculiar for 30 years last past. wch I cannot do so perfectly without them. haveing for diverse years only made a Memorandm of what

[231] By his letter of 2 March 1704, doc. **10**, however, Ritschel understood it to be a separate peculiar of York.

businesse happend between Courts, I have thoughts of going thither on purpose abt that matter, wch may be serviceable to us.

I have granted 3 Licences since our last Court, two of them before I Received those you sent me, & got the stamps for the Bonds here in Town so that I have 3 of your Bonds & but no blanck Licences.

I suppose you received the Process & prsentmt given in Last Court be pleasd to take notice that all those prsented paid their Church sesse except Mr Shafto who pretends it was not demanded, & John Green who is but a poor man & says he will pay it when he gets money. However pray put them in the next Process Itm our sydesmen or Assistants, their Case wd be tedious to write & may better be discoursed at meeting. Itm Bingfield & St.Oswald Chapel Wardens, We did design to have admonished the several persons presented for not comeing to Church sometime before & agt Easter, but the weather here has been so very sharpe till of late & our Church so very cool, that it did require more then an ordinary zeale (wch could not be expected from them) & so have deferred it hitherto, least they might make that a prtence for staying away, other things continue in statu quo after our last Court & I canot think of any thing more needfull to trouble you wth save to give my humble service with syncere respects to Mr Chancellor, the rest will be best adjusted by our personal conversation at & before the Court, you may depend upon my care & diligence in this affair. I am

Sr Your very humble serv't
George Ritschel

75. 30 July 1714 **Ritschel to Jubb**

Dear Sr Hexham July 30th 1714

I Reced yours of the 7 June wth 4 Blanck Licences & Bonds, Stephen Lathan not app[ear]ing (& some other reasons) have made me deferr an answr longer then I intended, this being the B[on]d I have made for you.

I am very sensible how much you are engaged in constant business, & that my lres to you have been prolix, & thrfore was the more desireous of personal conversation to see you at Hexham to prevent that trouble, thr being diverse things I wd discourse with you wch I am not willing to write.

Our Apparator made a certificate of those he cited to appr at our last Court wch Mr Burrell took with the Process, as I understood him to send them to York. I have made remarks upon your paprs to the best of my remembrance and returnd them herewth.

There hath not been any proceedings agt any of our Criminals since our last Court (nor have they paid any Fees; & as for those who have pd their Ch: sesse believe me Sr it were to no purpose to demand any of them) haveing resolved to let all things continue in statu quo, till you should come yourselfe, so that if you canot come before winter I conceive it more propr to deferr the keeping of a Court till the spring, for that Mr Burrell doth not much trouble himselfe how matters go with us.

The disordr in St John Lee pish are occasioned (as I take it) by the 24ly acting as they do, & their method of chooseing Ch:wardens wch is very irregular. I conceive the best way will be, whenever you come into the North to give the heads of that pish an invitation to meet us, & reason the Case calmly with them & Try if we can bring them to a temper & settle the affaires of that parish in an amicable mannr, otherwise I doubt they will create us a great deal of trouble.

I have sent you A Reprsentation of the Deplorable state etc wch was made after Whitsontyde, when I last calld the 24ly hoped they wd give me occasion to alter it, wch they did for the worse.

The roofe of our Clockhouse, wch doth close up the arch undr the Steeple, on the west syde of the Church is extreamly ruinous, the West Quarter being destroyed by the Scots & the Quire being now the body of the Church it will not only spoil the Clock but be very offensive to the congregation in bad weather, when the wind is in the west I designd to have mended it the last year, but that the weather changed and prevented it, & have told diverse of the Four & twenty that if they will repay me what I have disbursed I will lay out as much more as will do it, wch wd be about 48s besides the materials wch are all ready & pd for and also make a new style and Gates; but they refuseing to meet, nothing is like to be done, unlesse Mr Chancellor shall think it propr for him to ordr or direct me to do it; & shall be pleased to assist me to get my money; If it be his pleasure, pray let me know it assoon as you can, for that the soonr its begun the better. I have returnd you back some of the Licence Bonds, because of the late additional stamp, & if it be needfull shall send the Licences also. Pray give the enclosed wth my service to Mr Mawde. I design God willing to go from NewCa: next week to Durham & if I meet with Mr Burrell or any thing fit to be added shall give you an acct therof, & remain

Good Sr Your very humble serv't
George Ritschel.

Sir

Be pleased to give my humble Service to Mr Chancellor I do not wholy dispair to see you at Hexham before winter. otherwise wd have sent your Fees for your Marriage Licences. but if you canot come before that time shall send them pr next opportunity.

76. 5 August 1714 **Ritschel to Jubb**

Sr NewCastle Augt the 5th 1714

I have had some discourse with Mr Burrell abt your Marriage Licences & if I send your whole fees doubts he shall loose the 3s4d apiece you promised him, & thrfore desired me to lay out the money for the Stamps (wch I am not unwilling to do) & send your Fees & reserve his as they shall happen.

Mrs Rowell delivered her husbands paprs to Mr Burrell senr & thoe we canot yet find what related to Ch:wardens in Hexham Peculiar yet I am pos[itive] that our Jurors did app[ear] & were sworn till the late Revolution; but our 24ly or New Vestrey have in a mannr wholy laid them asyde & how far it may be propr & expedient to continue them is one point I wd discourse with you.

He tells me he sent you the Process for the last Court as he remembers, & promised to try if he could find the Certificate our App[arator] made of those he Cited. But whenever we have a Court pray let the Process be read in the severall Churches as usual.
I am

Sr Your humble serv't
George Ritschel

77. 23 August 1714 **Jubb to Ritschel**

Mr Ritschell York Aug 23th 1714

Your last came to Me in due time, which I have Communicated to Mr Chancellor who joyns with me in the sendg of our thancks for the same. the great trouble you have taken in the affair of Hexham sufficiently evidence how much you have at heart the welfare of the jurisdiction and the necessary repairs of the Ancient Fabrick, wch we are heartily sorrowfull to find you so obstinately opposed in as you demonstrate, but be the priviledges of the four and twenty never so great and their establishmt in like manner Antique (which I prsume you'l scarce allow them to be) yet you will find that (notwithstanding their threatened petition to the Parliamt agt the late worthye Chancellor, whose old age I dare say was the only hindrance in redressing your Grievances) the Law (if fair Means will not prvail) will Compell them, or they being cont[umatious] the Pishioners joyntly with you to Elect the usuall number of Chwardens and Sidesmen or Assistants and those (being invited and called before you as surrogate of that jur[isdicti]on to take upon them their respective offices by vertue of their Corporell oaths (by the by this may serve for answer to Mr Burrells refuseing to swear the sidesmen the last year) and these being duely admitted into their offices, are impowered by Law to take care that the Church be decently repaired and made fitt for Divine Service (whether the four and twenty be Consenting thereto or not) and if they neglect to do the same the Court has power to Compell them thereto upon pain of Eclicall Censures. and when those measures are taken tho' the four and twenty will neither [*indecipherable*] nor lay any Assessmt, the Ch:wardens themselves upon such neglect may & will be obliged to Lye an Assessmt for the defraying their Disbursmts (as well upon the Inh[ab]itants as upon the Lands within the whole Parish) & fear not but the 24ly shall be Compell'd to Contribute thereto notwithstanding their priviledges or any Articles agreed unto by you, neither of wch can Devest the Ordinary of his jur[isdicti]on which in this Deplorable Case seems absolutely necessary to be expected tho' I must Confess I can not but joyn in your wish that things might be Compromised without it.

His Grace after haveing been here but five days went suddenly to London upon notice of the Demise of our Late Good

Queen[232] otherwise I would not have failed to have laid the whole matter before him in like Manner as I have done before the Chancellor who thincks himself not a little Concern'd to see Hexham Church put into Tollerable repaire, & if we had apprehended that the poverty of the people & the insufficiency of the Lands & Grounds situate within the Pish had renderd it impracticable without the assistance of other well disposed people to have been Collected by Briefe or the like, we should not have reced so many prsentments of the Ruinous state of that Church and never prceed to have it repaired which I must Confess I always, for the aforesd Reasons lookt upon as an Impossibility. And, after all, his late Grace being dead (in whose time the like prsentment was made) I think it most Prper to be very Prticular, as to the Ruins, in that next Prsentmt, upon which we will ground our prceedings if imediate Care be not taken to Repair them. thus farr in answer to your state of the Case &c , the matters relating to the Corrections I shall not Coppy concerning which I desired Mr Ritchells directions

as for the Repaireing the Roofe over your Clock-house and makeing a New style & Gates neither Mr Chancellor or I can give you any Encouragemt to undertake them it is what the Pish is obliged to and lett them take care therein, if it be neglected the Chwardens must answer it and if so see if the four & twenty have power to sever them from justice. I am very well satisfied they have not and it shall not be any threats of Petitioning the Parliamt that will be sufficient to deter the Court from prsenteing them. besides, as far as I can prceive the pish is Capeable enough to put the Church (at least so much as is necessary for the prformeing divine service in) in decent Rep[ai]r and therefore it is more than needfull to apply the Commutation money to that use in order to ease such obstinate people. The rest related to Licence bonds & Licence Fees . As to the Chwardens of Hexham being sworn I make no doubt of it they have been sworn time out of mind & lett the 24ly endeavour as much as they please to discontinue them they shall find it impracticable unless they have so much interest in the Parliamt (which they would have us believe) as to obtain an Act to exempt them from haveing churchwardens. I can give you no hopes as to expect me at Hexham this yeare but shall

[232] The new archbishop hastening to London after the death of Queen Anne was Sir William Dawes. Sharp had requested that Dawes succeed him: G.Norgate, 'John Sharp', *Dictionary of National Biography*, Vol 51 (1897), p.410.

endeavour to Concert matters with Mr Burrell so as the Business may be done effectually without me.

I am etc.

78. 30 August 1714 **Ritschel to Jubb**

Sr Hexham 30th Augt 1714

Yesterday I Receiv'd yours of the 23d Inst with five Licence Bonds and these return my thankfullnesse to Mr Chancellor & yourselfe for the encouragemt you give me. When I was at NewCa: I had twice a warm discourse upon the subject of our Church with Mr Wilkinson[233] Chiefe Trustee for Sr Willm Blackett who doth still manage his Estate, after he had perused the Representation I sent you, who did condemn the neglect of the 24ly to appear, the trueth is they want a head & so are not like to do businesse with any successe, for Mr Carr our Bailiff has now so quiote drunk away his limbs that he canot stirr, & as before he wd not act so now he canot app[ear], I shall make a new Essay and if it do not take effect shall take care that the Ch:wardens & Assistants be appointed for this prsent year & conceive you need not cite our old Churchwardens.

As to St John Lees I told Mr Wilkinson I expected to see you at Hexham & we wd go over thither & drop all bypast in a bowl of punch wch he did well approve of, & as the two Chapelrys do not pay any sesse to the repair of the Pish Church so the parish do meet & act exclusive of them, Bingfield are all Tenants & some of them Dissenters, & their method for the old Chapelwardens to choose or return new ones, seems now to be at an end for that they have not had any of late years, nor are like to have any more after that rate, & since you canot come into the North this summer & Mr Errington of Beaufront has so great an Estate in each Chapelry & the Corntyth of Bingfield, as also of Keepwick & Errington in St Oswalds belong to the Lecturer of Hexham, I shall go over to him thoe a Papist, & try if we can settle that affair.

---

233 John Wilkinson, Newcastle merchant, industrialist and coalowner, executor of the will of Sir William Blackett II, and agent to his son, the third Sir William: Hughes, *North Country Life, op cit*, pp. 165, 167-8.

I conceive its fit that Allendale old Chwardens be Cited & shall enquire whether James Armstrong got his housekeepr with child & her name. Those prsented for not comeing to Church & paying their Ch sesse were not Cited last Court & none of the fornicators appeard save Gibson (who referrd himselfe to the Court & that matter rests there) nor were any decreed excomunicate.

I have thoughts of being shortly at NewCa: & shall return your Licence Fees thoa I do not approve of your method for that it doth create a new trouble & charge. Be pleasd to let me know if any such Licences were sent from your Court to Mr Bentham, to marry Willm Lee of Hexham the Elder & Jane Gardner of the same Wid (before the 14th of April) and John Fenwick of Hexham tannr & Elizt Lee of Acomb spster on Whitson monday, when I spoke unto him abt the later he did trifle so that I could not tell what to make of it, If he can have such Licences upon occasion I conceive it will save me the trouble of sending to you. Be pleasd to give my humble service to Mr Chancellor. I am

sr your Humble Servt
George Ritschel

79. 23 September 1714 **Ritschel to Jubb**

Sr Hexham 23 Sept 1714

In answr to yours of the 9th Inst my new project in favour of our Church is not like to take effect as yet, however I shall not fail to do my part.

The reason why I wd not have you Cite our old Chwardens, for that they were always ready & willing to execute their office & do their duty, there was no sesse laid on for the Church in their year, & I do not know them to be guilty of any misbehavior.

Mr Errington was very well pleasd with my scheme (wch I have sent enclosed, wch I beleive will please every body provided they may have but one Chapel Warden) He also offerrd to contribute to the rebuilding of Bingfield Chapel (or to any thing else for the good of the Countrey) & did condemn Mr Wate for pulling down the walls thereof to build stables &c.

The Name of James Armstrong's housekeepr was Anne Davison whom he marryed after Xtmas. John Gibson Glovr (a youngr Brother) had a poor mean thatched house left him by his Father wch he was forced to take down & rebuild the last year, wch with the charge abt the bastard child hath run him so farr in debt, that he is able to pay very little; & being a sober young man & haveing had great hardship from the woman & her Friends, & the other topping Criminals haveing escaped, it were great pitty to be hard upon him & I conceive it more reasonable that the woman (viz Anne Bell who is now at NewCa:) should pay the £7 she got of him, she being a rich mans daughter, I shall try If I can get 40d of him wch I hope will be allowed me in part of the £18 I disbursed the last year abt our Church & wch I know not how to come by I received only 20s of Nich.Dixon & am like to loose the remainder unlesse I will sue him.

I have sent you herewth 7 Licence Bonds with the Fees, viz 6 guineas, as also Mr Benthams Case, & did write to Mr Burrell abt a Court the 1 or 2d Wednesday in November, <u>the day after</u> when he shall keep Court at Corbridge, and desired him to give you an acct throf

Finally I canot approve of Citeing our Criminals to York unlesse in some prticular extraordinary Cases for that it wd put you to so great trouble & charge & make them Clamour so much the more agt me, & I am apt to beleive few of them wd app[ear], but continue in their contumacy, & it wd not be worth the time to be at the charge of a Capias writ agt them they being generally the poorer sort.

The Case between Mr Bentham & John Fenwick

A marriage being agreed upon between John Fenwick of Hexham tannr & Elizt Lee of Acomb in the parish of St John lees, Mr Bentham applyed himselfe to the sd Fenwick to take his Marriage Licence from him pretending he wd grant it 5s or 6s or a noble cheaper then Mr Ritschel yet when he came to pay him took the same Fees viz 26s & 6d & he could nevr get a sight throf. When I spoke to Mr Bentham abt it; he said he had some Licences from Sr Edwd Blackett or Mr Ayslaby & it was 3 or 4 years ago & seemd not well to remember from whom he had them; I desired a sight of John Fenwicks Licence he said he had sent it back again. I bid him send for it, for that he ought to keep it for his own security. My sister offerrd to hold him a good wager, that he had no such Licence, wch he declined & said he wd do so no more & Finally alleaged his place was small & he must make the best of it; Fenwick & his Father & myselfe were of opinion that he had no such Licence & being desireous to know the truth throf the easiest way I perswaded Fenwick to arreast Mr Bentham to our syde Court or Court Baron wch [...] every 3 weeks, for the sd Licence Fees or 26s & 6d expecting he wd have repd it as he did in the Case of Lambert etc but he appeard at Court & two Atturneys for him, who alleaged he might have a licence elsewhere then from Mr Ritschel, & he alleaged that he had one but wd not produce it, whreupon I proposed that If he wd swear that he had a legal licence I wd be satisfyed, & he did swear that he did marry (the sd) John Fenwick by a licence undr the seale of the Court of York, wch diverse concluded he had procured since the marriage & therupon I mentiond the time. after I receivd yours of the 9th Inst I wrote to him & sent it by Fenwick, to demand a sight of that licence. desireing he would send it either by the bearer, or some body else the twesday after. He told Fenwick that when he had occasion for such Licences he did write to Sr Edwd Blackett for them; & his wife came to my house the twesday after & complaind very sore that I was so hard upon her husband, makeing it the effect of malice, & said if I wd go to St John lee Church I might have a sight of that licence, wch I take to be only a sham or bantre (for that I was not like to find him there) & desired that she wd either bring or send it, wch he hath not thought fit to do.

And since he hath so often made use of Sr Edwd Blacketts name in the like Cases I wd gladly know whence he hath his licences; for Mr Paton of Allendale told me he had told him he had anough of them, at least he never wants them upon occasion. I suppose it needlesse to repeat what I wrote to you abt him after our last Court. If you think fit to send Process agt him I shall take care to get it executed & returnd etc.

Fees Recd For Marriage Licences

	£	s	d
Chr. Dawson		15	0
Jos. Arthur		15	0
John Coates	1	0	0
Mr Ra. Lazonby	1	0	0
Mr Ja. Rickerby	1	0	0

Mr Lambert		18	4
Geo. Fairlamb	1	0	6
	6	8	10

Dawson & Arthur being in the Diocess of Durham & granted before I receivd yours to the contrary I have deducted Mr Burrells Fees in lieu & by way of reprizall for Frank Carnabys & if that practice were justifiable could soon be even with the Court of Durham for Stephen Lathan.

You will find 3 of the Bonds drawn by myselfe upon Stamps got here & haveing recd 8 Licences & 8 Bonds from you I have 4 of your Bonds & but one Licence; when you send more be pleased to send 3 blanck licences without bonds to answr these; Pray give my humble service to Mr Chancellor & send a formal acquittance to

Sr Your very humble serv't
George Ritschel

[*Cover:*]
For Mr Thomas Jubb
at the Registers Office nigh the Minster in York,
by the York Stage Coach
Note that there be six guineas enclosed. wth care

80. 29 November 1714 **Ritschel to Jubb**

Dear Sr Hexham Nov 29th 1714

I Suppose Mr Burrell has by this time returnd you the Processes & your Schedule of Delinquents with an acct of our late Visitation. I did not Cite Anne Charleton for that she did more proprly belong to the Diocesse of Durham nor Mrs Carnaby (who is another of her that had the Bastard Child) her sess being only 6d wch I had rather pay 10 times out of my own pocket than be lickt with the rough syde of her tongue; nor did I Cite such of those p[res]ented for not Comeing to Church, as might be like to turn Whiggs or Papists or create us any disturbance & so all was quiet & every body did approve of what we have done. Nor have I yet published the Excomunicacon you sent me, being entirely of Mr

Burrells opinion that too eager a prosecution of such scoundrel people doth often occasion reflections upon our Courts, & it may do as well sometimes to drop them especially since the facts were comitted so long ago. Collison is now in Jail (a very propr place for him) Thos Elliot & Nich Dixon who is lately marryed, who comuted, wd doubtless make loud complaints, if Chain & Diana Elliot should now be proceeded agt, since it canot be done without exposeing them afresh. I am apt to beleive people wd put a wrong construction upon it, & it wd not do us any service. & therefore I made the Advertizemt on the back of the Process wch was read, and those who did not appear are decreed to be excommunicated & these desire you will be pleasd to hasten the Excomunicacon agt them, I shall send for them to come to my house, & it will enable me to reprove them more sharpely, & I shall denounce it agt such as continue obstinate and contumacious. I am confident it hath & will do very good service, there be more such like offendrs who come not to Church I shall God willing in the spring take a list & go abt & admonish them & if they do not reform prsent them

Sr In answr to the first pt of your lre dated the 2d Octobr our Ch:wardens pay the Court Fees out of the Ch sess & place them to the Pish acct & they are allowd so that whenevr they do not pay them for want of money they are not comitted or lost, but become a Debt upon the parish wch their successrs take care to discharge at one time or another, & they have now paid off all arrears of Fees. I am confident it was formerly so in St John Lee parish & did not know it to be otherwise till now.

Mr Burrell Receivd all the Fees wch amounted to £3 1s 6d but wd not clear off the house where we kept Court, the Bill came to 3-1-8 besides 2s given to the Servts, so that I did treat at breakfast the 23d & pd 4 0 he gave me & I wd have sent the Bill if it wd not have made this a double lre or charge, but I have sent you on the other syde a Copy thereof as also my own Bill. And as I must acknowledge that you have taken a great deal of pains abt this Peculiar & have hitherto met with no encouragemt so I hope you will own that its as hard on my syde, that besydes my trouble I should be out of pocket. I should have been mighty glad if Mr Jubb had been here to have seen what mannr of people we have to deal withall, If Mr Mawde be not pleasd with what I have paid Mr Burrell for the Admon of Jno.Bell of Stotefields goods for he did charge more, pray tell him that those goods did properly belong to Mr Gibson the

LandLd for Rent. of whom they had them, & so needed not have taken Admcon, that its a very poor businesse & I doubt the poor widow & her six children, will none of them receive so much for their Dividend, & that I have not yet received the sd Fees that I have not a farthing for Hutchinsons Admon, & had but sixpence by Wid Jacksons Admon, whose Fees I pd before I Reced them, & that whenever I desire any abatemt he may depend upon it that the partys are poor & not able to pay any more.

Be pleasd to give my humble service to Mr Chancellor, & assure him that I shall take the same care of this Peculiar as if I made some considerable benefit by it, for we must do somewhat for conscience sake, & I suppose you are now convinced that it was not so much a prospect of advantage as a desire to serve the Country that made me desire to be concernd with it.

I have returnd you by Mr Burrell three Licence Bonds with the Fees as I take it we adjusted the matter abt the noble (& not 8d) I deducted upon Mr Carnabys acct (& not Stephen Lathan) for I never did take above 19s 4d Fees for your Court for such Licences, before yours 12th Xber 1713 - viz a Mark besides the Stamps. & desire it may continue so for the future for that people are apt to grumble & complain of any the least addition & I am often forced to abate my marriage fees to induce them to take such Licence, wch they wd not do but upon that Condition. Haveing now but one such Licence & Bond, be pleasd to send me halfe a Dozen of them for that they will be the same trouble & charge as two.

I am very sensible that John Gibson is so farr in Debt, that he is not able to pay any thing unlesse you think fit to Dismiss him for moderate Fees. Mr Paton gave now a different Character & acct of James Armstronge, & alleaged that his late Chwardens did give an answr to the Book of Articles, wch I am very confident they did not, I have sent under written the Names of those Decreed Excom for not appearinge & am in sincerity

Good Sr Your very humble serv't
George Ritschel

George Renwick	Henry Lambert
Margt. Crozier	Elizt. Wife of Tho. Sharpe
Anne Robson	Anne Oliver Wid
Anne Bell	Elizt. Maughen
Marg. Carnaby	Geo. Stokoe

Edwd. Streight	Willm. Elliot
Robt. Hutchinson	Willm. Fenwick
Geo. Renwick	John Carrick
Edwd. Shaftoe	Chr. Dobson
John Green	George Angus
Humphrey Bell	Tho. Hemsley
Susan his wife	Jane Kell
Geo. Collyson	Joshua Hudson
Robt. Thompson	
Anne his wife	

A Note of Expences abt Courts & enquireing after Bastard Children made the 23rd of November 1714

	£	s	d
Impr[imus] Given to Mr Tweddale to bear his Charges when he went into Cumberld etc		10	0
Besides wch he spent of his own money		1	6
A Horse 4 days 1s pr day		4	0
He deserves for his trouble & pains		10	0
Expences at NewCa: abt Mrs Mary Carnabys Bastard child		5	0
About Court Nov.4, 1713			
Given to Geo.Yarrow junr our aged App[arator]s son who then did act for him, to bear his charges		3	6
pd Jno.Litle for goeing to Allendale		1	0
A Messenger to St John Lees			3
Yarrow Demands for Horse hire		5	0
He deserves (at least) 5s of each parish for Citeing so many personally		15	0
Abt Court the 22d Nov. 1714			
Pd the Post for Bringing the Process etc from NewCa:		0	6
Itm wch he pd there for bringing them from York		0	6
A Messenger on purpose to carry them to Allendale		1	0
Ditto the Book of Articles to Bingfield		0	6
A Messengr twice to St Johnlees for & with the Processes		0	6
Expences in treating at Court the 23d Nov		4	0
Given to our poor aged Apparator		2	6
	3	3	9

Nov 21 1714	s	d	22d		s	d
Ale	1	0	Ale		6	9
A pint of W.wine	1	0	Mum			7
A bottle of Clarett	2	6	6 bottles of Clarett		15	0
Brunt Brandy	1	2	Tobaccoe			6
Tobacco		1	Punch		4	11
Victuals	2	0	Brunt Brandy 3 gills		3	6
	7	9	Victuals for 11 men		11	0
			More for 4		2	8
				2	4	11
				2	12	8
			Horses oats & hay		9	0
				3	1	8

Nov. the 23d 1714

Recd then from Mr Peter Burrell the full Contents of this Note
Pr Tho. Baxter

81. 17 December 1714 **Burrell jnr to Jubb**

Sir,

Herewth you have the Vis^{on} Process 3: Licence Bonds & 3: Prsentmts as alsoe a Note given me by the Apparit[or] of Comutacons made & the sumes therein menconed reced by Mr Ritschell. As for the people menconed in your Process & Decreed Excomunicate according to my informaton are not all worth 1s most part of the poor people in Hexham are decreed Excom & some of them appeared & really fit to give one a surfeit blind & lame wth terrible odious smells, such ridiculous things certainly before this time was never made use of; - As Im'e informed Mr Ritschell was the occasion & I doe assure you that appearance of soe many poor filthy beggars as came there to the Court is a great reflection not only upon the Court but the people attending it, Ritschell himselfe attended all the beggars every sunday in the time of gathering Nutts & had 2: p[er]sons att each end of the Towne to take the poors Nutts from 'em wch they did & gave them to Ritschell who kept all their collection & made use of them as Ime told soe that he was the receivr I spoke to Mr Ritschell abt the Comutacons I suppose lately made he prtends all is applied to the use of the Church, & that Church will be a sconce[234] for all Comutacons & dismissions soe long as he's concerned You was pleased to mencon in yr last that all Fees shoud be refunded where Licences are granted in prjudice of the Jurisdiccon herein you receive a Licence Bond of Mr Sheild of Humbersled granted by Mr Ritschell & both the parties within halfe a mile of Durham & not only soe but married in a publick house in Hexham & as the people of Hexham informes by Mr Ritschells Cur[ate] there be severall other Licences granted both att Hexham & Yarrm 20th our Reg[istrar] has an acct of but too tedious to mencon. You'l find in the Process whats reced att the Vis[on] wch in all amounts to £2-6s 6d & my charges wth Mr Ritschell & the Gents invited to dinner amts to £3-0d The Acquittance I left wth Ritschell who promised to send it you. As for the Fees of the 3: Licences I have 'em with 7: you had before makes in all 10 Licences & to Deduct soe many Times 3s 4d will make £1-13s.4d & what I reced from Ritschell is as below. This account of what I heard att Hexham according to the informatons I met wth you have a true relacon of above. I am

Sir Your humble Servt
Pr: Burrell

Durham Dec 17th 1714

	£	s	d	
Reced of Mr Ritschell	2	19	6	for 3: Licences
Deduct 10: times 3s 4d	1	13	4	
remaines	1	6	2	

I hope out of the £1-6s.2d you'l add soe much as will make upp my expences & Il'e freely give my Journey in.

82. 23 December 1714 **Ritschel to Jubb**

Sr Hexham Xber 23d 1714

I Receivd yours of the 6th Inst wth 6 Licenses & as many bonds, & shall take for every of them 20s 6d. You need not wondr at Mr Tweddales charge if you do but observe that in such Cases, such

[234] possibly as in 'sconce bowl', ie. the church as a receptacle for payments.

persons do not spare money to baffle our Courts, & had rather give a great deal more, another way sometime after a Cumberld Gent being at my house, promised to send not doubting but he could send me a particulr acct of that Gunshole child, [235] but found himselfe mistaken, & six weeks after sent me an acct that so much money had been spent to conceale it, that it was not possible to make any discovery, & perhaps ere long we may have another like instance, if it may be worth the time to fateague ourselves abt it. As to the Aparitors Citeing the Delinquents & Chwardens prsonally, you will find it was according & pursuant to your own directions If you kept a Copie of that lre you sent me Dated the 25th of June 1713, to give me advice, that you Had come to termes with Mr Burrell, & had writ to him with a Visitacon process & gave instructions abt that affair. otherwise you may depend upon it, he wd not have done it.

I wish I had the Excomunicacon agt our late Delinquent before Xtmas wch wd be a favourable opportunity to prswade such of them as are tractable, for threatnings alone will not do with some people in some Cases. If you have not receivd an acct of our late Visitacon from Mr Burrell. Be pleasd to write to him abt it, for that if we threaten people & do not do it, they do but laugh at us and despise our Courts; I shall expect in your next to hear somewhat from you abt Mr Bentham, there is lately another like instance & he told the Chwarden whom I had spoke to to prsent it, that he wd justify that marriage. Robt.Sharpe our Presbyterian Schoolmr apprd at our last Court, that party wd alleage that the late Act to prevent the growth of schism[236] doth not extend to such Schoolmrs & that there wd shortly be a General Pardon, & Why should we trouble him; We told them we should reprsent the matter to the Court of York & let them do what they thought fit therein. I hope Mr Chancellor will be pleasd to take it into serious considration & Suppress both him & Jos.Gibson our popish SchoolMr. Pray be Pleasd to give my humble services to Mr Chancellor I wish you both a good Xtmas & happy new year & many of them & am

Sr Your humble Servt
George Ritschel.

Pray give Wts enclosed to Mr Mawde.

[235] Gunshole is on the north bank of the River Irthing, east of Brampton

[236] Schism Act 1714, which was intended to prevent the spread of dissenters schools, but never properly implemented as Queen Anne died on the day it was due to come into force, 1 August 1714: Hoppitt, *op cit*, pp. 234, 310.

83. 31 March 1715 **Ritschel to Jubb**

Sir Hexham 31 March: 1715

Yours of the 10th, I reced the 12th of Feby with the Excons. In answr wr.unto. Mr Burrell reced only £2-6s-6d from the Ch: Wardens but I accounted 15 shillings he reced of certain Criminals viz Nich Errington 10 shillings Wm Robson & Jn Oliver of each 2 s: 6d.

I've always condemned extravagances at such times, as inconsistent with the nature & design of such visitations, as also travailing upon the Lord's day to keep such Courts upon Monday, for which reason I have been more favourable to those presented for the breaking ~~of~~ the Sabbath and not comeing to church.

As to the paying the visitation dinnr etc out of the Comutation money, for my pt I shall rather choose to want my dinner that day than any pt of it should be applyed to any such use.

I formerly had my dinner gratis for my trouble and the Register took the fees but Mr. Burrell having made reflections at Court 4th Nov 1713 that I ought to contribute to pay for the dinnr. I thereupon resolved to do so for the future and take my dividend of the fees, and invited some acquaintance here in Town the last Court designing to have paid for them, and acquainted Mr. Burrell therewith, but when the Bill came in next morning & the fees wd but do. I let him take them all & pay it.

The three Gentn whom I invited went away presently after dinner & I am sure were not 6d a piece extraordinarys, & if I had taken my dividend or the 4th part of the fees, might have pd for them and myself and put money in my pocket wh[ere]as it cost me 4s-0d.

I did not take your directions on 25th June 1713 as a standing rule and after desired it might not be so.

I have no Comutation money in my hands nor recd any since Jackson and Dixon, which was certifyed, otherwise wd not have failed to have given you an acct thereof.

John Gibson is now gone off I believe he wd have pd a small matter according to his ability, but I did not receive nor demand any particular sum of him, because I had not a particular order from the Court of York.

I know how such Comutations ought to be made, and wd not have done so much therein (as I did in some Cases) if things could here be done so regularly as they ought to be, for I may truly say that of later years I have been both Surrogate Registrar & App[arato]r within this Peculiar at least have all the trouble) and haveing such persons to deal with, none can blame me for being cautious.

Mr Jackson (who removed to Durham) used to threaten what he wd do. I took it to be either jest or bantre, but its like he was in earnest, for being here upon the 9th Inst. I was taken with a writ of Speciality at his suit and gave Bail Bond. I shall make Affidavit that I owe him nothing to discharge my bondsman, and when he Declares shall send you a Copy thereof, and I hope Mr Chancellor and Mr Jubb will assist me to make my defence, if that cause can be defended nothing shall be awanting on my part for that the rest will doubtless follow the example, if he got the better.

As I Remember he did alleage it was contrary to Law to take money upon any such acct, if it be so and if cause cannot be defended, I conceive it will be left to comprimise that matter as easily as we can, and I hope Mr Chancellor will be pleased to send an injunction to our Churchwardens to repay me that money, as also about £10-6s-0d more I have since laid out upon the necessary repairs of our Church in expectation to be repayed by such Criminal money wch I now begin to dispair of, for be sure our late proceedings will make such offenders more cautious.

I did not design to have returned the 3 Licence Bonds by Mr Burrell but that he desired it, and had not engrossed the memorial of them with the fees in my book. & it being night he did it himself and charged what he formerly used to do, & I pd him all his demands, but since you insist upon it have sent 2/- herewith.

As to the 8s-0 you mentioned etc I reced & deducted only a noble for & from Dawson & Arthurs Licences wch were granted before I reced your directions to take 20/- for every Licence which was 8d more than I formerly did take. It was by way of reprisal for Mr. Carnaby's Licence, wch Mr. Burrell alleaged at our last Court. He had & did allow me the Court before, but when I was positive that he did not allow it, he was satisfied & I concluded that matter was ended, & did not expect to hear any more abt it, & that noble must be deducted from Mr. Burrell.

Shields and Shafto live very nigh Durham wch made Mr. Hilton[237] take it the worse, they came to Hexham to be married by a popish priest who wd not do it without a Licence (wch I believe is more that Mr. Bentham wd have insisted on) but being a reprisal as Mr. Hilton took it for Stephan Lathan, I conceived he should not insist upon it, but if he do I desire you will allow it lest he prosecute the Gentleman.

I suppose you will believe I have had some trouble with the Excom but I am very well pleased with it, for that (God be thanked) they have done so much good, I sent to every of them yet in the Country (except Mrs. Carnaby who is of a temper not to be spoken to) & did not denounce our petty Schoolmasters.

George Stokeld. aged 74 has given it over. Tim Bell had left the Countrey. James Aynsley wd take Licence but he is so poor that he hath not & canot get money to pay for it. His parents are Comon beggars, Robt Sharpe came with great submission willing to do anything he could to teach our Ch: Catechism & send his Scholars to prayers, viz. those who do & will come. He is a reall object of charity (as is Gibson) I told him I wd represent the matter again to York, & considering the times I conceive it not improper to deferr it till we see what the present Parliamt doth.

All those presented for Fornicon are denounced except Jane Chain and Margt Crosier who did their penance (in their ordinary habit) upon Ash Wednesday wch was very satisfactory for the Congregation and all that heard of it, I did endeavour to persuade more of them but they wd not.

As to those presented for not paying their Church sess Edwd Streight & Robt Hutchinson are dead John Green had given a note to one of Sir Willm Blackett's Stewards to pay it and deduct it the next pay. Shafto paid. Renwick is very poor.

Those presented for not coming to Ch have promised & begun to reform & amend. I read a paper when I denounced the Excom to advertize them & all others who have been remiss in their duty therein wch has had very good effect, & none of them denounced save Geo Collison & Geo Stokoe, who sd they wd come, but I told them plainly, that having spoken so often to them for so

[237] Durham proctor and registrar, 1708-28: Shuler, p.vii-viii.

many years to no purpose I wd certainly denounce them, unless I did see them in Church upon that day etc.

I sent also to John Carrick (& the rest etc.) who as I am since informed, went to Mr. Carr our Bailiff (who must be consulted in every thing) to take his advice. one would have thought he would have advised him to have submitted, hearing nothing from him I denounced him, the next day he came with two along with him to make his submission & desires you will send his absolution as soon as you can.

Persons Denounced Excom

Henry Collison	Dorothy Johnson	Mary Carnaby
Margt Wood	Diana Elliot	Geo Collison
Willm Ellis	George Renwick	Geo Stokoe
Margt Todd	Anne Robson	John Carrick
Mary Summers	Anne Bell	

St John Lees

I have had no small trouble with them to very little purpose. I sent the Excom to Mr. Bentham & desired him to acquaint & admonish the several partys, & if they did not & would not come here & submit (of wch I wd & did give him an acct to denounce it agt them the first Sunday in Lent (the day I had fixed to do it here) at what time he was indisposed and desired further time.

Joshua Hudson came & alleaged that he pd Mr. Bentham 26/- for a Licence & 10/- for his Marriage Fees, & therefore I thought it unreasonable either to denounce it agt him or demand any Dismission Fee & wrote to Mr. Bentham not to do it.

Chr. Dobson & Tho: Hemsley came the week after, and did but trifle with me & went away without doing anything. Hemsley was saucy & sd If he had the Excom he wd have burnt it; two days after meeting with Dobson here in Company, we did persuade him to pay 2s-6d for his dismission Fee wch was all I desired of him, & Hemsley being not willing to denounce them, Geo Angus came also& pd his Fees, but complained of hardship.

Last of all came Mr. Bentham & brought the Excom. I gave it him back again to denounce it agt Hemsley, if he wd not & did not come & pay his Fees, he alleageth that he spoke to Mr. Bentham two months before he marryed to publish him.

Mr Bentham saith he did it the first time upon St James's day (when he was sure to have no Compa. or Congregation) I have enquired of diverse of the neighbourhood who frequent the Church & none of them will say that they ever heard that Hemsley was published nor wd he himselfe or Dobson affirm it.

You must know Sr that it hath been an old practice of Mr Bentham to publish people at such times & after such a manner (some say in latin for halfe a Crown) that those who did frequent the Church knew nothing of it, I take Hemsleys to be pure trick & shall not now take his Fees but insist upon haveing the Excom denouncd & let him appeal & apply himselfe to the Court of York to get it taken off.

Mr Bentham was & is still very unwell. I desired him as a dying man to make an ingenuous confession as to those marriage Licences wch had created so much disturbance, he desired me for Gods sake, not to trouble him any more with those matters, & prtended that he had told me that some years ago at Sr Edwd. Blacketts instance he got three such Licences from the late Mr Chancellor. Jos. Hudson had one of them Jno. Fenwick another & he could not remembr the third.

Supposeing it to be so (for I do not much regard his Allegacons in such cases) I am of opinion that he did nevr fill any of them up but hath kept them by way of reserve, if ever he should be calld in question, & that they have served to marry all that have resorted to him or he could prswade, & will serve him as long as he lives for that purpose. And if you canot proceed agt him till the Chwardens have presented the partys I am of opinion you will never do it, suppose he recover his health.

For they being upon their oaths we canot blame them if they first enquire & examin the partys whether they had a Licence, whose answr being that they had one from Mr Bentham, & he telling them that he will justify such a marriage, we canot expect that they will prsent in such Cases.

I was told (& do not doubt of the trueth threreof) that upon the 27th of September last, he did marry Nicholas Rowell of Sandhoe, a man of good Estate in his Pish, & Isabell Addison his housekeepr (who was deliverd of a child abt the middle of Xber) in Rowells house that morning.

I spoke to Tho.Bell the Chwarden & his neighbour abt it, before our last Court, Rowell referrd him to Mr Bentham who told him he wd justify that marriage, & the Chwardens were sent out of Court to amend their prsentmt, but brought them in again wthout such amendmt & since the Court I desired Bell to desire Rowell to come & speak to me abt it, wch he refused.

George Bell a Cumberland Sparke has lately marryed Mrs Elizt.Hebdon of Wall in the Pish of St John Lees Wid & lives with her at Wall. I sent my Reader to him (when here in Town) to ask him abt his Licence, who being high flown did hector him at a fearfull rate, & told him if he had not been his Countreyman he wd have broke his head; & sd let Mr Ritschel & Mr Bentham lay that matter between them viz. as to the Licence, whence we Conclude that he had one from Mr Bentham at lest did pay for one.

Be pleasd to prsent my humble Services to Mr Chancellor, & if he thinks fit to ordr Process agt Rowell & Bell (ex officio) to app[ear] at York the first day of Easter terme, I shall not only assist you to manage that affair, but am willing to be at halfe the charge of the prosecution, for otherwise it will be in vain to trouble ourselves any more abt those matters.

If Mr Jubb do not design to see Hexham this summr I desire we may have a Visitacon Court before Whitsontyde to prevent Mr Burrells travailing upon the Lds day to keep it, he says he can spare no time but upon monday, the days being long he may come from Durham that morning, & go to Corbridge in the evening (as he once did) & prevent those chargeable night entertainmts.

And since Mr Jackson hath done so dirtily by me, Pray insert Elizabeth Hutchinsons name (the woman wth whome he comitted the Fornicon) in the sd Process.

I canot be pos: whether our Ch:wardens did prsent John Wilkinson & Mary Hodgson spr for Fornicon if not pray insert their names, thoa they be poor,

I lately Spoke to Mr Willm Pearson of Hexham prsented for Fornicon & advised him to Make his application to Mr Chancellor before the next Court, (who I hope will be more favourable in that Case for his names sake) wch he sd he wd do, but he hath been so unmindfull of his other concerns, that I doubt he will forget it, his Father left him a handsome Estate, but a heavy load of debt upon it, he has sold the one halfe & must part with the other, & when all his debts are pd I doubt he will have little or nothing left to himselfe.

I have sent herewith 3 Licenc Bonds with the Fees viz. £3 1s 6d & the 2s 0d wch Mr Burrell did charge short for the last three, as also 5s 0d I recd of Chr.Dobson & Geo.Angus (I could not get a farthing of any of Hexham Pish in all three pounds eight shillings & six pence I desire you will send me a formal acquittance on a peice of papr in full of the Fees for 13 marriage Licences granted since Court 4th Nov.1713 I assure you I am very carefull & exact in my accts to prevent mistakes, & I thank God I never yet had any. I have Recd 17 Marr Licences from you since you began this method of wch there be 4 yet in my hands not used, you may please to send me 3 more, for the 3 now returnd, with Carricks absolution etc.

I Recd Rich.Carrs Will undr seale in one enclosed from Mr Jo. Carter, Wherein he saith. Ive also receivd the Fees for the enclosed Probat of Carrs Will. the Ex[ecuto]r pd them to me & they are yet in my hands, pray let me know of whom he recd them, & upon whom the Excheq Office is settled.

I Return you herewth the two Excoms agt Hexham Delinqts this had come soonr but for St John Lees, I should be glad to see you at Hexham to have personal convrsation to prvent the writeing so long lres. If Mr Burrell had ever had so much trouble with this Peculiar (as I have) I should confesse he had good reason to complain & be weary of it but hope the worst is over. I am Sr

Your very Humble Servt
George Ritschel.

84. 27 April 1715 **Burrell jnr to Jubb**

Sir,

I Discourse yr Chap: relateing to the bargaine in yrs menconed who I find are better Jockeys then you or I can prtend to I was in hopes to have got you 5s but the Fellow insists upon't that 7:Guinn was the price without any consideracon of a returne & tells me before hel'e allow 5s hel'e take the Mare againe soe that Ime afraid the 5s is Demolished I gave you in my last an acct of what I recd att Hexham Which you herein have menconed below. The papers You sent by yr Clark I recd & was to waite of you att the Posthouse the minute after you took where I thought to have settled the small acct now depending. Il'e give Sureties and Thorneton t'other Tryall & am

Sir your humble Serv't in haste
Pr: Burrell

Fees recept apd Hexham Mich: 1714

	£	s	d
recept a Guard de Hexham pr 3:yrs Fees arrear	1	5	0
Allandale	0	14	0
Dismissions	0	7	6
	2	6	6
Disbt pr expenses	3	0	0
Recept a Ritschell pr 3: Lic	2	19	0
Due to me from Mr Jubb pr 7: L: pd by Ritschell	1	8	0
Due to me for 3: L: more out of 2=19s wch I recd of Mr Ritschell	0	12	0
Tot	22	0	0

Sr,

According to my computacon Im'e to pay you 19s you allowing me for 7: L: you recd of Ritschell & 3: I recd tho' I charge my selfe with the whole, soe that Ime to have allowance for 10: L: which is 40s.

Due to Mr. Jubb	£	s	d
	2	19	0
Due to me	2	0	0
Remains in my hand	0	19	0

I hope my charges will be considered which I leave to yrselfe.

[*in Thomas Jubb's hand*]

according to my Reckoning

2d May 1715. Mr Burrell is Debtor for moneys reced for my use of Mr Ritschell	2	19	0
Credit for his fees out of thirteen Certificates at 3s 4d each	2	3	4
21 July 1715 Reced by the [...] Debt	0	15	8

85. 13 June 1715 **Ritschel to Pearson**

Revnd Sir, Hexham June the 13th 1715

On fryday last I recd. a letter from Mr Jubb, wth his answer to wt I had wrot to him abt Mr Jackson (vizt.) I am sorry that Jackson has brought his action agt you & heartily wish the prsence of the Register or his Deputy (wch as I remember you writ was awanting when his Comutation was made) don't prove a fatal omission, in any other circumstances (as takeing a pecuniary mulct[238] in lieu of corporal penance) theres little question but you have done what you may justify in Case it was taken in such manner & before such persons as the Law directs. Mr Jubb (afsd Mr Register of York) was acquainted with the whole proceeding in that affair, & in a letter dated 20th Nov 1712 he tells me one of your Proctors showed him a letter (I take it was from Mr Jackson) to enquire after these proceedings wch he informed him of, & he prmised to advise Mr Jackson forthwith to pay his note (this is as I take it to submit to your Court) wch he did, before wch time I had sent you his note & returned him & Dixon into your Court to be proceeded agt therein if you thought fit, & Mr Jubb then had or might have had him in your Court of York & proceeded agt him as the Law directs, if those proceedings were irregular & wd not justify Mr Ritschel, he might have amended them & your worship countermanded your order specially after that Mr Jackson had sent a threatening letter, so that if there be a false step made herein. I conceive Mr Ritschel is not wholy to blame, who acted according to the directions of your Court, & think it hard, that he should suffer for it.

---

238 A fine.

I designed to have gone to Newcastle this day to have taken a Councils opinion in the Case, but that my Attorney advised me first to write to your worship I conceive the point will be abt your order 6th Nov. 1712 vizt./

Revnd Sir

I should not have deferred so long the returning an answer to your last letter, but that I have been in dayly expectation of having some application made to me in the affair therein mentioned, & wd have been glad (in Case either of the parties themselves or any other in their behalf had come to me) to have been able to acquaint you with the final result of that transaction.

But as yet I hear nothing from any body, & therefore do herewith return you your two notes, & desire you to acquaint Mr Jackson & Nicholas Dixon that I have authorized & appointed you to receive the respective sumes of eight pounds & two pounds thirteen shillings four pence therein mencioned & to give discharges for the same. And when the money is come into your hands I am very well satisfied that it be applied to the repairs of your Church & do hereby order accordingly that it be so applied, & that within three months after it comes into your hands you and your Church Wardens do Certify my Ld Archbishop that in pursuance of this my order it has been so laid out in such and such particular repairs as you shall judge most necessary to be made.

Sr. If this your order will warrant me agt what I have done in pursuance thereof, I shall abide him a tryall (for he hath now Declared) if not. I hope you will be pleased to take care to keep me indemnified, I had a letter from Mr Jubb (dated 2nd Nov. 1713) in the Case of Mr Warburton, wherein he saith (vizt) you need not be under any apprehensions of danger from the Suites Mr J. W. his friends threaten you with on account of any proceedings of this nature and I much lesse expected any in the present Case for performing your order. And since that money was actually & faithfully laid out abt Hexham Church, & cannot now be recalled, If it must be repayed to Mr Jackson These request you wd be pleased to order it to be paid out of that fund of Criminal money you keep to prosecute obstinate offenders & such special occasions. Pray let me have a speedy answer that if there be occasion I may advise with Council, before my Attorney takes journey for London. I am with sincere respects

your Worships Mt Humble Serv't
George Ritschel

86. 17 June 1715 **Pearson to Jubb**

Dear Sir, June the 17 1715

I herewith send you a peevish letter from Mr Ritschel, with my Answer to it : wch if you approve of it I desire you to forward by tomorrow-nights Post. I cannot see any Reason why he s[houl]d Expect to be indemnified by us, for his own Lackes & mistakes. But, if you think otherwise, I desire youl also write to him your Self, & soften what I have writ, in such manner as you think best. I wish Mrs Jubb & you an happy meeting. We have been extremely obliged to her and her Son for the little they have afforded us of their good Company. I am,

Dear Sir, Yr affect. & humble servant
Will. Pearson

87. 25 June 1715 **Ritschel to Jubb**

Sr Hexham June the 25th 1715

The last I have from you is dated the 2d of May wch I did not receive till the 10th of June at night. I suppose Mr Chancellor acquainted you wth wt I wrote to him upon the pt of your letter wch relates to Mr Jackson I Receivd his answr on wednesday & went the Monday to an able Council in NewCa: (Mr Serj C--- b---t)[239] who doth advise me to get an act of Court undr the Seale of your Court dated at the same time when such act should have been made according to the Canon. And he gave me a late instance for it, wherein himselfe was concernd as a Council at Durham Assizes viz. -----Brasse of -----Esq had marryed a Daughter of Mr Mascalls of Durham[240] wthout Licence Mr Smith Official had taken £2 of him by

[239] John Cuthbert, sergeant at law & recorder of Newcastle: Hodgson, *Six North Country Diaries*, *op cit*, p.85.

[240] 30 Nov 1710: Thomas Brass married Elizabeth Mascall at Esh, County Durham. Elizabeth was probably the daughter of Thomas or Richard Mascall of Durham: Hodgson, *North Country Diaries, 2nd ser*, op cit, p.92.

way of Comutacon, out of Court without makeing any such act as required by the Canon. Brasse afterwards brought an action agt Mr Smith at Durham Assizes for the sd 2li. Smith produced an Act of Court as required by the Canon undr the Seale of the Court (wch my Council tells me was made in the time of that Assize, but dated when it should have been made) that the Judge wd not admit of any dispute abt the sd Act saying that they ought not to question the Records of other Courts no more then others ought to do those of their Courts & so that Cause went for the Defendt & he further says he beleives that practice may not be unusual in such like Cases & I assure you he is a very sober religious good man. ------- My Attorney had given me the same advice upon the sight of your letter & I did not acquaint my Council therewth till after he had given his wch he did upon hearing of the Case, & it seems so natural that I am apt to beleive that If I should go to more Council they wd all give me the same advice.

And therefore these request that you will be pleasd to send me by the post (assoon as you can that I may acquaint My Attorney at London therewth) such an Act of your Court as required by the Canon in Mr Jacksons Case undr the Seale of Your Court dated at the same time when it should have been made, (and you need not fear that either my Council Attorney or selfe will expose the matter) The womans name with whome the sd Mr John Jackson of Hexham Solicitor at Law Comitted the Fornicacon is Elizabeth Hutchinson of Hexham Spinstr. I baptized the Child the 19th of Octobr 1711. its name is Anne. He gave his Note abt Easter 1712. Mr Chancellor's Ordr to receive the money is dated the 6th of Nov: a Proctor came to you the 20th & promised to advise him to pay etc. wch he did the 24th of the same month of November 1712.

My Attorney Mr Jno.Aynsley of this Town, designs to take journey for Londo[n] on monday but canot possibly go by York, otherwise wd have seen you & argued the point wth you if there had been occasion he tells me there is nothing at all in it, & you need not scrouple the doing it, that Wheras Mr Jackson was treated as a Gent. & it was omitted at his request to prevent the being exposed, & he hath now done so dirtily by us and made an advantage threreof to put a trick upon us, its an act of Comon justice by way of reprizal.

Sr. In answr to what Mr Chancellor prsumed that I haveing been so long concernd understood these matters & they were regularly done I never did look upon our Court of Hexham as a Court of Record or such as is supposed by the 123 Canon[241] for that we have no Seale, & keep no office etc. but only as a Court of enquiry to transact some small matters, & transmit those of a higher nature to be finally determined by the Court of York, as we do Wills & Admons. (When I was last at York in Octobr 1699) & gave Mr Chancellor Watkinson an account of the State of this Peculiar, he was pleasd to say with some Concern that we had not so much as the face of a Court or a Shadow of justice, since wch time I have made some Essay myselfe to take off that odium for my own satisfaction, but to tell you the plain trueth We often have Courts when I do not know where to find so much as a Memorandu made by the Register that any such Court was kept except his Recept in my Book for the Fees I had taken for him, for wch reason I always acquainted Mr Chancellor or Mr Register of York with the transactions abt Comutations, to supply that defect for my own security, knowing very well that I never wanted some who wd have been glad os such an opportunity, Well hopeing that yourr order & directions therein wd have warranted me agt what I did in pursuance thereof, as well as justify me when reflected upon.

This Sr is what I hinted to Mr Chancellor, that If there be a false step made I am not wholy to blame, haveing done nothing in my own name, & so much as did proprly belong to me to do in that affair, the final determination whereof did not belong to Hexham --- so that when Mr Jackson gave a Note to Mr Chancellor to pay £2 to some pious & Charitable uses. Provided his Worsp should approve thereof I conceive he thereby submitted to the Court of York, wch should have been recorded there, & such an Act made thereupon as the Law requires (for I do not know any other Court or place where it could have been made so as to be produced as Evidence in any of his Maj[ties] Courts) & I desire it may be so for the future, & then there will be no dispute abt your Fees. Be pleasd to give my service to Mr Chancellor & acquaint herewith.

Sr I have been tedious but I hope you will the more readily pardon this trouble for that I am like to have so much upon this occasion, yet must renew my former Request wch my Attorney expects you will not deney, to send me such an Act of Your Court as aforesd undr the Seale of Your Court, & I shall not only pay you

---

[241] Canon 123 ordered that no judicial act could take place without the presence of the registrar or his deputy: Smith, p.17.

what Fees shall be due for the same, but gratify you for your trouble herein & take it as a particular obligation upon

Your very humble Servt.
George Ritschel

88. 18 July 1715 **Ritschel to Jubb**

Sr Hexham July the 18th 1715

I thank you for yours of the 11th Inst. & send back your draughtes filld up & certifyed. Qre If it be not propr to Specify the sum (viz.£2-0s-0d) comuted. I showd it to my Council, who doth not take it to be altogether of the same nature wth an Act of Court & would have me prepared to prove (If there should be occasion) Mr Chancellors Order to receive the money & apply it to Hexham Church & that it was so actually applyed wch later thoa not strictly needfull yet may be a satisfaction to the Court; the other he saith may best be done by Showing his Worsp his letter & ordr by some who go the Circuit & his owning & the partys swearing that he did own that he did write such letter & ordr to me will do in that Case, & therefore I must begg that favour of his Worsp. Pray give my service wth due respects to Mr Chancellor. I am, Sr

Your very humble servt
George Ritschel

89. 20 January 1716 **Ritschel to Pearson**

Revnd Sr Hexham Janry the 20th 1715

Mr Jubb acquainted me (when at Durham in Novembr last) how much his Grace my Ld ArchBishop & your Worsp were concernd both for the safety of my person & my Conduct, when the Rebells were at Hexham for wch these return you my hearty thanks. As to my person I know not of any here that had just cause to fear any ill usage from those neighbouring Gentlemen who could not stay long & were to leave so dear pledges of their good behaviour, their wives & children to our mercy, on whom it wd have been easy to have revenged any insults or injurys after they were gone. Their behaviour was different to what it has been reprsented in some places, oblegeing to every body, & they haveing no powr to press or compell men to lift themselves it was doubtlesse their interest to oblege if possible to allure & perswade people to joyn wth them, the design of their comeing to Hexham was to encrease their number, but met wth no small disappointmt for not one Church of England member of any acct only 3 of the meaner sort [...] of them for bread did joyn them at Hexham, or belonging to this place.[242]

As to my conduct I conceive it to be such as no man can justly condemn, & whereas some malitious persons have given a very bad character of Hexham at London I appeal to any impartial judgmt whether so few joyning wth the Rebells, & so many refuseing notwthstanding their alluremts & obligacons be not a testimony of our good affection to the prsent Govermt at least that we are not enemys to it.

Mr Jackson did not bring on his tryall, but lest he may do it, or prtend to do it at our next Assizes, my Attorney (Mr John Aynsley the Bearer) conceives it wd be propr your Worsp wd be pleasd to own your ordr etc before him, that he may witness the same if theer shall be occasion.

I have sent your Worsp enclosed Mr Pearsons submission, his Father left him two pretty small Estates worth abt £150 pr annum but such a heavy load upon them that it was not possible for him to retreive them, he sold the one, & has now so little if any benefit by the other, that it wd be a hardship upon him to pay more then £5 (& I wish he may pay it at the time appointed) & therefore hope your Worsp will be pleasd to accept thereof. These wish your Worsp a happy new year and many of them. What I have more to add is that I am, with due respects

Your Worsps Most Humble Servt
George Ritschel

---

[242] Ritschell's account may be contrasted with that of Patten in the third edition of his *History of the Rebellion*, (1745), pp. 25-6.

90. 21 January 1716 **Ritschel to Jubb**

Sr Hexham Jan^{ry} 21st 1715

These return you my hearty thanks for your kind entertainmt at Durham I Receivd 4 Blanck Licences & Bonds & have filld up and returned one of the Bonds wth the Fees, & have now but 5 of either sort in my hands.

I have sent Mr Pearsons submission to Mr Chancellor who no doubt will acquaint you wth it he had lately another bastard Child & I have put both together, perhaps you may expect a greater sum but beleive me Sr this is as much as he is well able to pay, I wish you a happy new year & am

Sr Your very Humble Servt
George Ritschel

91. 20 April 1716 **Ritschel to Audley[243]**

Rt Worspll Hexham April 20th 1716

These congratulate your succeeding the late Worthy Dr Pearson as Chancellor of York, & wish you long life & health to enjoy that dignity, & also return you my hearty thanks, for that you are pleasd to continue me Comissary of HexhamShire. I shall God willing manage this Peculiar with the same care & diligence I have done hitherto, & if all things are not as they ought to be, it shall not be my fault.

Sr, As to the enclosed, the Quakers in Allendale (where they have been numerous since the begining of that sect) have of later years built them two new meeting houses, the one in East & the other in West Allen, & have burying places of their own adjoyning thereunto, & methinks its great pitty but those of our Church should have the same conveniencys; & they may justly upraid us if we suffer such places built for the service of God, to go to ruin or be

[243] Dr. John Audley, Chancellor of the Archdiocese of York from 1716. A young man when appointed by Archbishop Dawes to replace the incompetent predecessors Watkinson & Pearson in 1716: Till, Study, p.219. See Introduction, p.18.

made a stable, wch one of their Speakers did once acknowledge ought not to be, and thoa two new Chapels have been built of late, the one at Allenheads & the other at ColdClough, at the head of each dale for the Conveniency of the Miners, they haveing no burying places there, & they belonging to Sr Willm Blackett Barrt whose heires may pull them down & dispose of the materials to what uses they please, whenevr those lead mines shall wear off I conceive it needfull the sd Chapel should be kept in repair, & the best way I know of to have it kept up & in repair, will be to have the yard belonging thereunto made a burying place, wch I assure your Worsp will be a very great ease & convenience to the Miners at Allenheads & that pt of the Countrey, it being so great a fateague in the winter season to carry their dead to be buryed at Allendale Church, they had such a design & desire some years ago, but it went off. I suppose it needless to add any more upon this subject this comeing upon so good a design & occasion I prswade myselfe it will meet with a kind reception, & obtain pardon for this trouble from

Your Worsps Most Humble Servt
George Ritschel

Sr If it be needful to acquaint or trouble his Grace my Ld ArchBp with this affair, These humbly beg your Worsp will be pleasd to give my duty with sincere respects to him, The Neighbourhood canot tell me the name of the sd Chapel; I am apt to believe it hath been dedicated to St Peter the Apostle, for that they annually keep a feast, or publick meeting from all parts, in the sd yard upon the 29th of June.

[*Cover:*]

To the Rt Worshpll Dr Audley
Chancellor of York
These prsent

[*Rear of cover, in a different hand, possibly Audley's:*]

Enquire
To What Parish the Chapel doth belong.
What Minister has us'd to perform
Divine Service in it: and Administer the Sacrament

Whether any salary or Stipend us'd to be paid him: and by whom
Whether the yard belonging to the Chapel has been us'd for a burying place, and was ever fenc'd in.
Whether there is any record or memory of the Chapel and the Yard's ever having been Consecrated.
Whether they can make an Assessment to repair the Chapel or must depend upon Voluntary Contributions.
Whether they ever had any Chapel Wardens.
If they know what Gentleman or what Estate us'd to pay the Eleven Nobles

92. 9 October 1716 Ritschel to Jubb

Dear Sr

In answer to that pt of your lre dated the 26 of May wch relates to Mr Pearson When I see no hopes of a visitation Court this summr (for I have not seen nor recd any lre from Mr Peter Burrell of Durham these 18 months) I thought it best, not to defer it any longer, but to take a Bill for £7-0s-0d, as he agreed at first, for that if there had been such visitation I am very pos[itive] he wd not have made any such request, but rather have evaded it wch he easily might have done, & if I had not done so & Mr Robinson favourd me very much herein had got nothing.

I have sent you herewth Forty shillings Your Court Fees, & hope Mr Chancellor will be pleasd to allow me the five pounds receivd for Comuteing his penance, in pt of the eight pounds ten shillings I was actually & bona fide out of pocket (besides my great trouble, the last year in defending the Cause agt Mr Jackson, who did not bring it on this year. I assure you I have not had so much as a bottle of wine or a pair of gloves from Mr Pearson upon this account.

As to our Church & parish affaires I told our 24ly there should nothing be awanting on my pt to keep things in ordr, & that for the future the old Ch:Wardens should be dismissed every year, bet[w]een Easter & Whitsontyde, & accordingly this year the old Ch:Wardens (for our sydesmen & Assistants are dropt) gave in their Accts & Prsentmts & the new ones (thoa not sworn) did enter upon their office, and expect to be dismissed before Whitsontyde next.

I Suppose you will readily grant, that the not keeping Visitation Courts duely according to the Canons has been one cause of the disordr in this Peculiar I am sure it has made our Courts & Prsentmts to be very much disregarded, and therefore desire, that for the future, that if Mr Burrell canot or will not come himselfe he may appoint some to do it for him.

Those in Allendale complain very much, not only of the hardship to serve so long, but also that it doth occasion so much confusion as to their poor but I am apt to beleive St John lees will not complain if we never keep another Visitation Court, those Ch:Wardens have not paid any Fees of late years. If they may not be compelld & it be only matter of choise, the Registers Case wd be hard if the rest of the Peculiar should follow their Example.

I send you herewith a Licence Bond Certifyd wth the Fees, & am sorry Mr Pearson had no benefit thereby for it did not nor is like to take effect.

Sr, This is all I have dispatcht since the last I sent you, nor can you expect many from me so long as Mr Bentham continues his former practices herein wch he seems fully resolved to do; in May last he marryed four Couple of the parish of Allendale viz Jacob Brown a Quaker & his housekeeper Itm James Brown his Brothr & his housekeepr, they were Church women and wd not be marryed but by a Minister of the Church of England, Itm Edwd.Heatherington of West Allen Taylor & ---------- Itm Joseph Adamson Master of Allendale Freeschool, & Mary Daughter of Tho.White

I sent our Apparator into Allendale to enquire after such matters - who did sumon them to come before me that I might be better Certifyed concerning them, the two Quakers came & alleaged they knew not but Mr Bentham had a faculty or powr to do it. Heatherington told him that Mr Bentham had promised to keep him indemnifyed & he wd insist upon it & said he wd not come. Joseph Adamson likewise refused to come & insisted upon a Licence he had from the Court of Durham wch Mr Bentham after showd me, it was granted by Mr Smith Official & directed to the Minister of Allendale, and both the partys were put (as they were) within the parish of Allendale formerly they used in such Cases to put the one of them in some parish within the Diocese of Durham. I could soon make a reprisall but that I never could approve of such practice & a little before gave one a flat denyal as being an act of injustice to the Court by depriveing them of their Fees. I am apt to beleive the reason why

Adamson did not apply himselfe to me for such Licence, because White was her Fathers only child & heir & he wd have had her to have marryed another man & Adamson knew I wd not grant him such Licence without her Fathers consent, otherwise should put him upon takeing a Licence to teach School, as the founder directs.

I conceive its somewhat hard that John Carrick could nevr yet have his absolution, wch he so much desired & I have so long expected, & since its not worth the time to take out a Capias Writ[244] agt any of the other Criminals I wish some of them could be perswaded to submit, & have absolution & be dismissed paying their Fees. Be pleasd to give my humble service to Mr Chancellor. I am in sincerity Sr ,

Yours etc. George Ritschel

Sr Hexham October 9th 1716

The Bearer Mr Aynsley our Friend somes upon a prticulr occasion viz. a Certain Gent. here spoke very ill words of him, wch if they had been true might have endangered his liberty if not his life & Estate for wch he brought an action & got judgmt by default, & now comes to have a writ of enquiry for damages, you know that in such like Cases of malice the estimate is to be taken from the intention & not from the effect, If you can be any ways serviceable to him herein it will very much oblege

Your Most Humble Servt
George Ritschel

Mr Aynsley or Mr Shaw have your Fees viz. 2 guineas a pistoll[245] & sixpence - pray send an acquittance.

[*in Jubb's hand*]
12 Oct. Recd with £3-0s-6d of Mr Ainsley.

---

[244] Effectively an arrest warrant.
[245] French gold coin in English circulation. Although decreed in 1701 to be worth no more than 17shillings, the receipt attached to this letter shows that Jubb accepted it at the previous common value of 18 shillings: Kenyon R., *Gold Coins of England* – 1884, p180.

[*Cover*:]
For Mr Thomas Jubb These

93. 6 September 1718 Andrewes to Jubb

Sir Hexham Sept 6 1718

You will perceive that I have done nothing more, than persuading half a dozen Churchwardens to come in, be sworn, and save themselves from the anger of he court, but as for fees I cannot incline 'em to pay any, the churchwardens of St Johnlee, I am told, are willing to pay £2 8s 4d, but doe insist that it shall comprehend their Chapelries of St Oswald and Bingfeild. Those of Hexhamshire are instructed to refuse; except Edward Green, who has deposited his part in a neighbours hand, because I would not Receive it without the whole, and desires not to be named in the process; Allso Wm. Chicking of Bingfeild says, if you are determined that those chappels shall not be included in the fees of St John Lee, he had rather pay the[m] out of his own pocket then be troubled, and that they have never been used to gather rates for those chapels; therefore be pleased to declare your pleasure, without looking upon Green or Chicking as criminals. I have enclosed a small note of the delinquents, wch you may compare with your own roll, and the presentments, I have marked with a cross the names of the submitting persons above mentioned. The moneys I have Recd come to £2 4s 8d which you have the particulars of at the Bottom, and wch I now send with the Bonds, and my Certificates to Mich., be pleased to return me a receipt of them.

As to Mr Laidman[246] Sr Wm.Blacketts curate, he is now willing to submitt himself to be licenced by the authority of not finding his patron inclinable to dispute that power which he asserted for him, when he denye the pulpit 6 weeks to his Graces Licence, but he is now concernd he did not take the opportunity of your being at Hexham, and would take it as a favour if he could be excused takeing a journey to York on purpose by haveing it deferred, or contrived to be done in this place.

Tis Impossible your court should be readyly obeyed, or this Jurisdiction quickly ordered, till you have made the officers of this

[246] John Laidman; see ABN.

court Leet sensible, that their Lord has not that power, in Ecclesiastical affairs, which they assert in his name as Licenceing Curates, directing your Officers, disposeing of Pews, granting faculties to erect Gallaries, etc. which they are now busie about. Mr Chancellour would not have so much wondred at Mr Lowes the Curate of Allendales answers, had he seen his licence, which runs in as Authoratative a style as to preaching and administring Ecclesiastial functions, as he himself could have granted, I have sent in these paypers a coppy of Mr Benthams Licence, by which you may judge what notions they have, and power they pretend to; as allso a coppy of a grant to Mr Ritschel to erect a pew or Gallarie for himself & successors, if Sr Wm.Blackett has this power I would apply to him for the confirmation of it; But else desire this favour from the court of York, that I may lay out a little money for the convenience of my self and successors, the place is by the pulpit, most convenient for the Minister and will not distrub or displace anyone Its what Mr Ritschel intended, and I wish had finished. If Mr Chancelleur does Judge that his Grant of this vacant wall between the 2d and 3d pillars, will authorize me to build a seat notwithstanding any opposition from the lord of the mannor or his officers, I should be glad of the favour of it, because I am informd that a person intends to ask this liberty of Sr Wm, and to set aside this grant which has been allready made to Mr Ritschell.

Pray doe me the favour to present my most obedient service to Mr chancellour, and my friend Mr Lamplugh,[247] pardon this Long trouble from, Sr

Your very humble servant
Tho.Andrewes

Moneys Recd and sent	£	s	d
Mr Lowes exhibt		1	4
Mr Benthams exhibt		1	4
Tho.Harrissons licence	1	1	0
John Tompsons licence	1	1	0
	2	4	8

the farthings I will place to next account.

[247] Advocate at York: Till, Study, pp. 191-7.

94. 13 Oct 1718 **Andrewes to Jubb**

Sir Hexham Oct 13 1718

I am concernd, I must trouble you with the old complaint against my neighbour Mr Bentham, who I am well informed has married a couple of persons in his parish, that have been faulty as to the crime of fornication, the man (I think it him) had been twice enquireing of me what would be the price of a Licence, but thinking it to much, tryed Mr Bentham, who married them without Banns or Licence, upon trust for 20s, but the man haveing lost his child, and willing to save his money, Refuses payment, and Mr Bentham threatening to lay him under a severe prosecution, this person (a Turner by trade) applyed himself to a friend of mine for his advice in this matter; and I am inclined to think may make good proof of it. I must allso acquaint you of a method he has, which is as much to the same purpose of marrying without Banns, which is this, upon the encouragement of an advanced fee, he publishes 'em in his Lattin, and so marrys em upon it and the parish Don't know one word of the matter and all this he Dares, notwithstanding Mr Chancellour gave him that severe admonition against it, and was never yet Licenced otherwise than by Sir Wm Blackett and his Steward. Pray direct this as you please I am your very Humble servant.

Tho Andrewes

I have disposed of an other licence & 4 remaining with me

95. 27 October 1718 **Andrewes to Jubb**

Sr Hexham Oct: 27

Tis now a month since I sent you in a paquet all the paypers of your proceedings, when you held your court in this place; with 2 guineas inclosed, and two bonds for two Licences, that have issued out: I sent Mr Shaw a pacquet by the same post, and have received answers, which makes me hope that what I sent you has not miscarryed; About 3 weekes since I received a complaint, and sent you an information against my neighbour mr Bentham, for an irregular marriage, but upon more particular enquiry I find, that the demand he made was not for extraordinary marriage fees, for tis supposed the Banns were published, but he insisted upon 20s for commutation, for the crime of antenuptial fornication, and to secure 'em for being presented in your court, and brought into greater expenses; a practice that he has been long since famous for, twould be well if he could be persuaded to leave of these irregularities.

I must beg leave to be absent from this place about 8 or 10 weeks, and think to set out about ten days hence, therefore if there is any business that I can di[s]patch in your service before I goe, be pleased to give me what orders you think convenient, and they shall be punctually executed by

Your most Humble Servant
Thomas Andrewes

96. November 1718 [248] **Andrewes to Jubb**

Sir Hexham Nov [...]

I have enclosed to Mr Chancellour Dr Squires opinion of Mr Ritschels case, which seems to explain and prove our old abbey now a parochial church, notwithstanding the Bailiff of this town assumes the liberty to erect Galleries, controle the churchwardens, obstruct parish business, and church repairs, which payper when he has perused or made use of as he pleases, pray return it to me again, that I may place it to other of Mr Ritschells paypers.

The very vacancy that Sr Wm. Granted to Mr Ritschel, was allso granted by the court of York, and I should have been very well pleased to have found the seat finished to my hand, for now what was desired by him is much more necessary to my self, and the future Lecturers; for the seat Mr Ritschel and his father enjoyd was as they were curates to the Impropriator, and I suppose Mr Laidman may have the same right and occasion for it for the use of his wife and large family. I am not now so apprehensive that there is any intentions to deprive me of the vacancy formerly Granted, for the person who was goeing to build seems to compliment by placeing his designs elsewhere, and perhaps am flatterd as partly the occasion of

[248] Although the date is mssing from the original letter it must have been 1718 given mentions of Mr. Laidman, who was removed from the Hexham curacy in June 1719: BIA Pec.Hex/1 – sequestration order.

their Zealous expences, a hint I should not give, but as necessary to evince that I doe not write upon any disagreement amoung us. I shall be very much obliged to Mr Chancellour for his favour, when he has thought of it.

I acquainted Mt Laidman with your answer, and he did intimate that he would write to you, to know what would be the expence of a special commission, and he was desireous to take the most frugal method. If Mr chancellour will be pleased to empower Mr Richardson,[249] (who preaches the Lecture in my absence) to act by his commission as to the Licences, it will be very convenient and obligeing, my B[rothe]r will take the Blanks into his custody, and I dare answer will deliver them with all necessary caution, I shall [....] Mr Richardson with the instructions.

Of the Seven first Licences Recd, I have returned two Bonds, and I have now three By me that are allready executed, which shall speedily be sent; so that I can leave but two blanks in my B[rothe]rs Hands, if he wants before I return, he may write.

Mr Chancellor expressing his favour towards the delinquents that would yet come in, I have ventured to swear Robert Foster a new churchwarden of Hexhamshire into his office, which be pleased to note in your court proceedings.

At my Return, I will contrive to call at York, If you will be so kind as to deferr the correction process till then, and shall be ready to obey any farther instructions.

I am your Humble Servant
Tho. Andrewes

97. 9 March 1719 **[Wm] Richardson to Jubb**

Sir Hexham March the 9th 1718

I thought it was my bounden duty to tell you, that there are two Criminal Women in the Parish of Allendale, as I'm well inform'd, - three in my Chapplery of Hexhamshire, & one here, but has not as yet brought forth. I am sure some in my district will

---

[249] Revd William Richardson; see ABN.

commute, wch (if they do) pray remember my decaying Chapple. I hope yu'll see Mr Andrews shortly, and give him what directions yu think proper in this affair. Mr Lademan has not yet appear'd, since I wrote to yu. He writes to his friends here, that he can't opportunely attend this Cure in Person 'till nigh Michaelmass; He expects (as I'm inform'd) that yu'll send his Licence by Mr Andrews, - wch I hope yu will never grant;- for surely, if any can justly be call'd a Delinquent, he may be in the highest sense. - I can't possibly get a Farthing of him, neither can his wretched Curate; he has neither honr nor honesty in him; - I hope yu'll excuse both the freedom and frequency of my writing, when I tell yu that there are such just complaints from the Church agst him, and such reflections from the Conventicle, that I want words to express it; - It is a grand reflection upon Sr Wm.Blacket, and I wish yu may not partake of it too by your silence. - I heartily wish yu health and happiness, and shou'd be exceeding glad to hear from yu about this vacant Curacy; I'll spare neither Cost nor pains to have supply'd by an honest hand. - I am in the mean time wth great sincerity

Your most obedient & faithful servt
William Richardson

98. 29 March 1719 **Fenwick *et al* to Jubb**

[*in Wm Richardson's hand*]

Sir

Having taken into our serious & most deliberate consideration the shameful discharge & management of this our Curacy of Hexham, - we find ourselves bound in duty & conscience to make a true representation of it to you, & by so doing we can not avoid the presenting both Mr Laidman & Mr Dallace his Curate (as he calls him) The first for his great & notorious & wilful neglect of, - the latter for his scandelous, ignorant and offensive performance of the Pastoral Duty. Mr Laidman has only appear'd twice here since Michaelmass - the duty has been perform'd by his Scotch-Curate all this while, but to the great offence & scandal of the whole Congregation. - The Sacram[en]t of the Lord's Supper has only been administer'd here once since Whitsuntide last:- whereas the constant custom was once at Michaelmas, - twice at Xtmas - and once immediately before Lent. - And now at this solemn season It was always administer'd three several Sundays, but Mr Laidman has not yet appear'd, notwithstanding his Curate gave warning for it by his own orders and directions. This very day a considerable number of country-people, besides many Inhabitans here, came to receive the Sacram[en]t and were disappointed. - There is at this time very great & just complaints agst Mr Laidman, and we hope you will take it into such serious consideration, as we have done, and [deleted: you will infinitely oblige] Do us what justice, as lays in your Power, and you will highly oblige.

Hexham March the 29th 1719

Your most obedient & faithful Servants [*all sign*]
John Fenwick,
George Hubbuck,
Wm.Jefferson,
Ralph Thompson
Church-Wardens

P.S. We must not omit to acquaint you, that it is the general opinion here, that Mr Laidman's Curate has neither orders nor Licence. Mr Richardson presents his best respects to you.

[*Cover:*]
Mr Thomas Jubb Register
near the Minster of York
post pd This with care.

99. 5 April 1719 **Fenwick *et al* to Jubb**

[*in Wm Richardson's hand*]

Sir

We must once more give yu the trouble of presenting Mr Laidman for his neglect and omission of his Duty. - For notice was given for the Sacram[en]t for this day, & he neither appear'd himself, nor procur'd any in his place: - A great man of the Inhabitants here went to neighbouring Churches to receive, and many more were disappointed. - We hope you will bring him to a right sense of his Duty, and fix the Cure upon a more certain, and regular botom, - wch will be very acceptable to

Your obedient & faithful Servts -

John Fenwick,
George Hubbuck,
Wm. Jefferson,
Ralph Thompson

Hexham April the 5th 1719

[*Cover:*]
Mr Thomas Jubb near the Minster of York This with care

100. 5 April 1719 Richardson to Jubb

Sir

Your's came to my hand very safely on Tuseday last, for wch I do not only thank you, but every body else to whom I did communicate it. - This after-noon I have read the Process. - And I must beg of you to assist me agst Mr Lademan, who is indebted to me for a quarters salary ever since Michaelmass last. It is the fourth part of twenty mark: - I have frequently demanded it, and he has frequently deny'd the payment of it: - I desire yr assistance (whenever he appears before you) On getting this small summ, for wch I shall not be ungrateful. - Mr Aynsley presents his respects to you, & do yu be pleas'd to accept the same from

Your most oblig'd & faithful Servt
Wm. Richardson

Hexham April the 5th 1719

Tis every body's opinion here, that the nomination to this Curacy is in his grace the Archbishop. - I humbly and pressingly beg yr helping hand to be recommended to his grace; I have by me (as formerly mention'd to you) a testimonium both from this Town & my neighbouring Brethern. - Pray be pleas'd to give me an account whether Lademan appears on Thursday or no.

101. 14 May 1719 Richardson to Jubb

Sir

Your's came to my hand very safely yeasterday, and I have communicated it to those Persons yu mention in it. - The way and means Mr Laidman took for the obtaining of the Licence were thus, - He addresses me by the Person of Mr Allgood (a confess'd Non-juror) I expressly told the Gentleman I cou'd not grant any Licence except one of the Party did appear, and take the oaths according to the instructions. he did desiste - However Mr Laidman in person makes application to Commissary Andrews, - from whom he receives a blank Bond and Licence, and comes to my house betwixt the hours of nine and ten, where he tells me expressly, that he had given five hundred pound bond to the Commissary, in order to keep me harmless, wch bond was not executed, when I made my address to the Commissary. - He told me, that he would fill up the Licence, & take the Surrogate's fee, wch (I suppose) he has done, and notwithstanding my telling him the ill consequence of so doing, - he says he is proof against you, a common term of his -- This is a true and faithful relation of this affair, tho I might say a great deal more as to the circumstances of it. - My tender of my duty to Mr Chancellor is what I desire of yu & do yu be pleas'd to accept the best affection

of Yr obedient & faithful Servt
Wm.Richardson

May - Newcastle the 14th 1719

[*Cover:*]
To Mr Thomas Jubb Register near the Minster of York
Pd This wth care

102. 14 May 1719 Henry Andrews to Jubb

Sir Hex 14 May

I saw yrs to Mr Richardson, and am sorry that Mr Laidmans getting the licence is so great a concern to yr Court, I shall acquaint yo wth the affair as justly as I can - on Monday Sennight late in the

Evening Laidman came & desired a licence, I sent for Richardson who ws gone to Bed, Laidman acquainted me wth the Persons Intending, who both were personally known to me & to be sufficiently att age to dispose of themselves, the Gentlewoman being towards, & the Gentleman above 40, & no ways related, This made me think I might safely trust the Licence & Bond in Laidmans hands as far as Richardsons house where he told me he would goe & get them fill'd up, Laidman & Richardson haveing particular quarrels (as I understand since) fell out, & he did not fill up the licence etc as I expected, I am sure out of any honest Principle did he refuse it, when I come to know the affair, & that the Bond etc was not filled up, I sent for Laidman who was no where to be found, wch may be presumed was his particular direction to the People of the house where he lodged, it being about 12 att night, the next Morn I sent very Early to him & he was actualy gone there was word left that I must needs speak wth him, & that if he intended to be goeing never so early I would be up on purpose I did not apprehend the lea[s]t disturbance in the affair from any, my wifes Illnes in Lyeing inn, & my own indisposition att that time made me not thoroughly consider, I trusted Laidman & Richardson who are equally undeserving, not to say worse of their Cloth, I have Lately dispos'd off all the licences except one, & an old Fellow out of Allendale Last tuesday told me he should have occasion for the same next Monday I've recd what fees belong to yr Court, & Richardson has for his trouble those allotted to my Brother for his own use

I am Sr yr servt
Hen. Andrewes

my Brother I expect in a few weeks downe & I am certain things will be better regulated among such a vile Crew.

103. 15 May 1719 John Douglas[250] to Jubb

Sir

I am favoured with yours 9th instant writt to the reverend Mr Richardson of hexham about Mr Laidmans base and disingenious intentions it was attempted a month before to obtain a license from Durham; when they heard whose daughter she was they would not grant the same without consent on this they applied to mr Laideman who obtained from Comissary Andrews whether by corruption or what other way I know not a blank License for that purpose who brought the same to Mr Richardson to Signe he refused it I believe however Laideman came directly forward with that blank license to newCastle in order to marry them for I know where the blank license was seen and produced in Newcastle by Mr Laidman who came hither the 5th instant to marry them Mr Richardson was so honest and just that he pursued & followed Laideman the next day from hexham and came to Newcastle to acquaint me therewith but then it was too late for they were married that day by a license (though Laideman was here) obtained that day thro stratagem from Durham which license was brought to Doctor Ellison[251] Vicar of Newcastle who refused to marry them not withstanding the license knowing it was not with my consent however another Clergy man in newcastle did doe it if he had not mr Laideman was ready to perform the office; this is the honest account I can give you of the affair And that mr Laideman was very zealous and forward in the whole matter he is a scandalous unworthy parson; I return mr Chancellor and you hearty thanks for yr good interest not doubting your Justice in punishing offenders and wherein I can be serviceable you may command

Your most humble servant
John Douglas

Newcastle 15th May 1719

---

[250] John Douglas, (c.1640-1727) one of the Newcastle men who bought land in Northumberland, in his case at Matfen, Aydon and Halton. His daughter Jane, aged 32, married Capt Edward Tyrrell on 6 May 1719 at St.Nicholas Church, Newcastle: H.Craster, *History of Northumberland*, Vol X, Corbridge, (1914), p.406.

[251] Rev Dr Nathaniel Ellison, vicar of St. Nicholas, Newcastle, 1694-1721: E. Mackenzie, *Historical Account of Newcastle*, Volume 1, (1827), p. 283.

104. 8 June 1719 Richardson to Jubb

Sir Hexham June the 8th 1719

Since I now plainly see that yr Court hath for very just & good reasons depriv'd Mr Laidman of this Curacy, & I hope too yu'll also shortly discharge or dismiss his scandelous & illitorate Deputy, shall I presume without offence once more to beg of yu to recomend me to the ordinary for the supplying the Cure during the Suspension, wch if I may be admitted to perform, I shall take it as a pledge of the greatest honr & favour imaginable, - for wch I shou'd never be unthankful, nor unmindful of, and I trust wth God's blessing attending my diligent & conscientious endeavours I shou'd discharge or perform the Duty, both to yr satisfaction, & benefit of the people, and wth pleasure and comfort to my self; - And this I presume to say, because I did for five years successively (tho' indeed wth some little assistance from Mr Ritschell) officiate as Curate of Hexham, and as Afternoon Preacher for almost these nine years wth some tolerable reputation. - Your advice and assistance at this juncture (tho' pray excuse my freedom) will be of the most advantageous consequence to me, and assure your self, it shall not be long unrewarded, let the issue be what it will. - I shou'd freely and willingly wait upon Mr Chancellr upon the least notice, if yu think it proper, or to take any other method yu shou'd be pleas'd to advise me to. - I heartily pray for your health, and happiness. - And am wth sincerity & regard

Your most obedient, & faithful Serv't
William Richardson

Two lines from yu wth yr convenience will be very acceptable; -And, pray hasten the removal of the Scotch-Curate for I wast words to express how unaccountably he performs the office.

105. 12 June 1719 Cowling[252] to Jubb

Sr NewCastle June the 12th 1719

I perceive that Mr Lademan is threatened wth a prosecution from your Court for not taking a Licence to Serve the Cure of Hexham, & he having no acquaintance in York desird me to acquaint you, that he did at Easter Last resign all the interest he had in it to Sr Wm Blacket, who promis'd him in his way to London to wait upon his Grace, & also make him a complim't of the Curacy, if he had any woud accept it. So that, if any, Sr Wm must be calld upon to answer any want of service in the Church. The truth hereof Mr Lademan is willing to assure you of by subscribing [*deleted*] his name. Pray my humble Service to Dr Audley, & believe me to be

Sr Your Friend & Servt
John Cowling
John Laidman

[*Cover:*]
Mr Thomas Jubb
in the Minster Yard in York pt. pd.

106. 13 June 1719 Andrews to Jubb

Sir Newcastle June 13 1719

I came to this place yesterday by sea, and had been sooner, but my intentions have been long hindered by northerly winds; I shall be now speedily be at Hexham, ready to execute your instructions with diligent attendance. Be pleased therefore to appoint your visitation, and send withal orders if necessary, and I shall dismiss the old officers and admit those late chosen, and regulate your jurisdiction as you are pleased to direct.

---

252 curate of St. Nicholas', Newcastle c.1715, and unsuccessful candidate for Hexham lecturership after Ritschel: Rev John Thomlinson's Diary, published in Hodgson, *Six North Country Diaries*, *op cit,* p.69.

Pray present my humble service to Mr Shaw, and let him know that he may soon expect from me the dispatch of what business is ready, and shall be informd of such as are not to be brought in by early admonitions.

Pray present to Mr Chancellor the obedient respects of your obliged and humble servant

Tho Andrewes

107. 18 June 1719 Richardson to Jubb

Sir

I am oblig'd once more to trouble yu wth this, in wch I must acquaint yu, that since my reading Laidman's suspension in this Church (wch was on Sunday sennight) none of the Parishioners will employ his Curate, either in baptising, marrying or in burying the Dead, but have requested me to perform the Duty, wch accordingly I have done; - And Yesterday he publickly declar'd (tho' without any provocation) that he will receive no discharge from any but from him, who first fix'd or plac'd him here, - and accordingly he receives all fees whatever, and dos those duties, wch are to be perform'd in the reading Desk & Pulpit. The people are very uneasie wth him, & have desir'd me to acquaint you wth it & they humbly beg yr assistance in the removal of him. - I hope yu receiv'd my Lettr wch was dated on Monday the 8th Instant, wherein (as I do also in this) pressingly desir'd of yu to recommend me to the ordinary for the Supplying this Curacy during the Suspension, wch if I may be authoriz'd to perform, I shall take it as the greatest honr & favour imaginable & for wch I shou'd never be ungrateful nor unmindful of: - Pray be pleas'd to write to me, & give me what directions yu think proper, for without 'em I neither can nor will do any thing. - Mr Andrews presents his best respects to you, he came to this place on Monday last. - I am wth sincerity & regard

Your most obedient & faithful serv't
Wm.Richardson

Hexham June the 18th 1719

108. 22 June 1719 Andrewes to Jubb

Sir Hexham June 22 1719

I wrote to you upon my landing at Newcastle, to acquaint you with my return, and I wait your pleasure when you shall be pleased to direct the admission of the new officers, St James Day was the day appointed last year, but not very happyly because of a fair that was some distance from the town, the most proper day of the week would be some tuesday, wch is our common market, that the country men may be drawn to town on more the one occasion, I should be very glad to see Mr chancelour and yourself here as last year, but if I hope to great a favour, the business shall be executed in the manner you think fitt to direct. I find here has been a small error In relation to a licence that Mr Laidman obtained of my B[rothe]r at 12 a clock at night, in behalf of 2 parties that my B^r^ knew to be of age, and very allowable; and sent him to Mr Richardson, to fill up and execute the Bond, & give the oaths; but the partys not being present, and my B^r^ Deceived, He carryd of the licence with him, however I understand tis not yet executed, and expect to have it again upon the return of the fees, besides which I have but one licence by me unexecuted. My B^r^ did not understand our our instructions, and Is Heartyly vexed that he should be prevailed upon by Mr Laidman, to entrust him with a licence, tho but to Mr Richardsons house. I am your obliged

and Humble servant
Tho. Andrewes

Pray present my Best respects, and Humble Service to Mr Chancelour.

109. 30 July 1719 Andrewes to Jubb

Sir Hexham July 30 1719

I was in expectation of seeing Mr Laidman at our Sessions, to have Recoverd from him that Licence, I dont hear but that he is inclinable to retore it, therefore dont now account for the fees of it, I have wrote to him since the Sessions, and have cautioned him against the use of it, and that it must me very hazardous to him if he refuses to return it.

Sr Wm.Blacket resents a little the sham he has put upon his nomination, and has referrd it to the parish to recommend whom they can agree upon, and the parish are urgent that I would accept the care of it, and Sr Wm is inclined to favour me with his nomination; but when the town have performd as they have engaged, I shall determine; till then the Sequestration is a very good title to Mr Richardson, who is employd by the churchwardens and I beleive must be my assistant, or I cannot alltogether undertake it. I send you the Bonds of three Licences, excuted by Mr Richardson, I have done nothing that way since my Return, Mr Laidman has one, and I now have seven by me; I must complain of some neighbours that are bold to marry my people without such authority, Here is one Mr Twedale[253] a curate of Thockrington, (which is a kind of exempt parish, belonging to a prebend of York) has married two couple of my parish without banns or licence, here is a third couple one John Coatsworth a joyner of Hexham, married, but will not declare by whom, tis reported he was married at Ovingham by one Mr Lyant; I think he should be proceeded against as a fornicator, till he proves his marriage, and then too he will be plainly guilty of antenuptial fornication; Here are allso two poor fellows named Jeffersons, Brothers, they are Roman Catholicks, and are married to women of the same religion, Tho they cant pretend to make any proof of it, but have made application to assure me, it has been done by some secret Roman catholick preist, but how allowable this, I submitt to better judgement.

I Now Return you the proceedings of the correction and visitation courts, where you may plainly see in both, the present delinquents, I allso send the Presentments as they were given in by the churchwardens, there is one cath.Gosling, a considerable and notorious offender, that has been the Strumpet of an Irish Gent some time, She is presented for her 4th bastard and in other respects a person of a very vile character, upon no terms to be excused; her Gallant is lately come over, and very much Slights the newes of the presentmts, and says he knows the worst of it, that tis but a 40s business; His name is - Capt - Burleigh.[254]

---

[253] Edward Twedale; see ABN.

[254] See I. Hancock, 'The Irish gent and his strumpet: the story of Hercules Burleigh', *HH*, 22 (2012), pp. 35-54.

The South Quarter of our famous old church is again presented out of repair, but how it should ever be repaird I cannot Imagine, they talk of getting a brief, (to excuse their neglect,) but make no progress toward it tho they had the opportunity of the quarter Sessions in the town the other week; the churchwardens collect a Sess about once a year of about 35 or more pounds, (and by their certificate will appear how much has been layd out on the account of Mr chancellors monition), the Bayliff as deputed by the vestry of 24 Receives what the churchwardens collect; they account to him; the people murmur at the great abuses that are made of this parish fund; and that no publick account is ever made of it.

I must send you a complaint against Edward Foster Late churchwarden of St Oswald, who Did indeed pay his dismission fees, but at the same time behaved himself very insolently, and uttered some expressions of reproach and contempt against the jurisdiction; when I demanded his presentments, he asked me whither he should present himself and sayd that twas not his business to run enquiring about the Country, that there was noe occasion for all this bustle and trouble we gave them; and that twas only to bring grist to your mill. be pleased to order as you think convenient concerning him

Mr Bentham desires to know what may be the expence of a provincial Licence, for a person at Beltingam in the county of Nor[thu]mberland, to practice Physick and Surgery.

Mr Lowes told me that he expected some answer In relation to an Excomunication, but I did not understand his business, and can only remind you, if you allready have heard it from him.

If you know where Mr Hewett Lives, (somewhere in a curacy near York), pray inform him that I am ready to pay him for his attendance after Mr Ritschels death, if I knew where he would order me. I summond Mr Ricarby curate of Allenheads but he did not appear, he has never yet exhibited any orders.

James Broadwood churchwarden elect for Allendale is a quaker, but he neither appears himself, nor sends any proxy to serve for him. I send you a coppy of the sequestration as ordered, and return you many thanks for the Liberty you gave me in the direction of it, I deliverd it as directed, to the churchwardens, and they all agreed upon Mr Richardson to serve for the present, I was unwilling to appear absolutely in the direction of it, as knowing it impossible to gratify every body, and I Lately understand that Sr Wm Blacket upon the account of different Applications that are made to him, is inclinable to leave the determination of this £20 per annum curacy to his grace the archbishop.

I have allso sent the particulars of the moneys received, upon your account, to this time; but Not haveing heard from Mr Shaw concerning my last packet, I am timerous of sending money by the post, and therefore at present shall only give a note of my hand for it, and will pay it at Durham, or newcastle, as you shall direct, or send it by coach or post as you please to order me. who am your

most obliged and Humble Servant
Tho Andrewes

Pray present my duty to Mr chancellor and my most humble service to Mr Lamplugh

110. 3 August 1719 **Fees account 1718-19**
[BIA Pec.Hex/3]

An Account Due to Mr Jubb since nov 27 1718

	£	s	d
For Wm Chickens Licence	1	1	0
For Wm Smiths Licence	1	1	0
For Wm Leadbitters Licence	1	1	0
Correction court July 14 1719			
Hexham churchwardens for not certifieing the repairs		6	0
Mahoons dismission fees		6	0
Rowel for default		6	0
Waugh for Default		6	0
Lee and Stephenson of St John Lee Dismission fees		8	4
Anno 1718			
for their neglect		6	0
Wm Chicken Dismission fees for Bingfeild anno 1718		8	4
Robert Dawson Dismission fees for St Oswald anno 1718		8	4
For his neglect		6	0
Tho Markinson for default		6	0
Visitation court July 14 1719			
Hexham churchwardens dismission fees anno Dom 1719		8	4
Hexhamshire churchwardens dismission fees anno dom		8	4

1719			
Allendale churchwardens Dismission fees anno dom 1719		8	4
St John lees churchwardens Dismission fees anno 1719		8	4
St Oswald churchwardens Dismission fees anno D 1719		8	4
St Maries Bingfeild church ward Dismiss fees anno 1719		8	4
The R[nd] Mr Lowes exhibition of preists orders		1	4
	9	1	4

Aug 3 1709
I promise to pay to Mr Tho Jubb, or his order, the sum of nine pounds one shilling and fourpence, being the sum of an account due for moneys received in his business, from nov 27 1718 to Aug 3 1719, Wittness my hand Tho Andrewes

111. 22 August 1719 Andrewes to Jubb

Sir Hexham Aug 22 1719

In the proceedings of the Last visitation court, you find among the presentments of the Hexham churchwardens, a presentment of one Catherine Gosling for the crime of fornication, the last was her fourth Bastard, the Gentleman by whom she is reputed to have 'em is now Returnd from Ireland, and again cohabitts with her, In the same scandalous way; his name is Mr Hercules Burleigh, he has some estate in this parish at which he keeps her; I write this that you may, as you think convenient, Joyn him in the proceedings of the next correction call;

I dont remember that the churchwardens took any notice of our new galleries, under the article of enquiry as to errection of seats and pews, there are now some Debates about the two more galleries that are to be errected, which puts me in mind of what I heard Mr Chancellour say to me, when I calld at York in my Journey to London, that he would excuse their former omission, and irregular proceedings, but should expect them to acknowlege his jurisdiction and pay their confirmation fees; five galleries have been built that will hold from 8 to 12 or more apeice, and two more are to be undertaken speedily, Joseph Tate the Bailiff of the mannor (who has built one for himself)[255] informs the Lord, that his privilidge, and the Lord, Sr Wm Blacket, Leaves these favours to his grant and direction, by wch I beleive he getts some small perquisites; they claim the whole Nave or Quire of the church, as a chancell repaird by the Lord, But dont understand, or consider that in Leiu of such repairs, the Lord has had, and sold, and at present enjoys the ground rents, of the houses built where the old parish church stood, which are pretty large.

When ever Mr Chancelour is pleased to confirm the Grant formerly made to my predecessor of the wall between the pillars next the pulpit, & for which monitions I understand have been allready read, I shall accept it as a very great favour done to my self and successors;

The affair of our curacy is not yet determined. Sometimes Sr Wm says he will leave it to his Graces decision, at othertimes that he will please the town, and give it to the person they shall agree upon, we are to have another vestry upon the occasion; the case is a person or two that dont much trouble the Church, are disgusted with Mr Richardson, and represent him to Sr Wm as one that has spoke reflectingly concerning him, tho the far greater part recommend and are disposed to favour him, I will only take care, that the Sequestration is obeyd till a licence from his Grace or Mr Cancellour supersedes it, for it should not be as it has been for these two years past.

When ever you are pleased to direct me to pay or transmitt the moneys due by note of my hand, I am ready to obey your order, in that, or what else you have to give in command to

Your Obliged and Humble Servant
Tho. Andrewes

112. 3 September 1719 Richardson to Jubb

Sir Hexham Sept. the 3rd 1719

I must humbly beg of yu to excuse both the trouble, and freedom of this: - in which I desire yu to return me wth yr first

[255] Bailiff between 1716-25: NCH III, p. 65.

opportunity the Testimonial, wch I sent you & wch is sign'd by the Inhabitants of this place. - being I have an immediate and a very pressing occasion for it The charges of the Post I shall at some opportunity or other return to Mr Andrews, who tenders his best respects to yu. - This Curacy continues still upon the bottom of the Sequestration. - And I must humbly ask your advice whether the Sequestrators can lawfully pay me at Michaelmass (at wch time the Curate's salary is paid him) not only the quarter's salary, wch will be due to me at that time, but another, wch I have wanted of Mr Laidman ever since this time twelve months, - wch the Sequestrators wou'd freely, if they cou'd safely do it. - Your advice at this time (tho' wth all the deference & regard be it ask'd) will be very acceptable to him, who is wth great Sincerity

Your most oblig'd & obedient Serv't
Wm.Richardson

113. 24 September 1719 Richardson to Jubb

Being apprehensive that my last Letter has not com'd safe to yr hand, - I Humbly presume once more (tho' I hope yu'll excuse me, for in good earnest I can't help it) to give yu the trouble of this, wherein I pressingly beg of yu to return me by the very first Post (if possible) the Testimonial, wch I sent you, For it wou'd be of unspeakable satisfaction to me, and it may be of good advantage too at this very time. I also humbly request yr advice, whether the present Sequestrators can legally pay me a Quarter's salary out of the twenty mark, due to me at Michaelmass last, now at this season, wch annually commences the time of the Curate's Payment that if I loose it now I must never expect a farthing from Mr Laidman, Your advice at this critical juncture will be very acceptable, and shall never by forgot by him, who is wth great veneration

Your most oblig'd & most obedient Serv't
Wm. Richardson

Hexham Sept. the 24th 1719

114. 29 October 1719 Andrewes to Jubb

Sir Hexham Oct 29 1719

I have Received the Blanck licence that was in Mr Laidmans hands, so that I have now six by me, haveing disposed of but two since my return; I shall deferr certifieing 'em till the return of more business, expecting in a little time your orders for your correction court. there is in my hand, £9 1s 4d which you have my note for the old account, and £2 2s 0d the two licences Since, which I am ready to pay or send as you are pleased to direct In the mean time I am your most Humble

and Obliged Servant
Tho. Andrewes

115. 7 March 1720 Andrewes to Jubb

Sir Hexham March the 7 1719

I have been long in expectation of your instructions for a correction court, to regulate the defaulters that were prosecuted and returned in the Last; the slower we are in our proceedings the more it emboldens those that act in contempt of them, I doe nothing but as guided by your immediate directions; The affair of Licences has proceeded slowly, I have disposed of but 4 since my return, so that I have still 4 blancks remaining by me, I now send you the 4 bonds that I have filled up, upon which are due to you £4 4s 0d, which added to the sum of £9 -1s-4d for which I sent a note of my hand, makes the whole now due to you £13 : 5s : 4d, which I am ready to pay, or send as you shall direct me.

My Neighbour Mr Bentham has made bold to marry a couple of the Bp of Durhams diocess in the county at large, but he has not presumed as I can find in our peculiar.

As I remember there were about 3 or more that I returnd, that doe live together, & that will give no account of their marriages, and value themselves upon their contempt. The other sunday, when I officiated, I published 3 citations from Mr Chancellours Court, the one concerning a seat between the 4th & 5th pillars for Mr Allgood, which as soon the day of appearance is over and a Faculty allowed, he is prepared to undertake; Between the 3d and 4th pillars is the vacancy that has been allready obtained from Sr Wm.Blacket, and a monition, as I understand, has been allready published in behalf of the Lecturer and his successors, against which I presume, there was no objection presented to the court, if therefore Mr Chancellour will be pleasd to determine this favour to my self and successors, which has been already sued for, I will, with his permission, provide materialls, and keep the workmen in the business as soon as Mr Allgoods is finished, or, as they are adjoyning it may be an advantage to the contrivance, and money saved to build in consort.

I was well pleased at the publishing these citations, and hope the court will be allways carefull of this their prerogative, I am sure tis the only means to prevent ill neighbourhood and partiality amoung our inhabitants, and be a means to preserve poorer familys from the encroachments of the more asumeing, and keep every one their own right and in good order.

Mr Allgood will be the seventh Galerie that has been erected since your self and Mr Chancellour was to visit us. There has been allso a raised tuomb set up in one of the Back Iles, about a foot and half from the pavement, which a little streightens the passage to burials, they doe these things at their own discretion, & I only mention them that you may as you please direct your enquirys to the parish officers concerning them; no preperation is yet made to support the ruinous part of this noble old church, which I am heartly concerned for; they often talk of obtaining a brief, which I wish was to be soon upon the collection, else our assistance may be too late to prevent the falling in of the south quarter, the workmen agree the timbers to be so very rotten and decayed, that tis impossible for it to hang long in this condition, and god knows what may be the destruction, & when the fall shall happen.

I should be extreamly glad if Mr Chancellour would give himself the trouble of a Journey, again to see this distant part of his jurisdiction, or if we are not to think of so great a favour, yet your personal assistance would be very serviceable and obligeing, if this is more then your encourgement from this place can encline you to undertake, and if the Last court I held was att all satisfactory to your directions, I can only say that I am allways ready to act by such Instructions as Mr Chancellour and your self are pleased to favour us withall, and hope we shall never want such good assistance to preserve us in some churchlike order, pray present Mr Chancellour with my most Humble respects, and obedient service, and allso be pleased to accept what is Due from

your most obliged friend
and very Humble servant
Tho. Andrewes

116. April 1720 Andrewes to Jubb

Sir Hexham Apr 1720

I held your court on the 8th of Aprill in the manner you will perceive by the correction call, George Lee, who is a renter under the Lady Derwentwater, is desirous to commute for his pennance as Mr Chancellour shall please to favour him. John Coatsworth shewd me his Licence which he had for his marriage from Durham, from Mr Smith the surrogate, and Mr Hilton the Register, for the marriage of John Coatsworth and Margaret Carr of the parish of Ovingham, and they were named by Mr Lyant Minister of Ovingham, tho he must know they were not of his parish, about the 10th of Decemb 1718, whoever took out the Licence, which he will not declare, must have imposed upon that office, and has forfieted his Bond, or is perjured, if they use the same caution in their office as is in ours; our Defaulter is very sturdy, as thinking himself very safe under such Licence. he is very sufficient, and where ever the fault is I hope you will make them sensible of it; or we shall soon have less use for Licences, If Durham can adopt our people into what parish they think fitt.

Robert Grey and Joseph Bunting with their wittnesses are ready to bear testimony against Mr Ed. Tweedale of Corsenside, in Northumberland, as you please to require them.

John Green the same that should have been in the Excommunication for not paying his fees, was complained of by Hen. Rochester for non payment of his Sess; so that I had time to put him into the Citation process, and the apparitor was at his house with it, but not seeeing him he left a note with his wife, as soon as Rochester was sworn he presented him, he was then calld and did not appear, so that he is now, for not paying his fees, for witholding the church sess, and not giveing appearance to the Citation, However I shall not enter him into the excommunication, till I have a line from you, I intend to write to Mr Shaw to sue out Birds absolution, tho I have not yet given out the Excom till farther orders about Green.

Mr Burleigh appeared and gave the account of himself as in the call, I forgot the County but think it is Down in the province of Ulster, the parishes name is Crumliny, and the minister Mr Patrick Darnons, if this can be satisfactory; those that know more of him say, that in Ireland he pleaded himself to have been married in England, he is known to have courted other women for marriage in this place since that time.

Ralph Brewhouse was with me since the court day [...] and has been admitted, I could not take his six shilling because he was not nominated till after last court day, and was never summond.

I shall send Mr Shaw the Dimensions of the Loft intended by Mr Chancellours permission, between the vacant pillars that he may obtain the dispatch of a regular monition.

I have Communicated the contents of Mr Chancellours Letter to the principal persons of our town in a vestry, which I hope will have some good effect, to Forward a brief, or better to exert emselves.

I acquainted Sr Wm. Blacketts Steward, with the affair of St Johnlee Chancell, before the court, He seemd to make a doubt whether the repair might belong to Sr Wm, Because some moietys of the Great tythes had been sold; that which the Mercers bought is to my knowledge free of all incumberances, as crown Rents, curates saleries, etc, Sr Wm Remains Parson Imparsonee[256] of St Johnlee, presents or nominates the Curate, and pays him a Reserved Salery, is possessor of the Gleb[e], and Small Tythes; the great[257] were sold by the Fenwicks, before his father made the purchase.

The Chancell is in a very scandalous condition, without pavement, wants plaistering on the walls, is in nothing but dirt and confusion, the walls and Roof are very good, and a small charge would make all the rest so.

---

[256] ie. in full possession of the church.

[257] Tithes of corn, grain, hay and wood were generally considered great tithes, while those levied on vegetables, fruit, hops, animal produce, and profits on labour such as milling and fishing were considered small tithes.

The Parish officers are to be chosen on Easter wednesday, and I should be glad to fix them in their offices as soon as is possible, because I am obliged to take a Journey to the south the beginning of the summer; Therefore must desire the favour of you to appoint your court as soon after Easter as you please, that I may not leave our business in disorder, I design soon after it to wait on you (god willing) at York, to bring all moneys that are or will be due, and to Clear the account which now stands as underwritten.

There are in the body of our church two old high raised tombs, one of an Umphrevel a Knight Templer, the other of one of the family of the Ogles, and seats being very much desired and wanted, there are persons of this place if leave for such an alteration could be obtained, that would levell the stones to the Ground, and place pewes over them I hope to hear speedily whither You Judge, that Green may be regularly excomunicated for his church sess, and not appearing, and have no more at present to trouble you with but the respects of your

very Humble servant
Tho. Andrewes

	£	s	d
the account as it now stands	13	1	10
Robert Fosters default	0	6	0
Ed. Shaftoes Default	0	6	0
Hen. Rochesters default	0	6	0
John Hunters default	0	6	0
James Broadwoods default	0	6	0
Ed. Kells default	0	6	0
Apr 11 Remains now due in the account	14	17	0

Pray present my most obedient service to Mr Chancelour.

I forgot to inform you Sr, that our scholemaster Mr Rotheram, has left our schole for that of Haydon bridge, and the governors have elected a new one, that at present is not confirmed by your Licence.

I return now as you are pleased to direct the process for the Last court, as allso that for the present

117. 6 May 1720 Andrewes to Jubb

Sir Hexham May 6 1720

I held your court at this place the 11th of Last month, and if there is no hast of the return, will bring the process, & Call as I have dispatched them, and the other paypers, with the account, and Cash, in my Journey for London; which I hope to begin within this three weeks, Mr Shaw has obtained absolutions for Bird, and Bunting and his wife, Jane Symson has performd her pennance, the rest except Stippell, who is in Jayl, are Excommunicate, and Except Grey and his wife, who were not pronounced, because they are very much concernd and observant, they are ready to preform the their declaration after the from of Buntings, which if you will give me leave, I will admitt them to, and accept of such fees as their small circumstances, can enable 'em to pay. they are truely honest, and ignorant of the fault which they were betrayd into by Mr Twedale of Thockrinton, who has married now a third couple as you will find by you presentments when come to hand, I am informd he makes application to succeed Mr Bentham of St Johnlee who is dead, he is no more then in Deacons orders, and I am apprehensive that He may now appear at York for Preists, But I hope Mr Chancellour may not be uninformed, that he has committed these three most irregular clandestine marriages in his Diocess, and is a common greivance to the whole country, besides by a drunken life, a disgrace to the Order he has allready obtaind, and will in all probability be a scandal to the Preisthood, if he ever obtains it. Mr Shaw has I presume instructions from one of our attorneys, to take out an absolution for John Green, but I must remind you that besides the fees of his ~~default~~ non payment of church sess, he owes you 6s for a default of non appearance when churchwarden, and Whither any thing in this case is due to my commission I leave to your instruction. Pray doe me the favour at Your Leisure, to examine your Register, whither an Excommunication was ever Granted against one Lee of Acoomb in the parish of St Johnlee, and whither he ever obtaind an absolution from it, I think his Xtian name is Thomas, and it may be within 12 or 14 years. In hope of an opportunity of more free conversation in a little time, I remain in haste

Your very Humble Servant
Tho. Andrewes

118. 25 May 1720 Andrewes to Jubb

Dear Sir Hexham may the 25 1720

I Recd yours of the 14 of may, with 4 more bonds for Exc[om]mt and admi[ni]st[ration], Rd Brewis has given bond and pd most of his fees, the remainder is promised in a week. I have excuted both the marriage bonds and licences and have not any of the sede vacante[258] stile if a demand should come. I have held the court as directed on the 20 past, but haveing been since a Journey to Newcastle, and now this festival, that I shall not settle my packet of the proceeding till the week after this. I am ready for every business that shall offer except licences which I hope you'll think to supply, which is all at present

from your most Humble Servant
Tho Andrewes

119. 13 February 1721 Andrewes to Jubb

Sir Hexham Feb 13 1720

I now certifie, and return five of the six licences which I received when I was in my Journey to London, and the other is bespoke, I shall dispose of it in a day or two, and must therefore desire a fresh supply as soon as may be. I have allso returnd the two excommunication instruments, that were published last summer, according to your last order. Rachel Spoor a poor Slutt is lately married to a sorry fellow without banns or license, allso the other three are still in contempt; Green the Farmer pretends he would pay some small costs if he knew them, but I cant much depend on him.

Capt Burleigh that pretended to be married in Ireland, has shot his servant, and is gon to Jayle for his tryal. Buntings fees for his declaration and Absolution which you could not remember, were payd by Mr Shaw his proctor, and I find by my Book I accounted with him for them; you promised to send me against Easter visitation, a declaration for Carrs clandestine marriage, and the form

[258] Marriage licences issued during the vacancy of a bishopric.

by wch I should decree him excommunicate, in case they refuse to perform it.

No care has yet been taken to amend the scandalous condition of St Johnlees chancell.

Mr Tweddale is the curate that has been ordered to be put into St Johnlee, and was sent into possession by an Innkeeper of this place, whom the Baliff of this manner sent with him; St Johnlee is a very large parish, containing 3 distinct villages, 4 or five Hamlets or townships with several large farms and three or four Gentlemens seats, Mr Tweddale is in Deacons orders as I have formerly acquainted you.

Mr Tomson[259] who was ordaind preist by his Grace last summer has left this town; and Mr Graham[260] a very sober Gent; and very orderly, By Sr Wm Blackets permission, succeeds him, he says he is in preists orders, but remains as yet unlicensed. This Donative power which they assume, is certainly not independant from the court of York, for this Estate was in the crown till the Reign of Q Eliz who sold or gave it to Sr Christ. Hatton, and in Her Reign a free schoole was founded, and by her made subject to his Graces visitation, the Lordship of the mannor remaind in the crown till much later, did not pass with the estate. The mannor, and I suppose patronage of these churches, was not disposed of by the crown till the reign of Charles the 2d, nor is the present Sr Wm Blacket a person that would give himself much trouble to assert what is claimed for him, I beleive he would scarcely defend his curates in takeing possession of churches before they have been sworn or licensed, their distance and meaness of there preferments has been the reason of this neglect, and now tis grown into a claim or usuage, Mr Laidman, Sr Wms Relation, could not spirit him up to his defence, and was forcd to yeild to your suspension, I mention these matters as being part of the subject we discoursed on when last together, and now I write it t'will be better under consideration.

Mr Lyant vicar of Ovingham has married a son of Mrs Benthams, to a young woman, both of this jurisdiction, without banns or License, they are since their marriage gon to live at a place calld Chester in the Street, between newcastle and Durham. The

---

[259] Rev. John Thompson, previously of Haydon Bridge, was appointed curate of Hexham in October 1719: NRO SANT/GEN/ECC/3/3/10.

[260] Revd William Graham; see ABN.

court of Durham has granted a licence for the marriage of Mr Charles Shaftoe of the parish of Thockrinton, a young man under age, and he is married against his mother & guardians consent, to a Gentlewoman who's cheif place of Abode was here at Hexham, but she was a few days, at her Brothers, out of this jurisdiction before marriage. they were married by a Scotch curate of this country. Thockrinton is in the jurisdiction of Dean & Chapter. Wm Ritson of Allendale a person of pretty good circumstances and condition, has the misfortune to have a bastard child fatherd on him by his housekeeper, I presume before Easter you will have some application concerning that affair. I think I have mentioned every thing that has occurrd of any moment, since I left your Jurisdiction, except that our parishoners have had the repairs of their church viewd by workmen, and certified by the Justices at their Sessions, and we are in some hopes to proceed with success.

When you have considered these matters, be pleased to give such directions as I am to be governd by, and I shall be very punctual to them, and am

Your very humble servant
Tho. Andrewes

our present account for these five licences stands thus, which I shall return according to your order.

	£	s	d	
John Fishers licence	1	0	6	
John Lawson licence	1	0	6	
John Cotesworths licence	1	0	6	
Charles Lonsdales licence	1	0	6	
Wm.Hinds licence	1	0	6	
	5	2	6	Debtor to Mr Jubb

Certified to the 13th day of Feb 1720

120. 16 March 1721 Andrewes to Jubb

Sir,

I received yours with the two blanck Licenses, by the post; and now it is near Easter I may put you in mind to send, with the other Licenses you mention, the process for the visitation; which I think would be most convenient to be had, about a fortnight after Easter, when the new churchwardens will be appointed.

Mr Graham the Gentleman who is now Curate of Hexham, has received his nomination under the hand of Sr Wm. Blacket, and is desirous to take a Licence from the Archbishop; but would gladly save the Expence and labor of the Journey, If a commission can be obtaind, and upon favourable terms to take his subscriptions and administer the oaths In this place. our Schoolemaster is under the Like circumstance, you have his nomination signd by the trustees of the schoole; t'will be an act of goodness and charity to them to direct their business, as it may be least expensive to them. Mr Graham is in preists orders, as I am informed, and appears to be a very regular sober well behaved person. when you have consulted Mr Chancellours pleasure as to these matters, what he Directs, shall be duely executed according to the best abilitys of your most humble

and obliged servant Tho. Andrewes

Hexham March 16 1720

22 March 1720
Sent 3 Licenses desiring him to waite your return for an answer to the other Particulars

121. 1 May 1721 Andrewes to Jubb

Dear Sir, Hexham May the 1st 1721

I now enclose and certifie three Licences, disposed of from the thirteeth of feb 1720, to may the 1st 1721, I had six, I certified five last time; you sent me two, and your Clerk three more, which made the number six again, I now certifie three, and have three blanks remaining in my hand this May the 1st 1721

I must desire the favour of you to send us our citation and process as you as you can conveniently, for tis convenient to dismiss our old officers, be pleased to leave a blank for the day, pray read over my last letter before you make the correction process, and Let me know whether I may ex officio cite any delinquents before presentment from the churchwardens,

I am your most Humble Servant
Tho Andrewes

The account as it now stands, May the 1st 1721

By The account given Feb 13 1720 due to Mr Tho.Jubb	5 2 6
William Johnsons Licence	1 0 6
Robert Rymers Licence	1 0 6
Richard Ords Licence	1 0 6
Due to May 1 1721	8 4 0

122. 11 May 1721 Andrewes to Jubb

Dear Sir

Hexham May the 11th 1721

I hope you have received by Mr Shaws packet, sent Last week, three Licences that I then certified and returned the Bonds, with the account as it stood at that time; I have since the dispatch of my last, disposed of the three Remaining licences so that at present I have not one blank by me.

I must remind you to consult Mr Chancellour as to the commutation of George Lee, the farmer that rents about £50 a year.

If he pleases allso to set a commutation fine on Wm Ritson, his crime is allso for fornication for he has had a bastard child born to him by his servant Ann Parker; he prays the favour not to be brought to publick penance; As to his circumstances he may be worth about £60 or £70 real estate per annum.

The Affairs of our parish doe much stand in want of the visitation process, if you can be wth us your self 'twill be best, if your affairs will not allow to us that advantage, you shall be assisted, to the best of my Judgement, by your most humble svnt

Tho Andrews

123. 19 June 1721 Andrewes to Jubb

Dear Sir Hexham June the 19 1721

The visitation was held on friday the second of this instant June, according to the process, and the old churchwardens were dismised and made their presentments, and all the new ones appeard and were admitted in very good order, all that were cited appeard, except Mr Lowes who sent word of his indisposition.

I understand Mr coatsworth who was clandestinely married by Mr Lyant to Margaret Carr, has sent to obtain the favour of being excused from his declaration that has been decreed him to perform; I hope tis to be by way of commutation, he has been pretty stiff with me, and is able tho' unwilling to make the required submission, I exact nothing more of him then the performance of the declaration you sent, and the fees you mention 17:8.

The Reason why Robert Grey and Susanna his wife were blotted out of the Excommunication returnd, was because they had some time since left this country, and belonging to the business of leadmines, are gon to some other distant country, we know not where; they were never published to be Excomunicate, because they did offerr to make their submission and declaration, but could not answer the fees; I could not certifie the excommunication as publishd against them, and I was unwilling you should be at the expence of a writt against persons not in being amoung us.

Mr Graham our Minister and Mr Johnson our scholemaster, intend some time this summer for York, in order to Qualifie themselves for his Graces Licence.

I received three licences from your clark, and Three licences that you sent your self, which made my number nine, with the three I had in hand; I now certifie eight of them, and have but one left, and shall want a speedy supply. you never yet gave me your orders to venture your moneys by the coach; as I have orders by Mr Shaw to enclose his with the business in the packet; I have allways hitherto found means of returning yours, I am ready to pay or send it as you shall order me, that in the packet was accounted for to Mr Shaw, as I understand you have settelld it.

You will observe amoung the presentments, two persons that were presented by one of the churchwardens of Hexhamshire for breaking the sabbath, by looking after their sheep on the wastes. but there allso comes to ballance it, a certificate from the principal and sober persons of the neighbourhood, of Best repute, to inform the court of York, that the fact was not so bad as represented, and that the churchwarden was more malicious then conscientious; after the court was over the cheif persons of the country addressd in their behalf, but as I could not stifle a churchwardens presentment; so I send allso, in their behalf, the certificate signed by their neighbours, most of which I know to be men of good repute.

I send allso a certificate put into my hands from Ireland, signd by Patrick Damon, and attested by three other witneses, which declares that Mr Hercules Burleigh was not married by the person, and in the manner he pretends him self to have been.[261]

I allso send you my complaint against six clandestine marriages, several of them have been by licences from Durham, they certainly never give oaths, not take bonds, but prononce or stile our inhabitants persons of some parish in their Jurisdiction and make no scruple of the business; I now enclose to you three of their Licences, wherin of the six persons mentioned, there are none but Issabell Hind of the parish of Bywell, but what are all of Hexham tho' stiled by them of other parishes, and the seals that are affixed you will observe bear not the least impression. the names in my list that have a dash under them are persons of this Jurisdiction. I cant say that Mr Twedale has offended since he came into this Jurisdiction but often enough before if he does you shall hear of him.

My B^r Brings a report from the conversation of some of church of Durham that his Grace should intimate some design of favouring our country with a visit If so t'would be a convenience to the three Gentlemen unlicensed and very much a satisfaction to my self. I belive the oldest person of this place never saw an Archbishop in it if his Grace proposes any such agreeable design pray let me have the earliest notice of it I am your most Humble Servant

Tho Andrewes

[261] Now in BIA Pec.Hex/1.

124. 6 June 1721 **Maughen Robson petition**
[BIA Pec.Hex/1]

Whereas Nicholas Maughen of Foggett and Simon Gibson of the Hill both in the parish of Hexham and County of Northumberland are presented or stand presented in the Ecclesiasticall Court of York for prophanation of the Sabbath by Seeking Sheep on the Lord's Day by the Information of Martin White One of the Churchwardens there We whose names are hereunto Subscribed Inhabitants of the Said Parish Do hearby Certifie that the Said Nicholas Maughen and Simon Gibson are our Neighbours and have always Carryed and Demeaned themselves Soberly & Honestly and so far from being guilty of the Crime wherewith they stand Charged and that they are Constant Frequenters of the Worship of the Church of England as by Law Established especially on that Day and that therefore we really believe the Information agt them is altogether malicious and what is further Induces us so to do is because this Informer is a Comon Disturber of the Neighbourhood and particularly of these Two persons having formerly had a Quarrell with the One and been at Law with the other and has ever Since threatened Revenge & has betaken himself to this Method to Execute it Dated this Sixth day of June Anno Die 1721:

[*all sign except where indicated otherwise:*]
John Rowlands Robt Sharpe William Bell Thos.Teasdale Robert Gallen Thomas bell Thomas Gallan Robert bell [*mark*] John Oxly His Mk John Simson [*initials*] Mathew Bell William Benson [*initials*] WB Wilm Madline [*initials*] Edward Mackay Nickles Rodhm Richd Errington Anthony Hull Edward Hopkinson [*initial*] E Thomas Parker his mark

125. 3 July 1721 **Andrewes to Jubb**

Dear Sir Hexham July the 3d 1721

About the 19 of Last month I returnd by the coach the process of the Visitation, and Presentments of the churchwardens, and eight Licence bonds certified, with a small packet enclosed to Mr Shaw; I hope they have been safely received, I have but one Licence by me, and shall not be long before I dispose of it, I should be informd whither (if the woman liveing out of our Jurisdiction and the man a dweller within our peculiar) a licence Ought to be obtaind from us, of from that Jurisdiction in which the woman lives, I know we may grant if they apply, but whither Such a person is faulty if he seeks one elsewhere. I send enclosed a certificate of the Declaration performd as enjoynd by Tho.Nichols, but how to get of him any money for the fees that I know are due on that account is the difficulty, he is very submissive, but not any thing before hand in the world, he is a joyner, but so ill a husband that necessity I fear must Incline you to make a gratis act of it. Mr Coatsworth time is lapsed on which he ought to have performed and certified his declaration; he is able stiff and clamorus; which behaviour will never make me his advocate; Mr Carr has promised me that Green the person excommunicated, shall speedily comply and pay his fees for absolution, I hope to Hear from you shortly In haste I am your

Very Humble servant
Tho Andrewes

126. 5 Sept 1721 Andrewes to Jubb

Due to mr Tho Jubb Sept the 5th 1721

	£	s	d
By bysiness allready certified and an account of the same given in June the 19 1721	19	0	8
Isack woodells Licence	1	0	6
Abraham Buntings Licence	1	0	6
Joseph Tates Licences	1	0	6
[*in Jubb's hand:*]12 Sept 1721 Reced	22	2	2

Dear Sr

being obliged to take a Journey to London in haste to serve a Brother that is Extreamly Indisposed I have herein Enclosd to you the sum above and have certified what business I have dispatchd and there Remains here in my B[r]s custody 2 bonds and 2 Blank Licences. which he will be carefull of. I am your obliged Tho Andrewes

127. 30 Oct 1721 Andrewes to Jubb

London Oct 30 1721
Blackmoors head in Stockmarket

Dear Sir

As I came thro^ York, to afford my assistance to a brother that is very unhappily indisposed in this place, I left my Packet directed to you in the hands of Mr Shaw, not having the opportunity of meeting with yourself, and being forced to take the advantage [*torn*]e next mornings coach.

I informd you that I had left two Licences in the Hands of my B[r], who tells me he has disposed of one of them, and has But one now remaining at Hexham, if you please to furnish them with a few more to serve in my absence, I have left him my instructions, and may depend that He will be very punctual in the observance of them, I am Sr your most humble servant

Tho Andrews

128. 12 July 1722 Andrewes to Jubb

Dear Sr Hexham july the 12 1722

I now certifie for three licences, and return the Bonds, and I have now remaining but five of the eight licences, I was to account for; they goe of but slowly at present. You say that where persons live in two jurisdictions they may take the Licence from that they choose to marry in, In parishes the fees allways are to be payd in that the woman lived in, and I understood the licence must be had from the jurisdiction in wch the woman lived; I did apprehend from mr chancellours plain directions, that I might Grant his prerogative licence to any persons that required it In this part of the province, tho both parties not of our Jurisdiction or peculiar.

You will observe sir by the correction call who did not appear, and who did, and were dismissed.

John Robson and Sarah Marshal are persons that continue now to live as man and wife, tho not belived to have been att all married, he has some land of his own and other he farms, they were personally cited, but contemnd it.

All the churchwardens were personally attending, and made their presentments, perhaps not so regularly as you would have them, but according to their blundring way.

In St John lee presentment the woman that had a child would never declared the father, and therefore not mentioned by the officers.

In allendale presentments Jane Sheild the woman is presented by the expression of offering violence, but her crime was beating one of her neighbours in the seat with her, in time of divine service, I understand upon the account of seat room.

In Hexham presentments you have a free living old Gent, that Dealt with the Jockies, and tryd in the open streets, and payd 'em for a Horse on Sunday morning in the face of the Ch: Wardens[262]

I return the Excommunication of [Mr Geo *smudged out*] John Cotesworth of Hexham, published and certified under Mr Grahams hand, it is now 26 days since he has been under the sentance, and I hope tho he sollicit well, and is able enough to commute, Yet his case being so notorious that he will be held to his pennance, which he has contemnd and refused in the last years court, according as I returnd it, you have the pennance it self now by you; he appears to be clearly excepted from the benefitt of the act of Grace, should it be otherwise it would be greatly regretted by all of this country that well know their horrid crimes and deserveings.

As for Ritson alias Richardson of allendale he is deserveing correction, and very sufficient, I hope you will make the most of him. I have admonishd Lee to take out his pennance or procure the favour of a commutation, or he knows the worst. Gallon I have not seen as yet.

---

[262] Hexham churchwardens' presentments 20 June 1722 include "Mr. Robt Allgood Esq. [1653-1740] for bying a horse on the Sabeth Day' BIA Pec.Hex/1. See Dodds, *History of Northumberland, Vol XV, op cit*, pp.198-200 & pedigree chart opposite p.201 for the various Allgoods and their inter-relationships.

Between friends you Guess right as to Mr Shaws proceedings,[263] ~~and~~ he says he has got a civilians opinion that the act will excuse these delinquens, tho they had pleaded, confessd, and were decreed pennance, but I hope tis such as in this juncture will not weigh with mr chancellour, I shall entreat him not to urge it far against us, and he advises me to state coatsworths case to Mr chancellour, when I Last conversed wth mr Shaw I was in hopes he would not be engaged for him, (you'll not make use of this as from me). you intimate if he is thus sturdy you can refuse him the favour of appearing by his proctor, I pray that no favours may be admitted him, but that our Ecclesiastical pennance may humble them by an open confession before the congregation, for this small offence, tho they have by art, intrest, money, and management, escaped the punishments due to poysoners and adulterers, for such Judge Price, now a year since, declared them to be most aparently, notwithstanding the verdict of a combined and corrupted Jury.[264] If these affairs should be concluded at York, I hope (notwithstanding the act mentions but 1s and 4d fees) our apparitor who has spent his time, and horse hire, may be considerd for his money Citations and processes he has served on them, or the wife and children will have the Least benefit of the act of grace of any Subjects. The punishment and amendment of bold, hardy, insolent offenders in order to deterr others from their examples, will be of good use to this place, and I desire no other advantage than what with the publick I shall partake in it, except the obtaining some credit to this jurisdiction, and the proveing my self observant of your needfull commands, as

Your much obliged and Humble Servant
Tho Andrewes

---

[263] Shaw, proctor and deputy registrar of the York Exchequer Court, was eventually dismissed for malpractice following a long drawn out case from 1728. He had boasted that his office was worth £1,000/year to him: Till, *Church Courts*, p.32, Study, p.34.

[264] Presumably Sir Robert Price, (1653-1733) lawyer of Lincoln's Inn & Baron of the Exchequer Court in London: S. Handley, 'Price, Robert (1655–1733)', *ODNB*.

129. 16 July 1722 Andrewes to Jubb

Dear Sr Hexham July 16 1722

I sent a packet by the Coach on Friday Last, with the proceeding of your Last court, three licence bonds, and the Excommunication of John Coatsworth, concerning whom I may allso inform you, that notwithstanding the sentance he is now under, he came into our congregation on Friday last in time of divine Service, and continued dureing the celebration of the Sacrament of Baptism, and had remaind to the end of the Service, but that Mr Graham the curate took an opportunity to call him out of the church.

I forgot to let you know in my last, that Rachel Spoor, and Cath Shield who appeard and were dismissed, pleaded poverty, and I could not get the 1s and 4d of them, if you please to excuse them, or proceed for fees hereafter. I have allso made a mistake in your accounts of 1s 4d. The fees of Tho Dawson, I apprehend, were omitted in the account I sent; but shall be rectified hereafter. Nor could I get the name of the woman that Tho Hutchinson has clandestinely married, but if a blank is left, I may hereafter insert it, I hope to hear when you have received the paypers, with any further commands to

Your most Humble Servant
Tho Andrewes

130. 19th July 1722 Andrewes to Jubb

Dear Sir Hexham July 19 1722

This is by John Coatsworths desire To inform you, that he is now willing to submit to the court of York, and that they will perform the declaration so long contested, and requests you to send it with his absolution, and he promises to reconcile himself by performing what you require, what your instructions shall be concerning them I will see duely executed and am your

Most Humble Servant
Tho Andrewes

I hope the packet of the Last court proceedings is allready with you

131. 6 August 1722 Andrewes to Jubb

Dear Sir Hexham Aug the 6 1722

I have received yours of the 23, with the two Excoms and aske pardon for my error In not takeing the 1s 4 of each person - & wish you had mentiond it in your instructions before the court, it will now be exceding difficult to retreive it, more then the sum is worth, some were paupers and could not pay, others are under prosecution for not appearing, and they shall be hereafter taken care of -, as to the Stocking affair that is in my power and shall gladly be set to right; I allso begg pardon, for haveing done before the receipt of yours, what in it you forbid me (ie) troubling you with the submission of John Coatsworth; Mr Shaw I presume will take care to proceed in his affair, according to the Legal method of your courts.

You orderd me in your Last, to send you word whether Richardson, alias Ritson, alias Wrightson was ever cited before the Last court, or did judicially appear and own his crime; In answer to wch I can only say, that he was presented by his churchwardens at the visitation anno 1722, and did immediately apply by Mr Shaw his proctor for commutation, in order to prevent his affair comeing upon the stage of the court in this place; and Mr Shaw by Letter informd me that the sum of £16-10s-0d was sett by Mr Chancellour for his commutation, with fees; which upon the comeing out of the act of grace he s[h]runk from paying, but he was never judically cited untill this Last court anno 1722, when he appeard, tho not then dismissed, for reasons allready given, tho I promised to endeavour that no process should come against him, till he had been heard in another court at York or this place, this I think is the whole of his affair; as to Lee and Gallon I have admonishd them by the apparitor but hear nothing of them.

I am Sr your very Humble Servant
Tho.Andrewes

132. 22 November 1722 Andrewes to Jubb

Dear Sir

I now send you the five Bonds, and certifie for five licences, the whole number that I have in my hands to account for, and shall be glad to receive a fresh supply at your first Leisure for fear of a demand; I allso send the Excommunications as published, the one at allendale, the other at Hexham, I dont suppose there will be any application by any persons therein mentiond, because they are such as have little regard about it, Mr Burleigh and John Robson are persons of some circumstance, and estates of Lands in their possessions, but will not be prevaild upon to free themselves from your censure by their submission, if it should be so that a writ should be taken out to compell them, pray let me know whither it is the same cost to have four or five mentiond in it as one, if it is no more charge when such a one comes against Robson and his pretended wife, the pauper excommunicates may be included as well the present as the former. Wm.Bell was put out before the Publishing, because an absolution was obtained for him and his proctor Mr Shaw I suppose he payd all fees.

You were deliberateing in your last, whither It would not be best to cite all delinquents to appear at York by their proctor, or personally; I very much fear that such method must conclude in the excommunication of all or most of the persons you are concernd with. I send you below the coppy of my account as it now stands, and shall be ready to pay it on demand or return it the way you shall direct

your most Humble and obliged servant
Tho Andrewes

the account

the Last Ballance	6	0	2	
Lonsdales Licence	1	0	6	
Richardsons licence	1	0	6	
Leadbiters licence	1	0	6	
Wighams Licence	1	0	6	
Ellwoods Licence	1	0	6	
Tho.Dawsons Diss fees	0	1	4	
Error by Stockings	0	6	0	
	11	10	0	Nov 22 1722

133. 14 January 1723 Andrewes to Jubb

Dear Sir Hexham Jun 14 1722

I enclose with this, the bonds for three licences that I now certifie for, but as I was obliged to make use of two written bonds, being urged to doe soe before the packet could come to hand, (it Laying some time on the road) I have now by me 5 bonds, and 3 licences, and must desire you in the next supply to send two bonds, short and then we shall be regular again.

You have given me a satisfactory account as to the writ de Excom: cap: I shall only add that Green, Burleigh, and some others I fear will chuse to live and die under their Excommunications and the parish must goe without the rates of their farms. and shall mention this one case of John Robson and Sarah Marshall, who tho their crime of comeing together as man and wife was before the act of grace; yet after that act they refused to appear to your citation, or to plead it; nay still continue to live as man and wife, tho they had never Any Banns, licence or marriage, otherwise then the permission of an Anabaptist Teacher, as they confesse; and insist upon the sufficiency of that as a protection from your court; and unless you have some discipline for a neighbouring curate or two whose poverty they hope may protect them, and allso for our antenuptial fornicators, who never think of marriage till the woman is near Laying in, and then they think to seek a Licence is but setting a seal and date to their disgrace, and haveing made Bold with the first act they may as well goe thro^ with all the rest; Mr Green an attorney that was a stickler in Coatsworths case, is now in this predicament, about a month before the dame Lays in, he owns a marriage, without licence, banns, or any celebration that I ever could learn. unless you can correct these proceedings our Licences will grow out of fashion, and the Country run into very unlawfull one.

I dont know what you intend concerning your correction court, whither you would have it now, or defferr it to that after Easter when the churchwardens are dismised and sworn; I am not inclineable to think if Wm.Richardson Leigh and Gallon were cited to York, it might bring 'em to some conclusion, as to their commutations that are depending.

The Ball[ance] of the present account is now 14 : 8 : 2 as you will perceive; which with Mr Shaws sum being to considerable to venture by a coachman, I have given him a bill for the whole in London, and shall desire him to pay your account as soon as he receives the money. if you will venture the risque of sending by the coach, I could send the money as often as I certifie. but else must wait the opportunity of a return. I shall endeavour to serve you according to direction, and in the Best manner that I can, and am

Your Obliged and Humble Servant
Tho.Andrewes

[*Cover*:]
To Mr Tho. Jubb at his office, York

134. 21 October 1723 Andrewes to Jubb

Sr Hexham Oct the 21 1723

I must acquaint you that I have Recd your process, and have accordingly appointed the court to be held on the first day of nov: we are incumberd with some fairs, and markets, Races etc, that renderd Latter part of this month a little inconvenient to the country. I must begg your direction whether I am to dismiss the three old offenders by the act of grace, for tis proper to make some end with them; you will find that all three were presented before the act of grace: Writson or Ritson for fornication with mary Parker presented may the 2nd 1721, he treated for commutation by his proctor for [*two or three words deleted*] before he was cited, or ever appeard, to prevent the Decree of his pennance, & appearing in the publick court, but last [...] after the act of grace he appeard in the court, and would have had his dismission upon the act of grace, but that I defferd it, and referrd him to York as haveing had his commutation adjudged him. he allso said that he was presented by a wrong name, that his name was Richardson, but he is all one and the same person, and fornication with mary Parker is his crime. pray let me know whether I shall take the act of grace fees of Lee Gallon & Richardson or whether you will think of proceeding futher against them; when our day is over I shall, at my first convenience, Return an account of our proceedings, in the mean time heartyly wishing you a perfect recovery of the Gout, I am your

Most Humble Servant

Tho Andrewes

My B^r is removed to Durham, has lately had a severe fitt, but is recoverd

135. 9 December 1723 Andrewes to Jubb

Sir Hexham Dec the 9th 1723

I have sent you a packet by the coach, which I hope will come to your hand some time this week, I have sent you eight Licence Bonds certified, which is two more then my Stock, I have had a run upon me for Licences since the court faster then usual, and have not one Licence in hand; nay I am two in debt which I shall fill up to Mr Graham, be pleased therefore to send me eight licences, and six bonds by the first opportunity that I may be ready for the next call.

I allso return you the process and call of the court, you will find one man has submitted to his penance but as he was special poor I could not get any fees of him, the young slutt he was concernd with, is in better condition, but stept out of the way.

There was allso a person presented by the churchwardens of allendale for refusing clarks wages, but he has since brought a certificate that tis payd, which youll find.

Mr Aynsly has promised to employ a procter to appear in Mr allgoods affair,[265] I think he uses Mr Brathwaite I have directed them to make up that default at York

The account that is now due to you is £10 10s 8d which I promise to pay to your order, or to convey to York according as you shall direct me in your next.

You may find possibly many errors amoung the presentments, which the officers coming unprepared are apt to make in haste which I hope you will excuse, and correct as well as you can, and allso the mistakes of your

Obliged and Humble Servant

[265] See doc. **128** above.

Tho. Andrewes

Pray present my humble service to Mr Lamplugh and all my Friends at York

136. 16 January 1724 Andrewes to Jubb

Dear Sr Hexham Jan 16 1723

I have receivd the Eight licences, and six bonds, so that I am now accountable for six licences.

I have spoken to Mr Ainsley Mr Allgoods friend, & he promised me to write to Mr Brathwait to appear for him.

John Green who was formerly excommunicated for non payments of his church sess and non appearance, is lately dead under that sentance.

I can not at present think of any method of returning the Ballance now due to you, and may possibly wait long for an opportunity, if you Can hear of any person in Durham or newcastle where you can order me to pay it; or if your are willing to venture, and will give me orders to pack it up in Gold by the coach, I will carefully & punctually obey them.

Robert Dickenson did appear upon your citation, but Tho at present he does not live in our Jurisdiction, nor has he since marriage; his wife was of the parish of warden in the Jurisdict of Durham, where they now Dwell, and in which parish they were married; don't place them in an Excommunication, he may chuse rather to perform a declara[tion] & pay the fees, then endure that disgrace tho' gon from us.

I heartyly wish you a happy new year with out Gout or other misfortune and am your

Most Humble Servant
Tho Andrewes

As for Taylor and his wife that are Papists, they are contented to submit to perform their Declaration which if you please to send, or directions for me to fill one up here

137. 8 March 1724 Andrewes to Jubb

Sr Hexham Mar the 8 1723

An opposition it seems is made by two daughters of Ralph Brewis, against the Decree of his nuncupative will, which I now enclose to you, with the inventory taken of his personal estate, which is not considerable.

The case is that Ralph Brewis an old man, had long since married his two daughters, and bestowd with them such portion of his effects as he could afford; he had allso settled his Eldest son John; Edward the younger son remaind with him in his Latter days, as his servant, or Rather Sharer with him in the whole management of a small farm that they rented.

When He ~~grew~~ was ill, not long before his death, he told Robert Fenwick the contents of his will as now Sent, which he can swear to, a day or tow after He told his Elder son John What he had done for Him more, and that Edward his younger Br was his Executor; He allso told his Granddaughter Margaret Brewis, what he had ordered for her, And that his son Edward his Execut' was willing of it.

Now tho' the two last mentiond persons are mentiond for Legacys in the will, ~~yet they are~~ yet they are content to wave their matters, and would offer their evidence that the old man intended and declared, that his son Edward who had Long lived and served him, should be his executor, to bury him, pay his debts and enjoy the remainder.

This was certainly the intent and declaration of the old man Ralph Brewis; tho liveing in the country, and declining faster than was expected, he had not opportunity to put it in writeing and duely execute it.

This nuncupative will was put into writeing 3 or 4 days after his death, By his intimate friend Robert Fenwick, and signed by himself and the other two as evidences.

This is what I apprehend to be the truth of the case, and desire you to give it what weight you can, in the behalf of Edward Brewis, who is like to be a sufferer by this neglect of his, and opposition from his married sisters, ~~which is~~

This is the whole I know of this matter, and by direction of Edward Brewis submitt it to your care, and am

Your Most Humble Servant
Tho Andrewes

[*Enclosed will, without inventory:*]
27 December 1723

By Order of Ralph Brewis of Grinston Law in the Chappelrey of Bingfield within the Parish of St John Lee yeom[an] as by my last Will & Testament before Robt.Fenwicke do Legate or Bequeath as Followeth

Imp[rimis] I will that my Debts and Funeral Expenses be paid by my Exec[utor] afternamed

Item I Legate or Bequeath to my Son John Brewis a Spotted Grey Mare & a Quy[266] called the name of Gerrard Quy

Ite I leave to Margarett Brewis daughter to the sd John One Bed with all the Furniture thereunto belonging one Black Brock'd Quy & one Linen Sheet

Item I Legate and Bequeath all my other goods & Chattells of what kind or property whatsoever the same be unto my Son Edward Brewis Batcheller & I do likewise nominate and appoint my said Son Edward Brewis my full and Sole Executor of this my last Will and Testament - revoking and disanuling all other Wills or Testaments by me heretofore As Witness the day and year first above Written

[*in another hand:*]
We whose names are under written, Doe know and beleive from what was declared to us by Ralph Brewis in the time of his sickness, tho well in his sences; that the contents above written was his last will and testament, and what he ordered should be done after his decease

Robart Fenwick
The Mark of John Brewis
The Mark of Margt. Brewis

---

[266] Cow.

138. 18 March 1724 Andrewes to Jubb

Sir Hexham March the 18th 1723

We were Ignorant how far the nuncupative will of Ralph Brewis might avail, wittnessed in the manner it was, for he declared the intent of his will at three several times, and to the persons seperately; but Edward Brewis is very well satisfied with your opinion, and Desires that you would prove that the administration may be Granted to himself and his Elder Brother, John Brewis, the only two sons of Ralph Brewis deceased, that they may settle his affairs, and account with their married sisters for the overplus after Debts and funeral charges paid; pray let me know in your next what you are to receive of Edward Brewis for this appearance, that I may Secure it to your account; I presume as they are the sons of the deceased, there is no occasion for a citation contra omnes as before to the will

I hope Sir, Unless Mr Chancellour will doe us the favour of visiting us this summer himself, you will provide that we may have our court within a fortnight or three weeks after Easter, before you set out for your summer Journeys, because it mightly hinders the business of the parishes to be so late in the year; I have Receivd a Letter from Mr Archdeacon Sharp,[267] who is now my neighbour, and he tells me in it, that when he visited cholerton a Church in his Jurisdiction, he had reason to suspect the orders one Mr Lang,[268] who has left Cholerton, and is now got into our peculiar as curate of allendale, Mr Lowes being much indisposed, and past serveing in the church; if his orders shoud be forged, t'would be sad to suffer him to goe on till the visitation.

I am Sr your most humble servt
Tho Andrewes

[267] Thomas Sharp, (1693-1758) rector of Rothbury and archdeacon of Northumberland from Feb 1723, son of John Sharp, Archbishop of York Shuler, pp. 195-209.
[268] James Laing; see entry in ABN.

139. 3 May 1724 Andrewes to Jubb

Good Sir Hexham May 3rd 1724

I am informd by John Liddle the guardian of Mary Leadbitter, that he is come to an agreement with her father in Law Wm.Leadbitter, so far as that he has given up as much land as she can claim dureing her mothers life, but as to personal estaste, and rents embezeld tis to no purpose to medle with them; but Leaves all that part to her self when she comes of age or is married, and therefore tis at present desired that the absolution of Wm.Leadbitter may be sued out, and sent with the charges of the citations and Excommunication, and I will take care to get you bill answerd, before the absolution shall appear, I hope by this time this may meet you safe returnd from London I am Sr

Your Most Humble Servant
Tho Andrewes

[*written at side in different hand:*]
answered deining to wait your return

140. 4 May 1724 Andrewes to Jubb

Sir Hexham May the 4 1724

I have Received your packett with the process for the visitation, of which notice was given last Sunday for the 20th of this month, as being a most proper day for it.

I have in a packet directed to Mr Shaw, enclosed a packet to your self, in which I return four executed Licence bonds, and have now two blanks in my hands of the six Last Received, we have had a long lent. and no demands at that season.

I return allso the declaration of Tho.Taylor and his wife which they were content to perform, but I have not been able to get any fees upon it, they plead inability, his condition is that of a common taylor, I have not promisd them any releasement, but shall find it exceeding difficult to get any thing

Dickenson and his wife were not married in our Jurisdiction his wife never was of our Jurisdiction as I am informd, and at present they both live out of it,

I have not as yet seen Edward Brewis since you have gaind him the favour of his administ[ration], but I have sent a message to him and as soon as I have dispatchd that business I will send you the Bond and fees according to the direction of your former

I thank you Sr for the time you have gaind, and the regard you have to the widdow Youngers circumstances that Bell has been to sharp for, his procter directed his attorney to bring the person who wrote and witnessed the will to be sworn before me, but I answerd that as the cause was now depending at York they must answer your interrogatorys, and be sworn there, it seems they have only sent you a coppy to York; the Handwriteing of this attorney if compared with his other writeings, shews him to be in the Hurry of an election; Had Wm.Younger sent for this attorney any time before Bell came to town, it would have had some credit in it, but twas done the same night he came, when the day before he had declared to two of his neighbours that he had a will at home to his mind, which he should not alter; and the very next morning after the will was made a very reputable person of this place, went to see him but found him out of his senses, and could not be Known by him; and I have been informd that the woman that attended him should say he was not in a condition when the will was made, but the widdows circumstances can not bring these persons before you; what was owing by the deceased will eat up the greatest part of the personal estate, and the widdows life in the house is of little value,[269] she is old; she had power to sell it for her provision in the well thought of will, but in this made at Alnwick the most valueable part is Bells.

How that will is to be executed by the widdow I can't tell, she can't swear she belives it his last will and testament; and she has no reason to renounce the execut' given in the former, the creditors are importunate for what belongs to them.

If you please to goe on as you propose, since John Bell appears against this will, lett him produce a Later, which he must prove in form, as it is free hand it requires three wittnesses; and then you will have an opportunity to interrogate them as to the capacity of Wm.Younger; and then the widdow must either submitt, or produce

[269] Andrews possibly omitted ‘interest’ following ‘widdows life’.

what she has to the contrary; I fear this John Bell will not be brought to any agreement of matters, he is under the direction of an attorney that keeps all his clients up to their mettle, John Bell has brought two or three small actions in our mannor courts against this widdow allready, to make her less capable for contesting this will against him.

I enclose to you in this packet the testimony of Wm.Robinson, Roger Wood, and Cuthbert Lambert, which they voluntarily gave, and were desireous to have sworn to it; but that I declined it, as not thinking my self authorized to take such affidavitts, if you please it may lay by you while this affair is depending, that you make what use you may have of it.

It was a sharp trick in John Bell to undoe a poor woman in this manner, and tis what none can well be secure against if he dies from home, I could take a pleasure in disappointing such practices if it were in my power You'll think me too long winded Clients [*two words obscured*] hope you'll excuse in your

Most Humble Servant
Tho Andrewes

[T*he will referred to:*]
In the Name of God Amen This is the last Will and Testament of me William Younger of Hexham in the County of Northumberland Skinner and Glover made published and Declared this twenty seventh day of February in the Ninth Year of the reign of our Soveraign Lord George by the Grace of God of Great Brittain France and Ireland King Defender of the faith etc Annoq Domini 1722

Imprimis I Give and Devise unto my Dearly beloved Wife Margaret Younger All that my Messuage or Tenement Stable and Garth to the Same belonging Situate Standing lying and being in Hexham aforesaid for and during the term of her Natural life. And I doe give and Devise the Said Messuage or Tenement Stable and Garth from and after the Decease of my Said Wife unto my Dearly beloved friend John Bell Skinner and Glover in Hexham aforesaid and to his Heirs for ever Charged Nevertheless with the payment of Three pounds to William Johnson and forty shillings to William Stokoe of Hexham aforesaid Skinners and Glovers to be paid them after my Wifes Death which I give and bequeath to them. Item I give and bequeath unto my Said Dear Wife all my Goods Chattles and personall effects, of What Nature kind or Quality whatsoever, And I doe hereby Constitute Ordain and Appoint my Said Wife Sole Executrix of this my last Will, and doe hereby revoke annull and make Void all former Wills by me heretofore made. In Witness whereof I have hereunto Sett my hand and Seale and published and Declared this to be my last Will and Testament the day and Year first above written:

Signed Sealed ~~and~~ published and Declared by the above named William Younger the Testatour, as his last Will and Testament in the presence of us who have sett our names as Witnesses hereunto in the presence of and att the Request of the Said Testator } William Young [*symbol drawn after name*]

William Bard   Tho. Wardell   James Stott

[*The testimony enclosed:*]

March the 5th 1722

We whose names are hereunto subscribed doe testifie and truely declare, that when we were at the Election at Alnwick, we did Admonish and put our neigbour William Younger of Hexham in mind to settle his affairs, and dispose of his worldly concerns, he being then much indisposed by a severe fitt of the Stone; but his answer to us at that time was to this meaning and effect; that 'twas what he had allready took care of, and that no body could wrong his wife; this he did Declare (to have allready done to his own mind and content) in Less than a week before his death at Alnewick aforesaid; being on tuesday morning to two of us, viz feb the 26 1722; and that he was then very ill of a painfull distemper of wch he dyed on friday the first of march following; in wittness whereof we have set out hands the day and year above written

Signed
In presence of
Tho: Andrewes
Wm Olivant

the mark of Wm Robinson
Roger Wood [*signs*]
the mark of Cuthbert Lambert

141. 11 May 1724 Andrewes to Jubb

Sir Hexham May the 11 1724

I have received from you a confirmation of the most afflicting newes of the death of our Late most valuable arch Bishop; and allso six bonds of several sorts, with the style; according which instructions I shall take care to dispatch all business in this peculiar & remitt it according to your Directions. I have at present remaining in my hand but two former licence bonds; those four that I have allready executed, were sent from this place inclosed in a packet, directed to Mr Shaw on the 4th of this month.

I must desire your instructions by the very next return of the post, what I am to doe in relation to the visitation which by the process under the seal and in the name of our Late Good Bishop, stands appointed to be held at Hexham on the 20th day of May, which is next wednesday sennight. I have spoken to ~~Ralph~~ Edward Brewis but he has not yet come in to give bond for his administration, his money is hardly ready but I shall Hasten him what I can. In the mean time I am sir

Your most Humble Servant
Tho: Andrewes

142. 15 June 1724 Andrewes to Jubb

Sr Hexham June the 15 1724

I have sent you a packet this day for newcastle, in order to be committed to the coachman; the proceedings of the court, 4 executed Licence bonds, and two administration Bonds executed In order for the return of the Seals, and I have one blanck Licence remaining by me. The Account stands now due 16 – 16 – 11 which I shall remitt to York according to your order, or in about 3 weeks time I may have the convenience of a good London Bill, therefore in your next let me have your directions

We cannot yet prevail with Bell to make an agreement as to the widdow youngers case, tho his attorney would incline him, if He and his wittnesses were cited to prove their Alnwick will, and to answer to such interrogatories as to the family of wm Younger, as might be proposed to them att York, tis probable he might on that motion think of an agreement, if not the widdow ~~must think~~ must then Resolve to answer them, or Drop her right;

The church wardens of Allendale have presented their predecessors for not makeing any account with them or the parish, but Mark Lee has sent in his account since the visitation signed by the church warden, and principal persons in his Devision, if it may avail to his excuse.

Ann Green, the widdow of John Green who died lately under an Excommunication, is allso presented for not paying the church sess, but she has payd it since the court, and being a poor inadvertent widdow I hope you may excuse her neglect. Philip Atkinson a poor man has stood in a sheet for his pennance, but can pay no fees, what I have been able I have got of others.

Archdale and walker who were presented for clandestine marriages, have proved themselves to have been married since that time, and by banns asked in their parish church; the officers Judged they lived suspiciously with those women, and therefore presented them. when you look over the proceedings you will observe how the business stands and if there is any thing farther that wants explaining, I shall very readyly answer your enquirys at present I shall trouble you no farther but with the respects of

Your most Humble Servant
Tho Andrewes

143. 2 July 1724 Andrewes to Jubb

Dear Sir Hexham July the 2 1724

I hope you have receivd my packets with the court proceedings, and licence Bonds &c which I sent some time ago, in which I let you know that I had but one licence remaining; which I have since executed, so that I am at present broke, and have only time to acquaint you that a supply is wanting, Mr Lang whose orders are suspected, (you'll observe) did not appear tho summond to exhibit, he is a very busy man for marrying persons at any rate, he has married a person to the sister of his first wife, both of this

Jurisdiction, but without Banns or Licence, & I have his certificate of it under his hand.

This is in haste from your most humble servant
Tho Andrews

144. 28 September 1724 Andrewes to Jubb

Dear Sir Hexham Sept 28 1724

I Shall send you my packet to York by the newcastle coach containing 4 licence bonds, one will, two administration bonds, and one curation bond, so that the only Blanks I have now by me are 3 Executor bonds, and one Blank Bond and Licence, which will speedily be disposed of, so that before you can supply I shall be clear of what I have, and ready for more. I am now your debtor as will appear by the account I send upward of 25s which I will pay to your order or send by the coach as you shall direct me, If I can have the conveniency of a london bill in a weeks time I will advise you of it; you are to busy I presume to consider this Mr Lang that now serves at Allendale without Orders, as Mr Archdeacon Sharp has good reason to apprehend, he marrys the country at any rate, and as I am informd his life and conversation is not sober, I hear many complaints of him which you will hear of from other hands, I am Sr your most humble servant

Tho Andrewes

You may observe by the case of Last court, that Mr Lang did not come to the visitation, tho I summond him and to Exhibitt his Orders, he takes care to avoid been seen or spoke to.

145. 29 March 1725 Andrewes to Jubb

Dear Sir Hexham Mar 29 1725

I now return the Excom against Wm.Leadbitter published and certified, and he must be pursued to the utmost, or he will very much injure the minor, his wifes daughter, the Guardian was in treaty with him the other day, and began to think of agreement, but be unaccountably fell into his loose humour, and defies all Law and honesty he is a very profligate extravagant sottish person.

If you and Mr Chancellour could visit us in your travells, I hope you would find a more regular court then you had Last time; but if you doe not think so to favour us, I shall be glad to receive your comands, and shall give you the best account I can of it. and am Sr

Your most obedient and Humble Servant
Tho Andrewes

146. 5 April 1725 Andrewes to Jubb

Dear Sir Hexham Apr 5 1725

As I apprehend a citation has been served upon one Tho: Dawson, administr' of Tho: Dawson deceased, in order to bring him to deliver an inventory and make an account, at the suit of his sister or her children, he was Admitted I understand after the return of a citation contra omnes,[270] and they expect a share of the residue when there is none, he hopes upon the sight of this account to obtain a plene administer.[271]

The appearance he supposes is to be the 9th of this month, tho^ he had no written payper left to direct him, I desire you to appear in his deffence, and have enclosed to Mr Shaw His inventory deliverd in upon oath, and if you want farther directions write to Mr Orde attorney at Hexham and when this affair is dispatchd you'll send me your bill that I may take care of your fees.

John Liddle desires you to send Your Bill for the two citations, and Excommunication against William Leadbitter; and desires to know in case he persists forty days, as he apprehends he may, what will be the expence of a writt to take and confine him; I hope to hear from you shortly as to our visitation and in the mean time am Sr

---

[270] against all.
[271] full administration.

Your most Humble Servant
Tho Andrewes

147. 15 April 1725 Andrewes to Jubb

Dear Sir Hexham Apr the 15 1725

I have Recd yours, but have not had opportunity to communicate the contents to Liddle.

I now enclose to you the will* of Tho.Kell in which he gives to his daughter Jane £20, payable 1678, and the second £10 payable 1681 which Legacys have never yet been pd, nor any part of them; the executor George & his mother are both dead; Georges his execut' was his widdow Isabel Kell now liveing; your advice is desired or that of some advocate, if tis not a clear case, whether this Legacy of £20 may be recoverd from Isabel the wife & executrix of George Kell. if so, be pleased to forward a process against her, at the suit of William Garlick (the husband) and Jane Garlick who before marriage was the Daughter Jane Kell mentiond in this will. these persons have hitherto been in Low Circumstances, and therefore not able to to sue for their Right, and what their hopes may be at this distance I can't tell. but am tho^ in haste

Your most Humble Servant
T Andrewes

[*in different hand, possibly that of the probate court registrar*:]
answered & desired to know whether the Extors took upon them Execution J[udi]cially & whether Survived & when Geo.Kell dyed & whether his wife who was his Extrix proved the will & look upon her Execution

[*in Jubb's hand:*]
*24 July 1725 Sent the Coppy of Thos. Kells will back to Mr Andrewes

148. 29 April 1725 Andrewes to unknown[272]

Sir Hexham Apr 29 1725

I am sorry for Mr Jubbs Laborious call to London, I wish his affairs over to his satisfaction and himself well returnd, your clients are very well satisfied that there were assetts sufficient left, you may best inform your self in Mr Shaws office whether George and his mother were admitted executors, we suppose they were; George Kell survived his mother, George Kells will was proved Sept 11 1719 and his wife Isabell took upon her the execution and gave bond penalty £40. I am affraid Mr Jubbs departure will delay our visitation, when he returns you'll be so kind as to remember him of us.

I am your Humble servant
Tho. Andrewes

[*in same hand as that added to previous letter*:]

Cur. prerog.[273] 1675

Grace the Widow of Tho. Kell of Acombe & one of the Extors onely took upon her Execution as to the other Extr his Son Geo. reservate potestate[274]

149. 31 May 1725 Andrewes to John Lambert

Sir Hexham May the 31 1725

I presume by this time you may be returnd from the Cleveland visitation, I have sent by the coach with a packet eight licence bonds, which I certifie for, to be ready for Mr Jubbs perusal at his return; all my stock are now spent, nay I have got credit for one which I must fill up to the minist[er] of Hexham, and therefore desire you to send me one licence, in number more then bonds in your next packet, to supply this defect.

---

[272] Possibly to John Lambert in the Registrars office, as per following letter.
[273] Prerogative Court.
[274] power reserved (ie. to the other executor, his son George).

I wrote to Mr Jubb & acquainted that Wm.Leadbiter was come to terms with John Liddell, and that we desired the absolution to be granted and an account of the costs to be sent.

As to the affair of Garlick with the Executr of George Kell, they are out of expectation; for tho George Kell did meddle and and transact every thing both in his mothers life and after her death, yet he never took a Legal administration; the mother Grace married a second Husband and died insolvent both, but George never sufferd them to have to doe with the affairs wch the Father Tho.Kell left, all came to him, crop etc, he acted for his mother, and when she married he still kept it to himself, pray let me have the expence of this search, which the unfortunate has to pay: my Humble service to Mr Jubb when he returns, I am Sr

Your Humble Servant
Tho Andrewes

[*Cover:*]
To Mr John Lambert at Mr Jubbs office near the Minster, York

[*added underneath address in a different hand:*]
6 June Sent Pr Coach to Mr Andrewes 8 Licences & 8 Bonds

150. 19 July 1725 Andrewes to Jubb

Good Sir Hexham July 19 1725

I have received the process etc and the court shall accordingly be despatched on Wednesday the 21, and shall speedily after return you such presentments as shall be then made, it was Robert Trueman and margaret oliver that was clandestinely and incestuously married by James Laing, I have it certified under his own hand against himself, and can give many instances of clandestine marriages since, but at present he is dismissed from Allendale, but he frequently visits Hexham and marrys persons at any rate in our publick houses. I have two late instances, but what I think should directly subject him to the penaltys in the act of uniformity, is his having celebrated the holy sacrament ~~often~~, as I understand he has, at Allendale, tho^ he does not appear to be priests orders. I will take care to serve him with your citation when it comes, and I dare think he will give you leave to do your worst, I wish we could be secured from him; the date of your citation may have as long a return as you can, that the apparitor may wait an opportunity to serve him with it.

Wm Nicholson has not performed any pennance, but his father who is a small farmer, did propose to sue for the favour of a small commutation, the son is a very young man, and unless his father can obtain some favour for him, he desires, as I understand, to leave him, and seek a distant service. I will consult the old man what he concludes to doe in it.

I must desire Mr Lambert of your office to return the will of Thos Kell, I mean the coppy I sent him, Garlick desires it as soon as may be. I have Mr Lamberts account of the searches and shall take care of ‘em.

You’ll not forget to send me Liddles account.

I am Sir your Most Humble Servant
Tho Andrewes

151. 2 August 1725 Andrewes to Jubb

Dear Sir

Hexham ~~July~~ August the 2^{d} 1725

I send as on the other side Tho Dawsons accounts Debttor and credittor as I receivd from Mr Orde, when this affair is determined be pleasd to send your account that I may get it discharged

I have Received on you account your bill for the dispute about Mary Leadbitters curation £1:2s:2d, and if you please you may now appear for the offender Wm.Leadbitter and sue out his absolution; and send it as soon as you can. I will receive the fees you charge before I deliver it, and return ‘em when you give me your directions.

I here enclose to you a certificate under James Laings own hand, which shews the true writeing of his name, and is prooff of his haveing married this incestuous couple.

I received in your Absence from Mr Lambert eight Licences, and eight bonds, which is one bond more then I wrote for, or have occasion for at present, I wrote for one license more then the number of Bonds to be sent, to answer to a written bond that I Last certified for; this affair may be adjusted by the addition of a single Licence more sent, which will me make me debtor for eight blanks of Both sorts; I intend to get your court proceedings sent to newcastle for the next coach.

I am Sr your most Humble Servant
Tho Andrewes

[*in Jubb's hand:*]

The Charge will be for Fee and Reg	7.10
Ab[soluti]on and ac't	3.10
Court Fees	4. 0
Letters	0. 6
	0:15: 2

152. 9 August 1725 Andrewes to Jubb

Dear Sir Hexham Aug the 9th 1725

I can't omitt this post at the instance of Wm.Ledbitter, to let you know that he has according to your order deposited 15s 2d the fees charged for his absolution; and hopes the favour of the court without the expence of a journey, he is sensible of his offence, but as you determine, I must inform him; I have Receivd the licence which answers my Bonds, and now if I am right charged as debtor for eight I enclose allso the presentment of Tho Robison the churchwarden of Allendale who is recoverd for his sickness which confind him to his bed when he should have appeard at the visitation, he presents one offender in his ward or part of the parish and has nothing more,

I am Sr your most Humble Servant
Tho. Andrewes

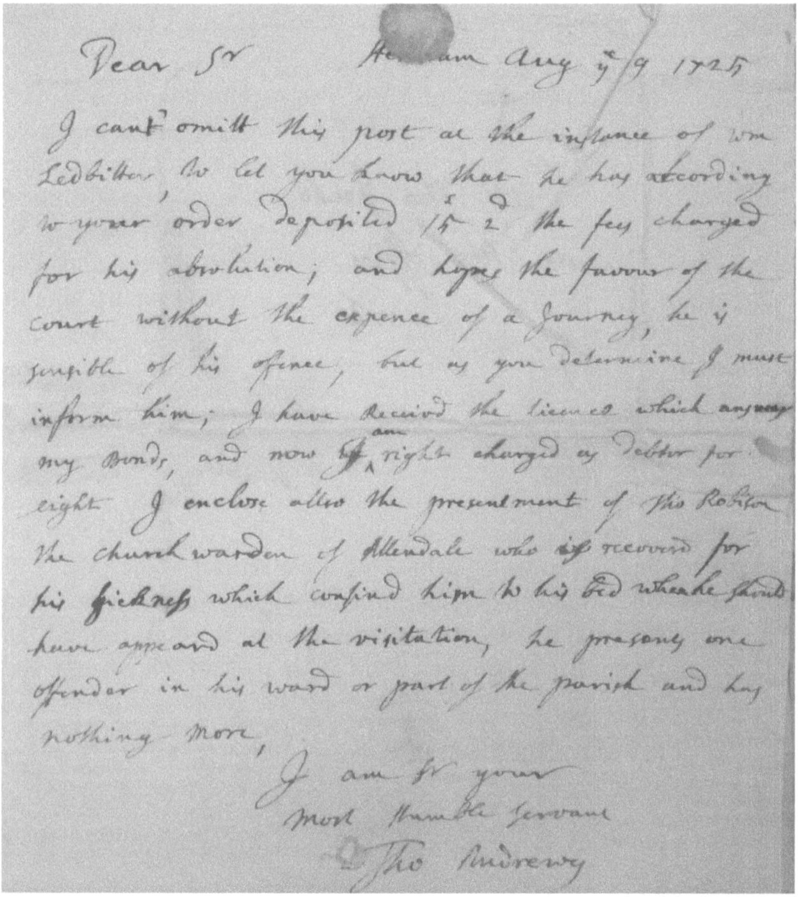

Dear Sr Hexham Aug ye 9 1725

I cant omitt this post at the instance of Wm Ledbitter, to let you know that he has according to your order deposited 15s 2d the fees charged for his absolution; and hopes the favour of the court without the expence of a Journey, he is sensible of his offence, but as you determine I must inform him; I have Received the licence which answers my Bonds, and now am right charged as Debter for eight. I enclose also the presentment of Tho Robson the churchwarden of Allendale who is recovered for his sickness which confined him to his bed when he should have appeared at the visitation, he presents one offender in his ward or part of the parish and has nothing more,

I am Sr your
Most Humble Servant
Tho Andrewes

Figure 12: Thomas Andrewes to Thomas Jubb, 9 Aug 1725, doc. **152** (Reproduced from an original in the Borthwick Institute, University of York, Pec.Hex/2)

153. 18 November 1725 Andrewes to Jubb

Dear Sir Hexham Nov 18 1725

I take the opportunity of Mr Shaws packet, to enclose to you and certifie for 7 licences and returnd Bonds, I have one Blank now Remaining in my hands, a supply may shortly be nescesary; as to the Ball[ance] now now due 20:10:4 I will pay it to your order, or return it as you shall direct, I have moved for a return to Mr Roberts Sr Wm.Blacketts son in law,[275] who are now my neighbours, and who married Mrs Key of York, and he sayd he should have such a sum of money at York, payable in about a months time, if that can be any service.

I have not yet Recd Tho Dawsons charges 1-5-9 but shall take care to call again for it.

I must desire you to appear in dr wards court in Behalf of Jane Sheild wife of John Sheild, who is under an Excom for not appeareing the day she was to take administ[ration] to the effects of her son nicholas, she is now determined to appear and renounce; and her son John to take the administ[ration] the effects are small. be pleased to get me her absolution, and I will take care of the rest. and am your most humble servant

Tho Andrewes

[*abbreviated notes in Jubb's hand written sideways:*]

1 : 11	Cit
5 : 4	ex
1 : 6	Cer
3 : 4	abs
5 : 10	&
: 10	ex
5 : 4	port
1 : 3 : 3	
2 : 40	Absol

[275] Andrewes must mean Sir Edward Blackett's stepson. Sir Edward, cousin of Sir Wm Blackett III, lived at Hexham Abbey with his wife, the widow of Nicholas Roberts, and her son Nicholas (1700-61), who married Katherine Kaye of York: NCH III, p. 297, A.W.Purdue, *The Ship That Came Home*, (2000), p. 86.

7 : 10 Feed of the cur
1 :13 : 11

154. 6 January 1726 Andrewes to Jubb

Dear Sir Hexham Jan the 6th 1725

I have R[eceive]d your citation, and calls for the correction court, which is appointed to be on the 19th of this month In the mean time be pleased to sue out and send me the absolution of Jane Sheild, and shall take care upon the recipt of it to take the sum you mention and if you please to send some blanks for pennance and Declarations, and Directions what to enjoyn profaners of the Lords Day, and what fees to Receive upon their acknowledgement and submission. and how to end with the churchwardens that were presented for not accounting, and what submiscion and fees for [...] Sheild for disturbing the congregation, and what of [...] the non appearing churchwarden, and what of the Refu[...] of clarks fees. and I shall receive accordingly. The Excom against the offenders 1723 were never issued out [...] and are very exact; that Wm Nicolson of the [...] was enjoynd a pennance, but proposed to sue for a suitable commutation, but I have not heard anything of him since; I have not been able to get a [...] Bill to return by; but Mr Roberts has instructed [...] to be payd him at York at candlemas, and promises [...] that time to return me what I have occasion for, when our court is over I shall return you a full account of all matters I shall call again upon this Wm.Nicolson, I have receivd before 3d May you Bill of Fees of Dawson, I have All the Licenses by me unexecuted you sent me last, no body has taken a wife against these Holydays; so that I need not as yet trouble you on that score.

I am Sr your most Humble servant
Tho. Andrewes

be pleased to forward Sheilds absolution

155. May 1726 Andrewes to Jubb

Dear Sr, Hexham the [...] May 1726

The citation I received from you was sent in order to be served upon Mrs Eliz Barton by Mr Allgood, who knew where she lived in the Bishoprick of Durham, but he found her gon from her friends, being married to one Thomas Shirley of Elvet in Durham and she to avoid her friends displeasure and [...] about this design is absconded, the messenger had not any instruction to have it published in the parish church, so that the return of this citation will be elapsed before [we...] get it served, Mr Allgood will acquaint you further of this matter himself.

You'll observe in your [... ... ...] George Brown but appeared [*line illegible through damage*] publish [*illegible line*] not at [... ...] advance by Dismission fee, I have since pd the 6 shill[ings] so please to strike his name out of the Defaulters [list].

We have had Mr advocate Bell who is now surrogate at Durham, at Hexham with Mr Archdeacon Sharp, they are travelled in their visitation northward your friend Mr Pye[276] was with them, but not very [....] under some gouty complaint in his foot our church wardens now being chosen, the old ones [... ...] glad to be dismissed, as soon as you [... ...] sure to send your process for your [... ...] have no more at present but [... ...]

Your most humble servant
Thos Andrewes

156. 10 October 1726 Andrewes to Jubb

Dear Sir Hexham Octob the 10 1726

After a long Bad weather harvest, which I have had to great share in, I have set down to order my paypers for York, first I return you according to your direction the Receipt you gave me at newcastle for 31-2-9, which you allso sent me at the foot of my

[276] Edward Bell and William Pye (d.1752) were both registrars and surrogates within the Durham diocese. Pye gathered several diocesan offices: Shuler, pp.258- 260.

account, haveing noe use for duplicates; I return you the pennance of Wm Nicolson, which you may remember stands as an accusation against Mr Twedale, who for the sum of ten shill[ings] payd to his wife, permitted Nicolson to perform his pennance before church time, and prevaled with the parish officers to signe what nither themselves not the parish were wittneses of.

I allso send the 4 licence Bonds now certified, which are all that were ~~all that~~ left Blank in my hands, & at present I am unprovided till you can supply. I have some time since Received Mr Allgoods £4-13s-0d which is in the account, and 6 shill[ings] for the Dismission of George Brown, who appeard and was admonishd last court, he has payd his dismission fees, and if you please you may strike him out of next correction call.

I now allso return our proceedings of the last court held Sept 7th, you will find a presentment made by Marmaduke Forest churchwarden of the Low Quarter of Hexhamshire, of a widdows son who being informd of two or three sheep that were strayd to the contrary side of the common, went to find 'em and drive 'em home on the sunday.[277] But the same officer I think deserves to be corrected for evident perjury, for a Farmer of note, tho of no great circumstances that lives near him, had a Bastard child born by his housekeeper, which he very readyly confesses, the whole parish is very well acquainted with it, and I cannot but think, he must have been prevaild upon, (tho upon oath to the contrary) to make no report of this matter to the Court, tis impossible he should be ignorant of it.

As to Mr Twedale, whose behaviour is certainly not to be mended, admonitions are of no force to reclaim his intemperate course of liveing, there are several matters might be objected against him, and nothing but poverty, and a wife and many children, to plead for him; I must submitt him to Mr Chancellours pleasure; I cannot but accuse his disorders, and greive at the same time to think he has a family to suffer with him. Let me act as I will in this matter, I shall get reproach either for Remissness, or severity.

As soon as your Leisure will permitt you to examine these and the former paypers, you will give instructions for the correction court, the persons formerly presented for their incestuous Mariages had their pennance enjoynd them, but they cohabit still together, and

[277] Forrest's presentment names him as Robart Bell, son of Elizabeth Bell. BIA Pec.Hex/1. See also doc. **159** below.

never intend to perform any pennance, you know best whether they should be now sentanced, or cited again.

I have no more at present but the respects of your most humble servant

Tho.Andrewes

My B^{r} presents his humble service

157. 29 May 1727 Andrewes to Jubb

Dear Sir Hexham May the 29

In a Letter dated Feb 29 1727 you sent me Mr Chancellours order, concerning Granting Licences only when one party was of this jurisdiction, by which he recalld his former directions; I have acted strictly in that business according to the instructions of that Letter, and shall continue to doe so; And at the same time you ordered me that if Mr Pye or any of his surrogates should encroach on us, and Grant their licences when both partys were inhabitants and subjects of our jurisdiction, that I should give information thereof, that you might assert your right in such cases; I am sorry I have the opportunity of informing you, that one John Loraine of Hexham barber and wiggmaker, was married by virtue of a licence from Durham, to one Jane Smith of Hexham, this I think was about october last; about 6 weeks since, as I am informd by Mr Graham minister of Hexham, one John Craigg of Hexham was married at corbridge by Mr Walton vicar[278], to Mrs Eliz.Copperthwait of Hexham, both subjects of York, by virtue of a Licence from Durham granted by himself About 1 month since Mr Taylor White son of Mr White, a Gentleman of a considerable estate in Nottinghamshire in [sic] the Borders of Yorkshire, who has never resided in the Diocess of Durham, otherwise then as a traveller for a nights lodging at an Inn, but has had his Education in the Inns of court, and is a young Barrister; and of late, for this 4 months Last past before this marriage, has resided alltogether in this peculiar; was married by virtue of a Licence from Durham, to Mrs Ann Errington a Lady of £2500 fortune, of Beaufront in the parish of St Johnlee, they were

[278] John Walton, vicar of Corbridge 1720-41, was a son of the infamous parson Walton of Knarsdale: Shuler, p.63.

married at corbridge, by Mr Walton, who has been made a surrogate as a check in our neighbourhood, he very well knew they were neither of them subjects of the Diocess of Durham, and yet he married them; If these are not evident breaches of the conference and agreement between our chancelour and Dr Sayer[279] in relation to marrying the subjects of each others Diocess, nothing can be such on their part, and the restraint lays alltogether upon us; yesterday I refused to give a licence to a couple when the man was of the Diocess of Durham, and the woman of the diocess of carlile, I was determind to be on the safer side, be pleasd to say whether I might not have done it in that case; but I shall not, without your Liberty, offer at reprisals, tho if let loose I could soon come up with them, they give no direction to their surrogates to administer oaths to the parties, the bond relates not to their habitations, so they put in what place it is for their purpose to name emselves of, wch gives them great advantage over us, who act by stricter orders, a person cannot be licensed by us under a fictitious name of a parish without takeing a false oath, which I would not suffer them to doe if I had the least suspicion of it, I submitt these affairs to your resentment as you think proper, if it has been a crime for the chancellour of Yorks surrogate to grant Licences as provincial, what must it be in the surrogate of an inferiour Jurisdiction, to Grant and to Marry with their licences, the subjects of the Archbishop knowing 'em to be such at the time of their doeing so.

When your affairs give leave our churchwardens would be glad to be released, and I should be glad to see you upon the occasion; who am your most obedient and

Humble servant
Tho Andrewes

158. 12 June 1727 Andrewes to Jubb

Dear Sr Hexham June 12 1727

I sent you a packet enclosed in one to Mr Shaw by last mundays coach with six bonds that I had dispatched, and the

[279] Dr Exton Sayer, chancellor of the Diocese of Durham 1724-31: Shuler, pp.vii, 91.

account, the Ball[ance] of which is 17:10:8 now due to you; now my B[r] is in the south, if you like it, I can shortly send you a bill which If you please to negotiate with merchants in York, will be duely payd at London.

I have had some thoughts of a Journey southward this summer, but would be glad to settle the affairs of these parishes as to their Churchwardens before I goe; if you could possibly spare time, I should be glad to have the processes for the visitation here, unless you have thoughts of letting us have your companys in person, there are two years or more behind as to proceedins against our offenders.

Nothing that can be sayd, can cure Mr Tweedale of St Johnlee from marrying of people clandestinely. there is great complaints against him from the clergy of the Durham Diocess, he has allso ventured to marry one couple of this peculiar viz Joseph Orde, and Jane Bowman of Ridlamhope in the parish of Hexham. Mr Chancellor will correct him as he thinks proper, I have no more at present but that I am

Your most Humble Servant
Tho Andrewes

[*in different hand, possibly John Lambert's*] -
15 June 1727 answerd & desi[r]ed him to wait Your return

159. 3 July 1728 Correction Court - Abstract
[BIA Pec.Hex/1]

Hexham

Thomas Stevenson & Isabella Henderson for lying under the suspicion of adultery	The man appeared but denyd any unlawfull act to have been committed when he travelled abroad with Is: Henderson and left his wife; the suspicion is yet against him, tho^ no bastard was begotten. The woman did not appear
Joseph Oliver and Mary Hardy for the crime of fornication together	The man appeared, the woman did not appear. The man pleads his innocence as to the fact as tis commonly believed that others

	were guilty and that the woman was dealt with to fix upon this man as the father
Joseph Williamson for absenting himself from his parish church and going to no other place of religious worship	He appeared and pleaded that as a surgeon he was often obliged to let blood &c on Sundays but of late has been more frequent; & promised not to be absent but when great necessity requires
Hexhamshire	
Marmaduke Forrest churchwarden for neglecting to present John Rolland & Mary Walker his maidservant for fornication she having bore a bastard child of which he is the reputed father	he confessd himself privy to the same but not certainly knowing him criminal, thought himself not obliged to present. A child was born and is yet living, but he still avoides making the presentment; he behaved him self very insolently in the court; and is presumed the criminal has dealt with Mar: Forest the CW on this occasion
Allendale	
Thomas Fleming and Francisca Welton for the crime of fornication together	They neither of them appeared
Thomas Robson & Margaret Armstrong for the crime of fornication together	They appeared and are since married a Declaration for antenuptial fornicn was decreed them
John Kirke for Drunckeness & disturbing the congregation in the time of divine service	He did not appear
St. John Lee	
Elizabeth Elliot for the crime of fornication with Hugh Addams	She did not appear
John Armstrong & Charles Lonsdale, churchwardens for the year 1726 to explain their presentments by naming the father of Elizabeth Elliot's bastard child	They appeared and presented his name to be Hugh Addams of Brampton in Cumberland

Before Thoma Andrewes, surrogate

In the presence of William Rotheram, John Goss

160. 5 August 1728 Andrewes to Jubb

Dear Sir Hexham Aug 5 1728

I have forwarded the paypers with all the proceedings of your court here; and have certified for and returnd 5 Licence Bonds; I Struck John Winter the young lad out of the excomunicat' process; and have received the £1 4s 0d the Dissmission fee you appointed; Mary Todd an extream poor woman who was excommunicated, came upon it and offerd her self to perform the pennance, which she did in St John lees church, and I must desire you to send her an absolution, and to consider her condition which is perfect poverty. Robert Gallon a churchwarden 1725, that should have appeard and given his presentments at the former court about two years since, was now excommunicated, he now comes and pleads that he was at that time under cure for a hurt he had Received by a carriage, that he had a rib or two broak, and could not attend and pleads ignorance as to sending in his presentments with the account of such his disaster, he beggs to know on what most favourable terms he may obtain his absolution.

I dont know whether the mistake is yours or mine as to Wm Lowden one of the churchwardens of Hexhamshire, Who should have been in the correction call for not appearing [*here is inserted above the line in Jubb's hand:* tho did appeare - for anything to the contrary] and entring into his office, if I enterd him that He did appear and took his oath at Admission it was an error, and I desire you to correct it in my visitation call of church wardens for the year 1726; He neglected to appear, and when the vestry sent a schedule signd to him to collect his Rates by, he entirely neglected it, and there has been no rates collected in his Quarter of the parish this two years, Tho cited to this visitation he refused to appear, a person unknown came to offer himself to make presentments, and be dismissed in his behalf, but one that had not been admitted, nor approved of by the parish, but I could not regard him as an officer that had never been elected, nor deputed by Wm Lowden, nor approved by the vestry; This Lowden is it seems a dissenter, a presbiterian and places himself above your Laws, and holds your authority in the utmost contempt; If he had appeard at the visitation Sept 7 1726 and Deputed one to serve as his proxy, and one the parish could accept, and he answer for, I know he should have been admitted; but he did not then appear, and I hope I have not forgot to make a memorandu that he did not, he has not regarded his office, nor did he appear upon this citation in order for dismission but holds us at defieance; I find him in one of the Excommunications now certified, upon a former presentment of some churchwarden 1725, which you have by you, I apprehend by my sent coppy of the paypers, that it was a presentment for non payment of church sess, & the next court 1726 in contempt for not appearing, and now under an Excommunication 1728, which was published soon after this visitation court was over, but he regards it not, as he goes to the meeting house, who are not cautious of receiving the Excommunicated persons; no person has yet been corrected that holds out under an Excom' this person is as proper a one as may be, he is both insolent, and of good condition, as to his circumstances, which makes him so, There are now in this Jurisdiction not less then 50 persons remaining under this sentance, so that unless, by some instances of persons further prosecuted, they are brought into some fear of such sentance, they will less regard it, or be contented under it, I have admonishd Mr Toppin,[280] and Mr Twedale, and mr Stokoe the Free scholemaster as to their licences; Mr Toppin prays that he may be dispensed with some time, being at present much unprovided for such a Journey, and I Beleive our scholemaster will hardly be able to answer your expectation of him; I thought Mr Twedale would have sollicited his own affair as to the suspension, but I understand Dr Bell surrogate of Durham has undertaken to serve him in it, Little knowing that he never Refused to marry any of his Jurisdiction that offer themselves to him.

You have heard that after I had refused a Licence to Mr Tho Shipley and Mrs Dorothy Wharton of Hexham under 20 years of age, for want of Guardians consent; they procured emselves to be Clandestinely married by Lang in Hexham the person the Archdeacon Sharp detected to have forged himself orders, but

[280] curate of Allendale, 1728-56, though his licence was confirmed only in 1734: NCH IV, p.81. See Introduction pp. 12-3.

aprehending themselves unsafe in that, a whole fortnight after they obtaind a licence from Durham, and were married as I understand a second time in their Diocess; Tho^ Mrs Wharton has lived and Resided this 3 years in Hexham they stile her of some parish in their Jurisdiction, and it has past with them. I presume you may have my Packet by that time this comes to your hand, If I have made any mistakes I hope you will favour me, and amend them, I am intending to take a Ride a little beyond Notingham about 5 or 6 weeks hence, and shall wait upon you if I find you at York; In the mean time I wait your commands here, and am your most respectfull and Humble Servant

Tho Andrewes

161. 18 November 1728 Aynsley & Carr to unknown

Sir

Yesterday a Citation, issued out of your Speciall Court, was read in our Church here, wherein all the Parishoners in General are Cited to appear att Yorke the twenty first instant, to show Cause why an Order or Licence to build a Gallery in the Church betwixt the second and third Pillars from the East on the North part of the Church : to adjoyn Eastwards on the second Pillar & westward on the third Pillar there, to containe in heighth fifteen foot & in breadth 8;foot, or thereabts should not be granted to Edward Heslopp Cotesworth & George Mitford & their familys to sitt kneel & hear service &c - NB: the word thereabts is intended to exceed 8:foot.

The Case is this

The place where Divine Service is now Done, is but small; being the Quire which formerly belonged to that Cathedrall Church: And consequently a great number familys in Town, not prvided with Seats: there is a Row of Pillars on each side of the Quire, and back Eyls behind those Pillars.

The Reading Desk and Pulpit Stand very nigh to to the said third Pillar, & there is now an open space between the said Eastmost & Westmost Pillars; where a Great Number of Pews, very antient & belonging to the Parishoners, are placed, and by reason these two Pillars are not filled up with anything, and are soe nigh the Reading

Desk and Pulpitt; severall of the Parishoners have erected Pews sometime ago to the very back wall of the Eyle, and by reason of that Arch being upon, & soe nigh the Reading Desk and Pulpitt, the people in those back seats can hear service or Sermon very well:

But incase this intended Gallery be erected, then those Pillars are therewith filled upp; Soe that those back Pews and a great many of the antient erected Pews between & adjoyning nigh to those two Pillars, will be altogether useless, and the persons who sitt in the same, will be altogether deprived of either seeing the Reading Deske or pulpitt, or hearing Service or Sermons

Besides that Gallary will be within halfe a yard in front of the Pulpitt, and those whose Sitt in Front, may read the very Sermon which the Parson preacheth aswell as himselfe.

Mr.Cotesworth & George Mitford, though two persons, are both of the same interest in this affair & Mitford is onely artfully named, as if he Joyned Cotesworthas an uninterested Parishon[er] in this matter. But Mitford is farmer of an house in Hexham belonging to Mr.Cotesworth, and hath noe other prtence to intitle himselfe to any seat in the Church: and if it appear he is, as his Farmer, well prvided for in that Church, than all his prtentions to a Second Seat must be wrong.

Cotesworth is a Single man, and lives in another Parish, viz. the Parish of St Johnlee, and keeps house there, and is well prvided with good Conveniences of pews in that Church:

His estate in Hexham is an house now Farmed by the aforesaid Mitford; & to this Tenement a very good Pew doth belong, wherein the said Mitford & family, & the said Cotesworth when att our Church, doe constantly sit, which will hold seven or eight persons, and scituat within six yards of the Reading Desk and Pulpit, in the very left part of the Church

And if this be soe I hope your Court will neither thinke it consistant with Justice or Conscience to give licence, to a single person, who lives & resides in another Parish: and who for his effects in Hexham already hath a larger share of the Church than most of the Inhabitants in Town; to erect that Gallary -- And the rather for that soe many persons must be thereby manifestly Injured -- And in case such Gallary were not prjudiciall (which Really will be soe) yet the Parishoners and Inhabitants in Hexham who are unprovided with

Seats, & who dayly pay to the repare of the Church; are surely better intitled to erect such Gallary: than Cotesworth can be.

Sir We doe desire on Receipt hereof you'l appear & enter a proper Caveat against the Building of this Gallary, And incase Cotesworth thinks fitt to prceed therein, that youl advise us thereof, & doe whats necessery therein; the Parishoners being determined to Contest that matter, We shall onely further add that we are on behalfe of ourselves and Neighbours Sr

Your humble servants

Jo: Aynsley
Tho Carr

Hexham Nov: 18: 1728

162. 27 August 1729 Andrewes to Jubb

Sir Hexham August 27 1729

I enclose to you by Mr Joseph Leeches packet the presentments of the churchwardens given in at your last court in this place, which by an oversight I had omitted to place in the packet when I returned the processes, be pleased to joyn them to those paypers. I wrote to you a about a fortnight since for a citation contra omnes to shew cause why the administ with the will annext of Hannah Fenwick late of Hayrake in the parish of Allendale should not be granted to Thomas Fenwick of Hexham Father in law of the said Hannah Fenwick which if you please to send to your

Most Humble Servant
Tho Andrewes

163. 9 October 1729 Andrewes to Jubb

Dear Sir Hexham Oct 9 1729

My Last was an information against the Office of Durham and their surrogates, for haveing Licenced three couple when none of the partys belongd to their Jurisdiction. This must present you with one complaint more, which makes the fourth since the injunctions I have Received from you; about three weeks since Alexander Johnson of Hexham a mercer of the Best shop and business of this town, came to me for a Licence to marry one Mary Fenwick, the Daughter of Tho Fenwick a grocer of this town who gives 600 fortune; Alexand Johnson was not of age, and would not communicate his design to his mother, who is liveing; nor to his Guardian by his fathers will, nor had he asked the consent of her parents, and under these circumstances I could not grant a minor a licence, till I had his parents consent; upon which he applyd to the office of Durham, obtaind their Licence, and was married at Corbridge; Mr Walton the minister of which place, whom I have formerly mentioned as surrogate to them, knew they were both of this place, and that the man was under age, and that I had Defferd their Licence, but by virtue of the Durham licence, he married them.

The six blank Licences that were in my Hand I have disposed of, and will send you the bonds by the return of the next carrier, I am at present without any blanks, I have Refused several when the partys have proved not to be of our Jurisdiction. If Mr chancellour pleases to take of the late Restraint layd on me, he has a sufficient opportunity; or as he pleases to account with them, I have given a most notorious Instance; They never give any oath as to the places of their habitation, and dont think 'emselves obliged by cannon to doe so, and If I were not to make that Inquiry, I could call all that come of the parish of allendale, for it is so that they use us. there is no condition of their being of any certain place in their bond, and so they act at liberty, & I am only under restraint which I shall not goe beyond, but as you shall direct

Your most obedient and Humble Servant
Tho. Andrewes

Our churchwardens have often urged me with the Length of their office, and Lay the hardship to my acount

[*Cover:*]
To Mr Tho Jubb at his office York

164. 1 January 1730 Andrewes to Jubb

Dear Sir Hexham Jan 1st 1729 / 30

I presume you have Received my packet with the visitation proceedings some weekes agoe, but I had not since then to write with them, there will want many allowances to be made in your account, I have followd directions to the utmost I am able, there are some so deficient of circumstances, as well as criminal, that I could get no fees; of some, as far as they were able, in proportion to their condition; of those that were of ability according to your instructions; except John Craigg and Ann his wife, (one of the couple married and licensed by the surrog[ate] of corbridge) they appeard at the court, made the required Declaration, but they are not by me to be prevaild upon as to fees, tho as sufficient as any I have had to deale with, I have Dund them by the apparitor since I have treated with them my self, and must now leave them to your correction, tis possible a citation will make 'em pay your dues, as they are in condition to doe it. My Demand upon em is 19s and 9d Your fees, and 1s for the apparitor. I Reced 6s apeice of the churchwardens of Hexham, for the presentment of the windows, which the parish thinks hard to make an allowance of; Wm Lowden alias Lowthain the dissenter, and the contentious churchwarden, who was sick and absent at the visitation has, since my paypers were away, been with me, and made his presentment on oath, so if you please you may dismiss him, there were former disputes concerning his not appearing nor bringing a proxy but you then advisd to drop the matter; Alexander Johnson was not to be prevaild upon to submitt to a declaration for his Clandestine marriage, tho dont pretend to disown the practice, as their circumstances are considerable, so they were forward enough to pay fees, but the submision the court requires, was what I was allso to insist on; Mr Allgood of Hexham our Baliff[281] undertook to sollicitt their cause with you, but what he has been able to doe I have not yet heard from you, nor him, so it rests as in the process, without declaration made, or fees pd. You'll see in the allendale presentments one against Mich.Armstrong and Ann his wife, they have importund me (to avoid citations and appearances) to be before hand in

---

[281] Lancelot Allgood (1691-1735), bailiff of Hexham 1725-35, third son of Major Allgood, rector of Simonburn, and nephew of Thomas Allgood, bailiff until 1713. NCH III, p.65, NCH VI, p.274.

receiveing their submission, so they have took out and performd a declaration of their crime, and I have charged 19s and 9d in the account you have; the Declaration shall come with my next certified Licence bonds, and if you please you may omitt them in the next citation process; I have (as you'll see) Blotted Isabel Henderson who is now married, out of the Excom, and have Recd 13s, wch I Beleive is the utmost she could doe to releive her self.

There are now some considerable offenders presented by the officers, and it would be convenient if their correction was to overtake 'em sooner then usually, they are sometimes a year before presented, another before cited, and perhaps a third before we have concluded with em, or more; so that they allmost think emselves passd over before we begin with em, and some times are removed out of the Jurisdiction. I think amoang the churchwardens there is not an old one now that has not made his presentments, nor a new one but what has appeard and been admitted, Mr Stokoe the new curate of St Johnlee is not Licensed, nor the new Schoolemaster that succeed in his place, if there is any thing in the proceedings that wants explaining I am ready to rectifie or give you the best account I can; The date of my letter obliges me to offer you the compliments of the season, and may you pass this and many years without more gout then is requisite for your health, and in all other degrees of Happyness; tho you will not bestow a visit on us, I am in hopes to make one to York this summer, I have calls into the south, which if my health gives leave I would gladly attend; & be so fortunate as to find you in my way, will be a pleasure to

Your most Humble and obedient servant
Tho Andrewes

165. 20 April 1730 Andrewes to Jubb

Dear Sr Hexham Apr 20 1730

I have at Last dispatchd, and now send you the will of Mrs Anna Swinbourn to wch Alderman Ridley has administerd by Decree of court, the weather and Roads have been bad, and he has had an ague, or it had been done sooner, when you have dispatchd what is requisite, send the Probat and your note of Expences to himself at Newcastle, and he can order your money to be payd in York.

The will of Mr George Robson of Ninebanks is now proved and at York, I expect the Probat to be returned very soon, but the Execut[or] Mr George Robson the son, haveing lands devised to him in it, Desires the original will may be decreed to him, so I desire you to take it out of court for his use, and to provide what is necessary in order thereunto.

The Correction court is over, and I shall dispatch the packet with those proceedings by the carrier that comes out the Latter end of this week, there is one Joseph Whitfeild that pretends innocence of the adultery of which by common fame he is accused, and I have cited him to appear at York on the 30th of this instant on pain of Excommunication, but I believe he will not, for the woman has performed her pennance, and confessed her fault, and the man Witfeild has since made an offer towards the same, and I believe he has not one sober person in this place that will say he believes him innocent.

There are some persons, that have, and more will appear by their proctors in order to obtain a commutation for their pennance but I must put you in mind, that when you receive of their agents for such favours, you doe not forget something for my apparitor, who after many rides and citations getts nothing in such cases, as to any advantage to myself in the case of criminals I never take, nor expect any, for they are generaly miserable sinners in more respects than one, miserably poor, as well as miserably wicked.

As for John Craigg and Ann his wife I have often demandd your fees upon the Declaration, which they performd for their clandestine marriage by licence from Durham when both of this place, but he will not pay any, tho he is in condition good enough for such fees, the sum demanded is but 9s 4d for himself as allso 9s 4d for his wife, and 1s for the apparitor, 19s and 8d in the whole, and I hope you will as you promised Cite them to York, which will doe me a credit, for they slurr me as if these fees demanded was my oppression, tho that I give my trouble gratis, and am asspersed into the bargain. Loraine and his wife have had sicknesses and are in low circumstances at present, I never told but otherwise, but that their fees are expected as soon as they are able, nor indeed I never pretended to accquitt any one, in any case, but only say I will represent their condition to your favour, and doe as well as I can for ’em, so that it will not break my word, if you are not contented; but it often happens to be the case, that tis better to punish them gratis, than to contest with such as has not Bread to eat, as in the business now sent is the case of several.

You have the case of Alex Johnson before you he is a double criminal, as to his Cland: marraige, for which he is now for performing a declaration; and Allso his fornication with Eliz Maughan, for which he would commute; I foremerly accquainted you with his condition, when he was married at Corbridge; He is a Mercer and may be worth a thousand pounds he deserves no favour; but what you please to express upon the sollicitations of Mr Allgood, shall be very well accepted as far as I have any concern in the matter, only don't forget something for the apparitor as you think fitt. I have not put the Excomm into the Minister of Hexhams publication as yet against him, but wait for further instructions; I think to provide for a southern Journey soon after Whitsuntide so desire ~~to desire~~ to dismiss the old officers before I goe, as soon as this packet returns pray forward the paypers for the visitation of the Churchwardens. I am Sr most respectfully yours

Tho Andrewes

166. 25 May 1732 Andrewes to Jubb

Good Sr Hexham May 25 1732

You'll find in your List of Excommunicants Elizabeth Maughan. The woman that was presented with Alexand' Johnson, who commuted. I have been applyd to by our Gentlemen that are Justices of the peace for this part of the country, who have an occasion for her testimony against a sett of persons concernd in coining, against whom they have made her a material evidence, they are importunate, that for the service of the crown this womans excommunication may be taken of, Least at the tryal, and now at her depositions it should be pleaded by the prisoners to their advantage, (and when assizes is over, you'll have opportunity to cite her again to her appearance if you please;) the Gentlemen desire this may be dispatchd because of Paypers that are directly to be sent up to the offices in London, In order for their proceedings. This the Bench desired me to signifie to the office at York, that the service of the publick required this woman might be made an unexceptionable evidence.

I find in the Rubrick for the Baptism of adult persons, that notice must be given to the Bishop, or whom he shall appoint for that purpose, that whom, I suppose may be his Chancellour. Now I am not assured whether I am sufficiently authorized, to allow and permitt the minister of Hexham, to examine and administer the office of Baptism to two persons that are above 14 and 15 years of age, they are the children of one Watson a Quaker, their mother of the church; she has instructed them in the catechism, and they are desireous to be baptised, their own father is dead. If I am sufficient for this I'll take care of it; if not, I must desire you to direct to Mr Graham curate of Hexham, such Licence as the Rubrick requires in behalf of one that is called Joseph Watson and his sister who is called Sarah Wattson.

When your affairs give you leave to draw up our instruments for the visitation of this peculiar, our officers would be glad of a discharge, and there are some criminalls that want your correction, but if your self can any time this summer be present, I don't care what time you chuse for it, which would oblige your

Most Humble Servant
Tho Andrewes

167. 19 February 1733 Andrewes to Jubb

Dear Sr Hexham Feb 19 1732

The court was duely held as you'll observe on 20th of Decemb Last, tho I have been hindred, & have delayd the dispatch of the paypers till this time, penances were to be performd, and citations to be signd; you'll observe amoung the paypers, a petition of the minister church wardens etc of allendale, in behalf a poor old man that was sometime since Excom for Contempt etc he was presented for not paying clerks dues, wch are now, as by Receipt sent, they petition his abso[lution]. Mary Rea a poor woman, who formerly had a bastard child, has performd her penance, she is now under excomm, she's an object of charity and hopes for an absolution as a pauper; and indeed the Rest that I have sent have been performd by Paupers of whom I could get no fees; but you'll observe one Mary Shaftoe, that was formerly presented for a bastard child, she was now in the call, but did not appear, she has not discovered the father, and as I am informd is well taken care of, and intends not to filiate, tis rumord to belong to young Gent of good circumstances in this place. There two more Gentlemen presented, young Fellows of this town that have about two or three hundred pounds a year, that have no business but to drink, Game, and divert themselves, and have been sometime traders amoung the weomen, but are now taken at Last, You'll find em in the presentments Robert Elrington Gent, and Wm Heron; Mary Shaftoes spark when you know him, and these two, are Lads of condition, you have allso a third now before you that should have appeard but did not, i.e. Robert Jennison Gent, He did reside in this town when he Had to doe with Ann Stephenson, and now maintains the child here, but at present he Lives in the County of Northumb, under the Jurisdiction of Durham, he is allso a Esqr of Late come to an estate of 3 or 4 hundred a year, they are a pack of idle sparks, and now you have opportunity to doe something towards their reformation, or at Least to shew the world, that discipline is not only intended to expose the poorest of sinners. I have sent you a bill Last week for £15 payable by Mr Tempest Rawlinson in st pauls church yard, 10 days after date, which I hope has been safely Received by you; you'll see by the account I have Received Mr Featherstons money, Mr Hunter has your Letter but I have not yet seen him, he is safe enough, I will speak to him the first time. Mr George Greens widdow says she has nothing to administer to, and that he dyed much in debt, & worth nothing, I shall doe what service I can in these matters; you had thoughts of seeing us Laste year, now here may be business to prevail with you to assist at the next court, the sooner the better After Easter, But this is all at present from your most Humble Servant

Tho Andrewes

[Cover:]
To Mr Tho Jubb at his office York

168. 26 March 1733 Andrewes to Jubb

Dear Sr Hexham March 26 1733

I am first to thank you for your free information of what was advanced against me, and your kind offices; His graces[282] haveing

[282] Lancelot Blackburne, archbishop between 1724-43.

for good reasons given his injunctions against this new method of singing, is sufficient to discourage the persisting in it, But since it has reached you in this manner, I shall give you a just account of it, and in particular what relates to my self. About Septemb Last a man came out of Yorkshire, I don't yet know his name, he addressed himself to Mr Knight when he was here, who knew his B[r] a singing man of your church, and before I knew any thing of such a person being in town, he had obtaind' a permission from Mr Graham to teach some scholars at vacant hours in the church, as being a place proper to try their voices; soon after he obtaind a Leave of Sr Edward Blacket, which was to sing them a Psalm in the church, this they performd for a Sunday or two, so that his first entrance was by the favour of that Family, after wch the master came to me, I referred him entirly to be ordered by Mr Graham, and cautiond' him as to the behaviour of himself and scholars, they have since that time increased to 60 or more, among which are the children clerks and servants of Mr Aynsley, and many belonging to the principal persons of the town, I have never had so much as a servant amoung em; the congregation generally seemed to express their approbation, and those that could not Learn thought it better to attend to good singing, than such as we had been used to, however my Lady Blacket on second thoughts came to dislike it, and then Mr Roberts encouraged an opposite party to sing against, and confound them, and threa[te]ned the clark to get him removed, if he did not chuse such Psalms as they were not acquainted wth and to roar his utmost to drownd their voices, these oppositions, and disorders contin[u]ed some time, and there was nothing but noise and confusion instead of singing, on a Sunday about a month since, in the Absence of Mr Graham, I offerd to rectifie this by giveing the Clark an order of what Psalms he should sing for that day, which were very regularly performd except the second Psalm in the afternoon, which by some contrary order was omitted; when I next visited, my Lady Blacket resented that I had concernd my self in this affair, asked me why I did so, I told her to put an end to the confusions that had been, but what authority had I, my reply was that I was surrogate, I hoped I might endeavour to compose these disorders in the best manner I could, she sayd that would be giveing up the point; for in reality it is growing into a * party matter, and there are some that may find their account in it. I have not been concernd since, or more than I tell you, and if it has been too great a streach of the surrogates power, to give directions to the parish clark, in the absence of the minister, what

Psalms he should sing for one day, ~~for one day~~ tis the only instance I have made use of it in this 15 years, but when specially directed; Three weeks before the reception of yours I was determined to concern myself on neither hand; and we have carried on our neighbourly correspondence with the Abbey[283] ever since, and were I to visit to morrow I don't doubt of a good outside reception; but to say the truth I wish they had never settled within five miles of this town, for her Ladyship is addicted to Government, that there is nothing amoung private familys, parish, country affairs, or matters in our church and congregation but she is very unhappy if she has not the ordering of them, and Mr Graham honest and good man, as he has ten pounds a year and table for reading Family prayers, must entirely act under direction to the offence and great inconvenience of many; nay most proceedings as to the jurisdiction must pass examination, & I have stood many a tryal in her Ladyships consistory, and bore a great deal of clamour from her son, for the Legal transactions of the court, not without such aspertions on your self as I thought to provokeing, and impertinent to communicate; and I should have but Little comfort in my part, if I were to suffer under the misrepresentations of a busy imperious woman, and the forward young Gent her son; for Sr Edward Blacket tho his name must be used, is not really the Resenting person. I shall observe your order, and you may keep this if you please, tho I don't confine you to secrecy, Least you should think I write any thing that wont bare a publick examination, they are well known in this neighbourhood, nor is there a family of any consequence amoung us that have not had striveings, and matters of debate amoung 'em, The umbrage they must take against me as being inclind' to countenance the singers must be from what passd in conversation with them, when I disapproved of the methods used to quiet the disturbances, that the use of a Justices authority in church matters would but provoke 'em, as by writeing up to the board of commisioners to get an Exciseman, a good officer, turned out or removed, for Learning to sing Psalms: by offering to take up the master and to pass him away as a vagrant, because in their books they find singers in the catalouge of vagrants; my declareing for some Psalm to be sung, wch they have given orders to omitt, between sermon and prayers, and that My self could not easyly perform both dutys without the benefitt of it. It has allways been my declard opinion against the admission of singing

[283] ie. with Sir Edward Blackett's family at Abbey House.

masters, as foreseeing such disorders as are now amoung us, and I shall not fail as I have opportunity openly to declare the Archbishops dislike of their method of singing to the exclusion of greater part of the congregation, and persuade them, if I can, not to persist in it.

I shall send by the Fridays carrier one Licence bond that I have executed, a penance that has been performed by a poor offender, and five Blank Licenses and their bonds unexecuted & the Last absolution that was published at allendale. Which you made a present of to two poor persons and this is all at present From

Your most Obliged And very Humble Servant
Tho Andrewes

PS * the Party matter mentioned above, Mr Aynsley makeing interest for the two old Knights of the Shire; Sr Edward etc for Mr Fenwick a new one; Mr Aynsley knows how to turn the usuage of these freeholders to his advantage, and therefore seems inclind to assist and support them and they may prove obstinate enough.[284]

169. 28 May 1733 Andrewes to Jubb

Good Sr Hexham May 28 1733

Some time in august AD 1726, or therabouts, there was a request made to Mr Chancellour by Mr Shaw as proctor, For the takeing down of an old tomb belonging to a family many ages since extinct in this place, that stood between the 2d and 3d pillars, on the south side of Hexham church, in the midst of the congregation, and for converting the place into a seat for the uses of David Johnston and his family, upon which a citation was issued, read, and returnd to shew cause why the said old toomb should not be moved, to a vacant place some few yards south ward, and placed under the wall on the south side of the Ile, The sexton then assureing, that the place Intended to received it was such as noe one had any pretentions to,

[284] John Fenwick was the unsuccessful Tory challenger to the Whig incumbents Sir William Middleton and Ralph Jenison at the May 1734 Parliamentary election: R. Sedgwick (ed): *The History of Parliament: the House of Commons 1715-1754*, (1970), p.295. Of more than 100 voters in Hexham only 32, including John Aynsley, voted for the two Whigs, however: *Poll Book, op cit*, (1841), pp. 172-83 .

nobody then appeard, or had any thing to object against, upon which an order under seal was obtained for the removeal of the toomb, and for placeing of it where it now stands, which order was performd, certified, and returnd, and then Johnson obtaind his Faculty for the enjoyment of his seat. But of late a small attorney of this place whose name is Shaftoe Downs, who very rarely goes to any place of divine worship, if any thing, reputed a dissenter, pretends to claim the ground on which this old Figure of a Knight Templer now Lays, as the proper burial place of his Family, and has commenced an action of trespass at common Law against the mason that set the toomb where it now stands; D Johnston is now dead, has Left a widow and many children, and not pleased to goe to Law with a vexatious attorney, yet must be obliged to defend the workman her husband employed, and had all regular authority from the court for doeing so, The Fees pd to Mr Shaw on the account of this seat, and were in all 3-9-6, for my own part I had only the pleasure of assisting a person who had been bred a dissenter, and was become a regular churchman with a convenient seat; Tho^ Downs his relations may have been burried in this part, yet I conceive he cannot make out any Legal right of a burial place, he Does not pretend A faculty for it, tis in the common pavement of the church, of wch the freehold must be in the minister and church wardens, If he had any right he should have claimd when cited, and the toomb was erecting; neither was there any dammage done, If his burial place, the ground was not broke. As I must be an evidence for Johnson, by what authority he moved this toomb to that place, so I must request you to entrust me with those two Instruments now in your office, the citation, and the instrument that empowerd him that was returnd or certified; I should think this not a matter triable at common Law, but if it comes on against her, we must assist her as much as we are able, and in all good time, that her pleaders may be instructed. I have executed the two Licences that you sent & am now vacant. Since the Law is Establishd on an english foot, and I have no commission but what was in Bp Daws'es time, and in Latine; whether it is not proper I should be better empowerd in these days of regulations? My B^{r} and his Friends in this place present their most humble service. Let Mr Knight know, Sr Edward Blacket has had good success in his newcastle cock-match, his cocks have won about £200;

I am Sr Your most obedient and
most Humble Servant, Tho Andrewes

170. 16 September 1733 Andrewes to Jubb

Dear Sir Hexham Sept the 18 1733

At the request of Mr Allgood, I here enclose to you the will of Mrs Ann Featherston proved this day, together with the Execut[or] bond, I have r[eceive]d the usual fees of the office for the probate £1 1 [...] s d the inventory respitted and must account with Mr Leach. If Mr Leach has any packet for me pray do me the favour to bring it with you, I expect your instructions by next post, Mr Allgood's messenger requires haste, I can only add, that I am,

Your most humble servant
Thomas Andrewes

I hope my last packet is at York by this time.

171. c.1733-4 Reputed papists
[*signed by churchwardens for either 1733 or 1734 & written in the hand of James Goss, Parish clerk at the time*]

The Names of the Reputed Papists

Mr. John Heeron; Mr. Thomas Kirsopp Thomas Jefferson Robert Jefferson Margt Spoore widd Joseph Studholme Cuthbert Lambert surgeon Phillip Jefferson apothecarie Ralph Ridley Mr. Richard Ellis Mr. Robert Rimer Edwd Browne Ben: Cooke Joseph Cooke Mrs Bridget Carnaby Mr Edward Charleton Phisitian

[*each churchwarden signs:*]
Thomas Baxter Wm Olivant Cuthbert ellot Edward Cooke

172. 8 October 1734 Mary Nicholson case papers
[BIA Pec.Hex/1]

James Nicholson Cordwinder, & Mary Clints was Married the 19th day of July Anno Dmi 1731[285]

[285] Date as given; possibly mis-transcribed from the registers by the court clerk, for the case only makes sense if the marriage took place in 1732.

Thomas Son of James Nicholson was Baptized the 28 day of March Anno Dmi 1732/3
This is a true Coppy taken out of the orriginall as witness my hand this Eight day of October 1734

John Goss Parrish Clerk

May this certifie whom it shall concern, that we, whose names are Underwritten, were Eye witnesses, when Mary the Wife of James Nicholson had the Misfortune to fall of Horsback from behind her Husband in the Road between Plenderheath & Brockenhough in their way to Hexham. There was a strong Frost at that Time, & the way being very slape & slippery was the occasion of her falling off, which was in a hollow, wain way, against the Edge of which she unhappily fell flat on her Belly, & for some time after lay [*word erased*] speechless, as tho' she were in a state of Death, not being sensible for a long time, & after she partly recoverd her senses, with a great difficulty & pain, as tho' sometimes this was in danger of falling in Labour by the way, got to Hexham; & with in a few days after Actually fell in Labour frequently (after her fall till the time of her being Deliverd) complaining of a violent pain in her side. We believe this fall hastend her Labour, & in reality was the occasion of her being deliver'd before the time usual to women with child: As witness our Hands the Eighth Day of October in the year of our Lord one Thousand seven Hundred & Thirty four.

Eliz. Surties Thomas Noble [*both sign*]

I James Nicholson do certifie that my Wife Mary was deliver'd of her first Child to me on Thursday morning between the Hours of one & Two, being the fiveteenth Day of March in the Year of our Lord one Thousand seven Hundred & Thirty 2 / 3

As Witness my hand James Nicklson [*signs*]

I Mary Stephenson, who perform'd the office of a Midwife to Mary the wife of James Nicholson, at the first time of her being deliver'd of a Child after she was ~~deliver'd~~ married to the said James, do certifie: That the said Child was brought to light before the time usual to women with Child: I could produce several reasons to prove this Matter of Fact; but I hope I may very well be excus'd from divulging Events appertaining to women in such a Condition, nor ought it in modesty to be required, except in private.

This I willingly certifie, As witness my hand the eighth day of October, in the year of our Lord one Thousand seven Hundred & Thirty four.

Mary Stephenson her mark

I Anne Clints, who was daily & constantly in the house with Mary the wife of James Nicholson from the time she had the misfortune to fall from a Horse, till the time of her being deliver'd of her first Child to the said James after they were lawfully married to gether, do certifie, That the said Child was not at its full time; & further to convince whom it shall concern, the said Mary had not made a proper provision for her lieing in: that is to say had not finish'd, as she intended, the cloase [clothes] necessary for the Child, nor so much as wash'd those few she had made. It is further manifest, that the said Mary had not undertaken so hazardous a journey as she did, had she thought her self so near her time: & I do verily believe that unhappy fall hastend her Labour & brought her pains upon her sooner than she expected or reckoned, for after she got home she continually complain'd of a pain in her side. The said Mary at this time being big with Child is in great Danger of falling into Labour, purely, as I do believe, upon the Thoughts of being falsly accus'd of Fornication, having allways during the time she was a single woman liv'd under a good Character & reputation.

This I willingly certifie, as witness my hand this Eighth day of October in the Year of our Lord one Thousand seven Hundred & Thirty four

Ann Clints her mark.

173. 11 October 1740 Aynsley to unknown[286]

Sr

One John White of Morpeth and Hannah his wife, one of the Daughters of George Lee late of West Acomb in the Parish of Saint Johnlee in the Diocess of York, have taken out a Citation against Mary Lee of Acomb aforesaid widdow, Relict & Adm[inistratri]x of the said Geo Lee (who dyed intestat), to appear at Yorke the thirty first instant to exhibit upon oath an Inventory of the Intestats personall estat, & to make Account & distribution thereof:

[286] Probably James Costobadie, York proctor, recipient of the next letter.

To this process I must desire you to appear, & Exhibit the Inclosed Inventory: and if any further proceedings, that you will take Care of Mrs Lee: I have alsoe put you a Schedule of the Intestats debts etc; by Mrs Lee his Adm[inistratri]x paid since his death: which I hope will be allowed her, & if soe: I think there will be nothing to distribut, those payments Surmounting the Inventory:

Besides theres a bond from Intestat to one John Salmon for £10 & interest for Severall years yet unpaid, which must take place before any distribution:

There is alsoe a bond for £200 and a mortgage for further security; of the Lands in Acomb, made by the intestat & all unpaid, And I take it; as this debt is upon the Wall estat by bond & mortgage: after payment of debts, all the Surplusage of the personall estat (if any be) must goe in ease of the reall estat.

And note that Whites wife on her marryage, was provided for by her father the Intestat, who paid or secured to her £40.

These things I thought proper to mention; that when its a proper time You may make use thereof.

I have never got Mr Jacksons discharge from Mr Teasdale; though often demanded: but he still makes one excuse or other; I wish you would in your next to me, make mention, that the Commutation money & Costs for Mr Jackson are paid; & the process for excommunication Stopt; that I may shew it to Mr Andrews. Your Complyance will oblige Sr

Your Humble Servant
Jo: Aynsley

Hexham Octob 11 1740

174. 11 December 1740 Aynsley to Costobadie

An account of the Charge attending George Lees death & Funerall

	£ s d
Paid for the hire of Severall men for three days in Seeking for his Corps, he being unfortunatly drown in the River Tine & expences	00:15:00
Paid for his Coffin	00:10:00
Paid for 80 quarts of Ale for his funerall at	

3½ d per Quart	01:03:04
Paid for Nine quarts of Brandy	00:15:00
Paid for 5 bushells of wheat for Cakes & bread for the guests	00:16:00
Paid for Cinamon & Cloves to prepare the Ale & Brandy	00:01:06
For Sugar to Sweeten the Same paid	00:07:00
For 9 pounds of Currens for the Cakes	00:05:03
For an ounce of Nutmeggs for Seasoning	00:00:09
For a Firkin of butter for the Cakes etc paid	00:19:00
For Cheshire Cheese for the Company pd	00:11:00
More for two Cheeses made in the Neighbourhood	00:03:00
For Tobacco & Pipes for the Funerall paid	00:04:00
	06:10:10

Sr

I have & as you desire [*word erased*] put you the particulars of the Charge of the Intestates funerall; who being a person of reputation in his Neighbourhood, is very low: I shall apply to the prosecutors Attorney and try to agree it or referr it, but White the prosecutor (who marryed Lees daughter) & is soe p[er]vers[e] a fellow that I have little hopes, & think it best before I apply to prduce the discharge: I think a bond of £10 unpaid, and another for £200 with a mortgage of Land unpaid, & if any prsonall estat more than will pay the Intestats debts. It will, I take it, goe in ease of the Lands, & not in distribution, if anything was over his other debts, which you see is otherwise. On Tuesday last Mr Abra: Teasdale gave me Jacksons absolution & not sooner, he says he paid you all his Bill. I am etc

Your humble Servant
Jo: Aynsley Hexham Dec: 11 1740

[*Cover:*]
To Mr Jacob Custobadie[287] at his House York

---

[287] A James Custobadie appears amongst the York Cause Papers as a proctor from the 1710s onwards – BIA, DC.CP.1710/3.

[*at side of cover in a different hand:*] Cop: of Acct Lee add White

[*Separate schedule:*]
A Schedule or Particulars of the Debts of George Lee late of Acomb deceased by him owing at the time of his Death to the Severall persons hereafter Named with an account of the Provisions made for his Children in his life time and of the payments made by Mary Lee the Widdow and Relict & Administratrix of the said George Lee Since his death:

	£	s	d
June 1 1739 Paid to Robert Salmon in discharge of a Debt due to him from the Intestat	4	2	6
August 17th 1739: Paid by her to John Wild for and in discharge of an arrear of Rent owing him by the Intestat for a Farm in Acomb	42	0	0
The same day paid Mrs Ann Carr for an arrear of Rent due to her from the Intestat for lands in Acomb	5	5	0
August 28th 1739: paid Edward English for a debt due to him from Intestat abt the Exchang of an horse		10	0
September 4th 1739: paid Richard Ellis for one years Interest of £200 due from the Intestat to the Executrix of Richard Eagleston and Secured by Mortgage out of his reall estat in Acomb and yet unpaid	10	0	0
May 27th 1740: paid Mr Richard Heron in discharge of a bond from Intestat to him	10	5	0
Paid Mrs Margaret Heron a Debt due from the Intestat for the Interest of £50 by Intestat owing to her	2	10	0
Paid to Isaac Woodall for the like for a hat sold to the Intestat by him		2	0
Paid Mr John Aynsley for a debt due to him for law busness for the Intestat done		18	6
Paid Mr Ellis for the Interest of the Said £200 more	5	18	9
Paid Samuell Taylor for leading timber for Intestat		5	0
Paid for funerall expences of Intestat	5	0	0
Paid to the Incumbent for his mortuary		10	0
Paid for the expences of the lrs of Administration	2	0	6

Paid John Surties for Smith's work wrought for Intestat		15	3½
Paid to John Hutchinson for the like		19	0
	91	1	6 ½

[*Footnote in a different hand:*]
Total sum of the Invent[ory] Exhibited is 85:12:6

[*Separate schedule:*]
The Accompt of Mary Lee Widow Relict and Admin[istra]trix of the Goods & Chattles of George Lee late of Acomb in the parish of St John Lee and Diocess of York Dec[eas]ed

This Accomptant Charges herselfe with all and Singular the Goods & Chattles of the Deced Comprized in an Inventory thereof made and by her Exhibited into this Venerable Court amounting to the sum of	85	12	6

Out of which this Accomptant has paid Disbursed and Satisfyed or Secured to be paid for the Funerall Expences of the said Deced, for the payment of his Debts and for taking Admon and other Necessary Disbursements in manner & form following (to wit)

First this Accomptant haveth Allowance for the Expences of Letters of Admon of the Deceds Goods and other necessary Expences in obtaining the same	2	0	6
Also paid for the Funerall Expences of the sd Deced for the Horsehire of severall Men for three Days in Seeking for his Corps, he being unfortunately Drown'd in the River Tine and Expences		15	0
Also for his Coffin		10	0
Also for 80 Quarts of Ale for his Funerall at 3½ pr Quart	1	3	4
Also for nine Quarts of Brandy		15	0
Also for five Bushels of Wheat for Cakes & Bread for the Guests		16	0
Also for Cinamon & Cloves to prepare the Ale & Brandy		1	6
Also for Sugar to sweeten the same		7	0

Also for nine pound of Currants for the Cakes		5	3
Also for an Ounce of Nutmegs for Seasoning			9
Also for a Firkin of Butter for the Cakes etc		19	0
Also for Cheshire Cheese for the Company		11	0
Also for more Cheese made in the Neighbourhood		3	0
Also for Tobacco & pipes for the Funerall		4	0
Also paid to the Incumbent for a Mortuary		10	0
Also paid to Robert Salmon in Discharge of a Debt due to him from the Deced	4	2	6
Also paid to John Wild for & in Discharge of an arrear of Rent owing to him by the Deced for a Farm in Acomb	42	0	0
Also paid to Mrs Ann Carr for an Arrear of Rent due to her from the Deced for Lands in Acomb	5	5	0
Also paid to Edward English for a Debt due to him from the Deced about the Exchange of an Horse		10	0
Also paid to Rich: Ellis for one Year's Interest of £200 due from the Deced to the Extrix of Rich: Egleston and secured by Mortgage out of his Reall Estate in Acomb and yet unpaid	10	0	0
Also paid to Mr Rich: Heron in discharge of a Bond due to him from the Deced	10	5	0
Also paid to Mrs Margaret Heron a Debt due to her from the Deced for the Interest of £50	2	10	0
Also paid to Isaiah Woodell for a Hat sold to the Deced		2	0
Also pd to Mr John Aynsley for a Debt due to him from the Deced for Law Business		18	6
Also pd Mr Ellis for the Interest of the sd £200 more	5	18	9
Also pd to Sam Taylor for leading Timber for the sd deced		5	0
Also pd to John Surties for Smith's Work wrought for the Deced		15	3½
Also pd to John Jenkinson for the like		13	0
	92	17	4½

This Acct also haveth Allowance for a Bond of £10 which is still unpaid to John Salmon & Interest for severall years	10	0	0
Also for a Bond of £200 due to the Extrix of Richard Egleston and secured by Mortgage out of the said Deceds Reall Estate in Acomb yet unpaid	200	0	0
This Acct further saith & haves Allowance for the sum of £40 pd or secured to be paid by the sd Deced to his Daughter while the Plaintiffe in this Cause	40	0	0

Also this Acct haveth Allowance for drawing the Inventory in this Cause Ex[ecut]ed for the Exhibition thereof Drawing & Ingrossing this Acct Advocate & proctor's Fees & for other Charges Expended & to be Expended in this Cause what the Worsf[ll] the Judge of this ven[erab]le Court shall think reasonable in the event of this Suit

Index

Letters are listed by author name.

In addition to an annual journal, *Hexham Historian*, published each year since 1991, the Society's series of occasional publications include:

Richard Britnell, Claire Etty and Andy King, (eds) *The Black Book of Hexham, A Northern Monastic Estate in 1379 with Additional Documents, c.1113-1536*, (2011)

Anna Rossiter, *Hexham in the Seventeenth Century: Economy, Society and Government in a northern market town*, (2010)

Tom Corfe, (ed) *Hexham Lives*, (2006)

Members of the Hexham Local History Society, including Sonja Bailes, Mark Benjamin, Jennifer Britton, Steve Casson, Susanne and Chris Ellingham, Greg Finch, Ian Hancock, Jim Hedley, Susan Ketelaar, Yvonne Purdy, Liz Sobell, Peter Rodger and Ted Wall, have transcribed and checked the letters in this collection from the original material held in the Borthwick Institute of Archives in York and the Northumberland Archives.

The project was overseen and the collection edited and prepared for publication by Dr Greg Finch, who has published numerous articles on the early modern period in the North-east of England and other aspects of English regional history during the past thirty five years. He is treasurer of the Hexham Local History Society, and helps run the Friends of the North Pennines' Dukesfield Smelters and Carriers conservation and research project into the regional lead industry.

www.ingramcontent.com/pod-product-compliance
Ingram Content Group UK Ltd.
Pitfield, Milton Keynes, MK11 3LW, UK
UKHW041858190726
13854UKWH00002B/971